Notes from a Working-Class Playwright

OTHER TITLES IN THE THEATRE MAKERS SERIES INCLUDE:

The Theatre and its Double, by Antonin Artaud and translated by Mark Taylor-Batty

Theatre across Borders, by Abhishek Majumdar

Notes from the Rehearsal Room: A Director's Process, by Nancy Meckler

Toward a Future Theatre: Conversations during a Pandemic, by Caridad Svich

The Uncapturable: The Fleeting Art of Theatre, by Rubén Szuchmacher and translated by William Gregory

Adrian Lester and Lolita Chakrabarti: A Working Diary, by Adrian Lester and Lolita Chakrabarti

Movement Directors in Contemporary Theatre: Conversations on Craft, by Ayse Tashkiran

Contemporary Women Stage Directors: Conversations on Craft, by Paulette Marty

Julie Hesmondhalgh: A Working Diary, by Julie Hesmondhalgh

Julius Caesar and Me: Exploring Shakespeare's African Play, by Peterson Joseph

The Actor and His Body, by Litz Pisk and introduction by Ayse Tashkiran

Steppenwolf Theatre Company of Chicago: In Their Own Words, by John Mayer

Revolutionary Messages, by Antonin Artaud and translated by Joel White

The Art of Resonance, by Anne Bogart

An Alchemy of Living Culture: Collected Writings on Double Edge Theatre, by Stacy Klein and preface by Jonathan P. Eburne

The Paris Manuscript: The Early Draft Rediscovered, by Michael Chekhov and translated by Hugo Moss

Notes from a Working-Class Playwright

Leo Butler

methuen | drama
LONDON · NEW YORK · OXFORD · NEW DELHI · SYDNEY

METHUEN DRAMA
Bloomsbury Publishing Plc, 50 Bedford Square, London, WC1B 3DP, UK
Bloomsbury Publishing Inc, 1385 Broadway, New York, NY 10018, USA
Bloomsbury Publishing Ireland, 29 Earlsfort Terrace, Dublin 2, D02 AY28, Ireland

BLOOMSBURY, METHUEN DRAMA and the Methuen Drama logo are trademarks of Bloomsbury Publishing Plc

First published in Great Britain 2026

Copyright © Leo Butler, 2026

Leo Butler has asserted his right under the Copyright, Designs and Patents Act, 1988, to be identified as Author of this work.

For legal purposes the Acknowledgements on pp. xvi–xvii constitute an extension of this copyright page.

Cover image © Tim Stubbings, 2023

All rights reserved. No part of this publication may be: i) reproduced or transmitted in any form, electronic or mechanical, including photocopying, recording or by means of any information storage or retrieval system without prior permission in writing from the publishers; or ii) used or reproduced in any way for the training, development or operation of artificial intelligence (AI) technologies, including generative AI technologies. The rights holders expressly reserve this publication from the text and data mining exception as per Article 4(3) of the Digital Single Market Directive (EU) 2019/790.

Bloomsbury Publishing Plc does not have any control over, or responsibility for, any third-party websites referred to or in this book. All internet addresses given in this book were correct at the time of going to press. The author and publisher regret any inconvenience caused if addresses have changed or sites have ceased to exist, but can accept no responsibility for any such changes.

A catalogue record for this book is available from the British Library.

Library of Congress Control Number: 2025936831

ISBN: HB: 978-1-3504-2947-5
       PB: 978-1-3504-2946-8
       ePDF: 978-1-3504-2948-2
       eBook: 978-1-3504-2949-9

Series: Theatre Makers

Typeset by RefineCatch Limited, Bungay, Suffolk
Printed and bound in Great Britain

For product safety related questions contact productsafety@bloomsbury.com.

To find out more about our authors and books visit www.bloomsbury.com and sign up for our newsletters.

For Bea

CONTENTS

List of illustrations   ix
About the author   xv
Acknowledgements   xvi
Note   xviii

1 The hidden play   1

2 Getting started   9

3 I know my place!   13

4 Tungsten carbide drills or what is a working-class playwright anyway?   27

5 Make it up as you go along!   36
   Ideas bank   38
   Titles   39
   Posters   40
   Borrowed images   41
   Conjured images   44
   Procrastination   47
   Freestyling dialogue   48
   And if you're stuck   53

6 I can play the lion too!   56

7 How to write a play   78
   The plot   78
   The setup: Disorder, piano and staircase   79
   The characters   85
   Repeated efforts and complications   89

Avoiding conflict   93
Reversals and twists   94
Winners and losers   96
Bending the rules   98
Breaking the fourth wall   99
Suspense and dramatic irony   101
The worst thing that can happen (the climax)   104
The resolution   107

8 The multi-locational life and times of (insert name here) and other structures   110

9 Ch-ch-ch-ch-changes!   118

10 Births n' rebirths n' rewrites n' bellyaches   136
Feedback   137
Model box   140
Do I really have to do a rewrite?   141

11 The magic toybox   146
Critics   160

12 What the f*ck is a dramaturg?   166
Elyse   172

13 Now and then   177

Appendix   182
Q & A exercise   182
The twelve-week course   186
Some plays and films   190

Bibliography   195
Index   199

ILLUSTRATIONS

The author and publisher gratefully acknowledge the permission granted to reproduce the copyright material in this book.

Chapter Two: Getting started

1	Butler's teaching notebook © Leo Butler, 2024.	9

Chapter Three: I know my place!

2	Tree outside bedroom window in the 1980s © Leo Butler, 2024.	16
3	Butler brothers at Christmas, 1980s © Leo Butler, 2024.	18
4	John Gordon Barber with greyhounds, 1952 © Leo Butler, 2024.	22
5	Judy Butler (née Barber) on doorstep, *c.*1953/1954 © Leo Butler, 2024.	23
6	Terence 'Bill' Butler in the 1970s © Leo Butler, 2024.	24
7	Day out in the countryside, *c.*1975 © Leo Butler, 2024.	26

Chapter Five: Make it up as you go along!

8	St Jerome by Albrecht Dürer (1471–1528), oil on pearwood, *c.*1496. Image reproduced with permission from © Ian Dagnall Computing/Alamy Stock Photo.	41
9	Ingeborg Arnoldi in 'Mutter Courage', 1968. Photographer: Fred Erismann. Public Domain.	43
10	'Redundant' (directed by Dominic Cooke, Royal Court, 2001). Photo reproduced with kind permission from @ Tristram Kenton.	43
11	'Lucky Dog' sketchbook #1 © Leo Butler, 2024.	44
12	'Lucky Dog' sketchbook #2 © Leo Butler, 2024.	45
13	'Lucky Dog' sketchbook #3 © Leo Butler, 2024.	45
14	'Innocent Creatures' notebook #1 © Leo Butler, 2024.	48
15	'Innocent Creatures' notebook #2 © Leo Butler, 2024.	49
16	'Innocent Creatures' notebook #3 © Leo Butler, 2024.	52

Chapter Six: I can play the lion too!

17	Young Butler at typewriter, 1980s © Leo Butler, 2024.	59
18	Meg Jepson teaching at the Sheffield Youth Theatre, 1980s (photographer unknown). Photo reproduced by kind permission of © Sheffield City Archives.	64
19	Sheffield Youth Theatre 'The Tempest' production, 1980s (photographer unknown). Photo reproduced by kind permission of © Sheffield City Archives.	65
20	Article on Sheffield Youth Theatre's 'A Midsummer's Night Dream' (cutting from *Sheffield Star*, 1985). Reproduced with kind permission of © SWNS Ltd.	66
21	Butler's Fish speech, Briar Rose, 1987 © Leo Butler, 2024.	68
22	Butler Biology Report, 1980s © Leo Butler, 2024.	69
23	Leo Butler, Marc Fretwell, Matthew Burgess and Huss Garbiya in 'Robyn Hudd: The Pantomime', 1992 @ Leo Butler, 2024.	74
24	'Runners' (1992) film poster © Leo Butler, 2024.	76
25	'The Magic Chocolate Box' directed by Beatrice Butler. © BeaPictures 2016. All Rights Reserved.	77

Chapter Seven: How to write a play

26–31	'The Music Box' directed by James Parrott © Hal Roach Studios 1932. All Rights Reserved.	78–80
32–33	'Star Wars: A New Hope' directed by George Lucas @ Lucasfilm/Disney 1977. All Rights Reserved.	81
34	'Happy Days', featuring Billie Whitelaw (Winnie), directed by Anthony Page © BBC 1973. All Rights Reserved.	82
35	'Raging Bull', featuring Robert DeNiro (Jake La Motta), directed by Martin Scorsese © United Artists. All Rights Reserved.	83
36	'Little Miss Sunshine' directed by Valerie Fanis and Jonathan Dayton © Big Beach/Bona Fide Productions. All Rights Reserved.	83
37	'Lucky Dog' (directed by James Macdonald, Royal Court, 2004). Photo reproduced with the kind permission of @ Tristram Kenton.	83
38	'Persona' directed by Ingmar Bergman. © SF Studios (Sweden) 1968. All Rights Reserved.	84
39	'2001: A Space Odyssey' directed by Stanley Kubrick © Kubrick Productions/Metro-Goldwyn-Meyer 1968. All Rights Reserved.	85
40	Bill Cubin and Nancy Wardell with the Sons of the Desert, 1988. Photo kindly reproduced with permission from @ Sheffield City Archives.	86

41	'The Live Ghost' directed by Charley Rogers © Hal Roach Studios 1934. All Rights Reserved.	87
42–54	'The Music Box' directed by James Parrott © Hal Roach Studios 1932. All Rights Reserved.	89–91
55	'The Lord of the Rings: The Return of the King' directed by Peter Jackson @ New Line Cinema 2003. All Rights Reserved.	92
56	A posed photograph of Anton Chekhov reading 'The Seagull' to the Moscow Art Theatre company, 1898. Public Domain image.	92
57	'The Weir' (directed by Ian Rickson, Royal Court, 1997). Photo reproduced with kind permission from @ Tristram Kenton.	95
58–59	'The Music Box' directed by James Parrott © Hal Roach Studios 1932. All Rights Reserved.	97, 99
60	'Funny Games' directed by Michael Haneke @ Wega Film 1997. All Rights Reserved.	100
61	'Persona' directed by Ingmar Bergman © SF Studios (Sweden) 1968. All Rights Reserved.	100
62–71	'The Music Box' directed by James Parrott © Hal Roach Studios 1932. All Rights Reserved.	101–102
72–73	'Psycho' directed by Alfred Hitchcock © Shamley Productions 1960. All Rights Reserved.	102
74	'The Music Box' directed by James Parrott © Hal Roach Studios 1932. All Rights Reserved.	104
75–77	'Do the Right Thing' directed by Spike Lee © 40 Acres and a Mule Filmworks 1989. All Rights Reserved.	105
78–81	'The Music Box' directed by James Parrott © Hal Roach Studios 1932. All Rights Reserved.	108

Chapter Eight: The multi-locational life and times of (insert name here) and other structures

82	Storyboard #1 © Leo Butler, 2024.	110
83	Storyboard #2 © Leo Butler, 2024.	111
84	Storyboard #3 © Leo Butler, 2024.	112
85	Storyboard #4 © Leo Butler, 2024.	112
86	Storyboard #5 © Leo Butler, 2024.	113
87	Storyboard #6 © Leo Butler, 2024.	114
88	Storyboard #7 © Leo Butler, 2024.	114
89	Storyboard #8 © Leo Butler, 2024.	115
90	Storyboard #9 © Leo Butler, 2024.	115

91	Storyboard #10 © Leo Butler, 2024.	116
92	Storyboard #11 © Leo Butler, 2024.	116
93	Storyboard #12 © Leo Butler, 2024.	117
94	Storyboard #13 © Leo Butler, 2024.	117

Chapter Nine: Ch-ch-ch-ch-changes!

95	Grass Hoppa (Rhydian and Dan Persad, Jim Smith and Leo Butler) playing on stage in the 1990s © Leo Butler, 2024.	121
96	'Alison! A Rock Opera' gig poster, 2013 © Leo Butler, 2024.	122
97	Rejection letter #1 @ Leo Butler, 2024.	124
98	Rejection letter #2 @ Leo Butler, 2024.	124
99	Rejection letter #3 @ Leo Butler, 2024.	125
100	Rejection letter #4 @ Leo Butler, 2024.	125
101	Rejection letter #5 @ Leo Butler, 2024.	125
102	Rejection letter #6 @ Leo Butler, 2024.	126
103	Rejection letter #7 @ Leo Butler, 2024.	126
104	Excerpt of Willy Russell correspondence #1 @ Leo Butler, 2024.	127
105	Portrait of Ola Animashawun, 2024. Photo reproduced with kind permission of @ Justine Themen.	131
106	Excerpt of Willy Russell correspondence #2 @ Leo Butler, 2024.	134

Chapter Eleven: The magic toybox

107	The cast of 'Decades' (directed by Eva Sampson, Ovalhouse, London, 2016) © Leo Butler, 2024.	147
108	Director Ramin Gray and the author in rehearsals for 'I'll Be the Devil' (2008). Photo by Ellie Kurttz. Reproduced with the kind permission of @ RSC.	147
109	The cast of 'Made of Stone' (directed by Deborah Bruce, Royal Court, 2000) © Leo Butler, 2024.	149
110	Robert Innes Hopkins' model-box for 'Redundant' (directed by Dominic Cooke, Royal Court, 2001). Image reproduced with kind permission from © Robert Innes-Hopkins.	151
111	'Made of Stone' rehearsal notes, 2000 © Leo Butler, 2024.	153
112	Leo Butler and 'All You Need is LSD's' co-directors Stephen Harper and Paul Hunter during rehearsal. Photo reproduced with kind permission of © Ben Wilkin at Benkin Photography.	154
113	Actors in rehearsal for 'All You Need is LSD'. Photo reproduced with kind permission of © Ben Wilkin at Benkin Photography.	154
114	'Boy' (directed by Sacha Wares, Almeida Theatre, 2016). Photo reproduced with kind permission from @ Tristram Kenton.	155

115	Email correspondence with Methuen Proofreader, 2016 © Leo Butler, 2024.	156
116	'Woyzeck' (directed by Roxana Silbert, Birmingham Rep, 2018). Photo reproduced with kind permission from © Graeme Braidwood Photography.	157
117	Leo Butler *Metro Live* Newspaper Clipping, 11 September 2001. Reproduced with kind permission of @ London Metro Newspaper.	158
118	'Redundant' in lights at the Royal Court Theatre, 2001. © Leo Butler, 2024.	159
119	'I'll Be the Devil' (directed by Ramin Gray, RSC/Kiln, 2008). Photo reproduced with the kind permission of @ Tristram Kenton.	162
120	Twitter feed on 'Boy' at the Almeida, 2016 @ Public Domain.	163
121	Clipping from *Evening Standard*, 13 September 2001. Reproduced with kind permission of @ Evening Standard Newspaper.	164
122	'Devotion' (directed by Liam Steel, Half Moon Theatre and Theatre Centre UK Schools Tour, 2002). Photo reproduced with the kind permission of @ Hugo Glendinning.	164

Chapter Twelve : What the f*ck is a dramaturg?

123	Leo Butler, Emilia Berger, Pierre Costa, Florencia Martinez, Begoña Ugalde, Camila Le-Bert, Nick Payne, Cláudia Jimenez, Andrés Kalawski, Elyse Dodgson, David Arancibia, Daniela Contreras, Bosco Alvarez, Gerado Oettinger and Juan Andrés Rivera. Santiago, Chile, 2012. Photo courtesy of © Elyse Dodgson archive.	173
124	Dominique Gumede, Nobantu Shabangu, Genna Gardini, Napo Masheane, Winsome Pinnock, Neil Coppen, Amy Jephta, Mongiwekaya, Mandi Vundla, Omphile Molusi, Leo Butler, Eliot Moleba, Tau Maserumule and Mpapa Simo Majola. Magliesberg, South Africa, 2014. Photo courtesy of © Elyse Dodgson Archive.	174
125	The author and Elyse Dodgson in Lima, Peru, October 2018. Image reproduced from the author's archive.	176

Chapter Thirteen: Now and then

126	The author pretending to write, 2025 © Leo Butler, 2024.	180

Every effort has been made to trace copyright holders and to obtain their permission for the use of copyright material. The publisher apologizes for any errors or omissions in the above list and would be grateful if notified of any corrections that should be incorporated in future reprints or editions of this book.

ABOUT THE AUTHOR

Leo Butler is an award-winning playwright. His plays include *Made of Stone* (Royal Court), *Redundant* (Royal Court), *Devotion* (Theatre Centre), *Lucky Dog* (Royal Court), *The Early Bird* (Queen's Theatre, Belfast), *I'll Be the Devil* (RSC), *Faces in the Crowd* (Royal Court), *Juicy Fruits* (Paines Plough), *Alison! A Rock Opera* (Royal Court/King's Head), *Sixty-Nine* (Natural Shocks), *Boy* (Almeida), *Decades* (Brit School/Bridge Theatre Co.), *Woyzeck* (Birmingham Rep), *Cinderella* (Theatre Royal Stratford East), *All You Need is LSD* (Birmingham Rep/Told By an Idiot), *Innocent Creatures* (NT Connections) and *Living* (Sheffield Playhouse).

He also writes and directs for screen, and, as a musician/composer, has produced albums and written songs for some of his own plays.

For more than twenty years, Leo Butler has run playwriting workshops and courses in the UK and across the world, in theatres and universities. He is Dramaturg for the Marlowe Theatre, Canterbury. For ten years, he was Writers Tutor at the Royal Court Theatre and helped nurture a new generation of playwriting talent.

ACKNOWLEDGEMENTS

There are many folks to whom I owe a huge debt of gratitude. Many are mentioned in this book. For one reason or another – never personal – many are not.

Firstly, I'd like to thank Anna Brewer at Bloomsbury for encouraging me to write this book in the first place, and for all her support and advice along the way. Likewise, Aanchal Vij and the rest of the Bloomsbury team. Enormous thanks to my agents Giles Smart and Lee Byrne. Also, Howard Gooding and Michael McCoy.

Other glaring omissions from the book who I'd like to thank, for lots of reasons, are Emil and Jude Marwa, Sarah Gilfillan, Omid and Sarah Armin, Georgia and Josie Armin, Dawn Persad, Dan Romer and Bronwen Morris, Gordon Sumner, Patrick Marmion, Tamsin and Matthew Dodgson. Everyone from the Sheffield Youth Theatre 1986–1990. Everyone from no. 6 and no. 18 Heverham Road. The Royal Court ushering team of 1999/2000. My colleagues at the Royal Court Young Writers' Programme: Clare McQuillan, Louise Alexander Stephens, Chloe Todd Fordham. My many support workers at the Young Writers' Programme, you know who you are. Deborah Shaw, Millie Brierley and all the team at the Marlowe Theatre, Canterbury.

So many directors I've had the pleasure to work with (alongside those mentioned in the book): Chris Sonnex, Rachel O'Riordan, Donnacadh O'Briain, George Perrin, Maria Aberg, Nadia Fall, Anthony Odey, Samantha Potter, John Tiffany, Gillian Wearing, Ned Bennett, Liam Steel, Abigail Graham, Tom Hughes, Lorne Campbell, Quinton Golding. And any others I've missed.

All my fellow playwrights who I've come to know as friends and associates.

All the actors who brought my words to life.

All the literary managers and dramaturgs.

The designers, stage managers, the casting directors, the crews. The ushers.

Anyone who ever bought a ticket. Or got a comp.

Every writer I've ever taught – and who have taught me so much – on courses and workshops in the UK and around the world.

All the theatres, universities and institutions that invited me to run a group or course. Or to write a play.

Lucy Morrison, for first planting the seed in my head. Brad Birch for his company, notes and advice. Marie Wood for her thoughts and advice. Hazel Stevens, Isabelle Defaut, Laura Woodward, Angela Terence, Paul McNally, Beth Astins, Charles Orrell, Mary Onions and Steve Waters for their thoughts and advice. Graham Saunders at Birmingham University for his thoughts and advice.

Matt, my sister-in-law Judith, and my niece, Clara Butler.

My parents.

Nazzi and Bea for everything.

NOTE

There are lots of excellent books that give advice on playwriting, but I thought the best, and most honest, way I could contribute would be to talk about my own personal experiences, journey and practices.

It also explores my process as a playwriting teacher, and, as such, the book is littered with practical exercises. I've tried to merge the personal with the practical, given that, in life, they bounce off each other anyway.

As much as it may be useful to anyone who is writing (or thinking of writing) a play, it should also be handy to anyone interested in playwriting or theatre making in general.

In fact, it may well be useful for anyone considering any type of dramatic writing.

If it's not useful at all, I hope you enjoy it anyway.

Just as French novelist, Stendhal, claimed '*it is the other arts that taught me the art of writing*', you'll find I've included lots of references to other art forms, especially movies, which have had a direct or indirect influence on my work.

1

The hidden play

In the summer of 1993, I left Sheffield to start a playwriting degree at Rose Bruford School of Speech and Drama in London. I'd just turned nineteen – slightly shy, acne-scarred, dressed in Stone Roses-inspired baggy jeans, and quietly confident that my precocious talents were about to set the world on fire. Three years earlier I'd stumbled out of state school with just the bare minimum of grades to enrol on a BTEC Performance Arts course at Norton College in Woodseats (a 50-minute bus ride on the No.76 from my parents' house in Pitsmoor). The BTEC was a two-year diploma and turned out to be one of the happiest times of my life, and once it was over – together with my best friend, Huss – it seemed that leaving home for Rose Bruford was the right thing to do; primarily because Gary Oldman had studied there, which was pretty cool, but also because 'leaving home' was the expected rule of thumb for children of '1960s baby boomers'.

The drama school was based in Sidcup, and it ran courses for actors, playwrights and directors, offering maintenance grants to students of all backgrounds (yep, this was way before the government abolished grants, and plunged an entire generation of youngsters into debt). Huss applied for the acting degree, but I couldn't make up my mind as I loved acting, directing *and* writing equally – basically, anything that allowed me to show off on stage. I remembered Mr Lockwood – my English teacher at secondary school – had told me that writing was a great career choice as you got to sit on your arse all day drinking tea, and so, as something of an arse/tea virtuoso, I plumped for the playwriting course. Luckily Huss and I were both offered places, and by the start of September we'd packed up, rattled down the M1 and found ourselves renting rooms in the suburbs of New Eltham. Having grown up in an area that is rich with diversity, it was a bit of a shock to be confronted with National Front graffiti on the bus stops and pub toilet walls.

Fascist scrawl aside, the first few weeks chugged along smoothly. The coursework was well-intentioned, with decent lecturers, and our classmates were – like most people who stumble into theatre – desperately uncool misfits who'd had a shit time at school. By the end of the first term, we'd established a tight group of mates (from such not-so-far-flung places as Stoke, Liverpool and Ilford) and we decided we'd find somewhere to live together as a group. My dad, Bill Butler, after years of graft at a commercial timber merchant – *'twenty years destroyin' the rainforest'* as he mordantly put it – took out a cheap-as-chips mortgage on a three-storey terrace in Plumstead; a working-class area, full of student accommodation and squats, which is just down the road from Woolwich Arsenal (where Stanley Kubrick filmed *Full Metal Jacket*).

Despite the house's considerable size, there weren't enough bedrooms for all of us, so E had to stuff his mattress into one of the corridors, house couple G & D had to pin a dividing curtain between their bedroom and the living room, while DM (who refused to wear shoes) was quite happy bedding down in the garden shed. The large attic room was claimed by my older brother, Matt, who had just finished a Creative Writing MA at Bretton Hall and was hoping to find some peace and quiet to focus on his short-story writing. Unfortunately, peace and quiet were non-existent at 18 Heverham Road, as it rapidly descended into a squalid halfway house of drug-addled students, small-time dealers and dole-queue mystics. It's unsurprising that Matt eventually moved out, or that so many of us ended up quitting (or getting kicked out of) drama school, as our commitment to partying far outweighed our commitment to work. We rapidly earned a reputation as 'naughty boys', or 'space cadets' or 'nobhead losers' (not necessarily in that order), and as far as academia was concerned, the writing – no pun intended – was clearly on the wall.

This was all a very long time before I had my first play produced, and despite my initial desire to 'set the world on fire', being suddenly out of my comfort zone and drowned out by a cacophony of wildly competing egos, my ambitions were put on hold. By the end of the second term, I admit I was putting in the bare minimum of effort. Consider this report from my tutor . . .

> **FILE:** I don't wish to go on about it, but have another look at the brief for the project. There is still a lot that you don't seem to have done. Your research material does not show an enormous advance upon the earlier portfolio. There is not a great deal on your conversations with teachers, observations of the kids' home and outside environment. On which kids have you based your characters? What changes have you made, and why? Are they fictions? (You were writing such scenes for Phil Young's class at the start of the term.) You have set it in Sheffield, for heaven's sake! Not where you have apparently been doing your research. (You have also not included your biogs or monologues.)

Or this . . .

> I beg of you . . . get another typewriter from somewhere or at the very least buy another ribbon. If it can't be read it can't be judged and from next year the marking will have to get serious and all this will count against you which seems silly when it's something you can do something about.

And finally . . .

> Rethink what is the main objective of the project. And you will surely see that you haven't really done it. Cast your mind back to my criticisms of your working process last term. You are still only marginally engaged with you chosen course.
> OVERALL MARK: A pass, but with concerns

In my defence, the 'chosen course' didn't offer much advice on the craft of playwriting, and, regardless of my dreadful grades, when we did get the chance to present our work in front of an audience, my own plays – daft comedies with titles such as *Buds of Truth* and *Giddy Little Kippers* – always went down a treat. Also, somewhat scandalously, several of our tutors left their posts (or were kicked out) in protest of the dodgy principal and his deliberate mismanagement of the school budget. But, as tempted as I am to rewrite the narrative, it's a bit of stretch to justify my laxness on political outrage or solidarity with the staff. In truth, I was lazy and entitled, and far too stoned. And this is where the story begins.

I'd been regularly smoking weed since I was about 16, but now I was deliberately overdoing it. Soon after we moved to Plumstead, we'd got our hands on a ridiculously strong batch of synthetic 'skunk' weed, which smelt and smoked great, seemed to be in never-ending supply, and which gradually took over our lives. I remember now, with some embarrassment, how I carried a large wooden bong in my rucksack to smoke between lessons or during breaks, as I couldn't bear a moment away from the stuff. We even attempted to graffiti the train station platform signs from 'Plumstead' to 'Skunk-stead', until we realized that it really wasn't worth getting arrested for, and, besides, we were far too spaced out to apply ourselves to anything beyond Scorsese and Kurosawa movies on the portable telly at home.

But then I started hearing a voice in my head. It came out of nowhere, sudden, and unexpectedly, and I nosedived into a kind of paranoid psychosis. The voice was sharp as butcher's knives, and utterly terrifying; I was convinced it was a demon, that I was possessed. I kept it secret from everybody, afraid that my friends would think I'd gone crazy and have me sectioned, which hadn't been part of the plan. As I went about my days, the 'demon' spouted horrific platitudes and prophecies about me, my friends and my family – its every word validated because it presided in a more enlightened dimension, way beyond the limitations of earthly matter, and it knew me better than I knew myself. As the weeks went on, the voice became my every second thought, my confidante and tutor. Death was its mantra, and it was quick to interpret the smallest interactions as proof of someone's evil intent, or to draw evil intent out of me. We'd be playing cards or watching a film, and all the time I'd be privately, frantically imploring the voice to 'be quiet', or 'shut the fuck up', begging it to leave me alone. But this only made it worse, egging the demon on.

Like most mash heads who are having their lives ruined by weed, I categorically refused to blame the weed, recklessly caning spliffs from the moment I woke up, all through the day, right up until the moment I passed out in bed. Inevitably, I was sleeping a lot more as being unconscious on my grotty single bed was the only guarantee of peace.

Then, sometime in the spring – as luck would have it – a two-litre jar of magic-mushroom honey arrived from Penzance. I'd taken acid in Sheffield many times before, but never mushrooms, and now we had a flagon of the stuff. Our supplier told us that we only needed half a teaspoon each and we'd be tripping our tits off for hours, so – somewhat inevitably – we necked a couple of teaspoons each and headed up to Plumstead Woods as the sun was coming down.

The mushrooms were strong, and the woods became outrageously alive – like something out of Tolkien or pagan myth. Trees were breathing, squirrels were squirrelling and the birds revealed themselves inexorably connected to an infinite cosmos – one which was also present on the swirling, geometric patterns on our clammy hands. A lot of new-age guff was spoken (in between fits of gasps and giggles), but, thankfully, the demon voice had been silenced. For the first time in ages, I was having a great time with my compadres, chattering and joking, getting lost along the newly transformed footpaths of the urban green space.

But then it went dark, in more ways than one. Dusk had passed, I'd somehow taken a wrong turn, and now I was lost and alone. *Where was everyone?* I scramble to a plateau, look across the horizon – beyond Woolwich Dockyard to the distant flashing lights of Canary Wharf – and there's a thunderstorm approaching. The fear sets in, everything feels *very bad*. Although I don't hear the voice, I suddenly feel its *presence* rising inside and around me. My whole body seizes up. I'm trying to avoid the storm at all costs, tramping away from the plateau, moving deeper into the woods, keeping my head down. But as I look down at the ground, I see a dark red shadow forming around me. The storm is at its peak, I'm scared, my legs feel like maracas. I suddenly lose control and stumble forward, dropping to my knees by a pale, branchless tree, and what happens next changes everything.

Something explodes inside me. The fear, and the burden of keeping that fear secret, cannot be contained any longer. Slumped at the foot of the tree, with the storm overhead, I jerk my head upwards and let out an ear-splitting scream. And the demon jumps out of my mouth.

I can still picture it now. It's tall and thin – naked, sickly pink, translucent, with elongated limbs and a large, hairless, pin-shaped head. I don't see its face – *if it did have a face* – because, as soon as its feet hit the ground, the demon sprints away through the trees, like a prisoner escaped. Had the storm passed? I don't remember. All I remember is the *thud thud thud* of its feet running across the dirt and into the dark

Was it a hallucination? Those kinds of hallucinations are, to the best of my knowledge, usually restricted to petrol sniffing or super-strong psychedelics like ayahuasca. Probably just my imagination fired by psilocybin and anxiety, right? Does it even matter? Probably not. The point is, I never heard that voice again.

Moments after the demon legged it away, I looked up and I was surrounded by my pals. 'What the fuckin' hell was that?' went the collective mantra. Were they referring to the scream or the demon? Who cares. The point is, they helped me off the ground and we found a secluded spot to build a fire where we spent the rest of the night talking shit and singing the wrong words to Beatles songs. And I never heard that voice again.

Twelve years later, in 2006 – and a lifetime away from that thunderstorm – I was commissioned to write a new play for the Royal Shakespeare Company. The play was called *I'll Be the Devil* and the opening scene begins like this . . .

> **Dermot** I saw the Devil last night, Ellen. He rode up out the Shannon on his horse. A great black Barbary she was, and him all burning red under his cloak. He asks me to sign his covenant with his claws pulled tight upon me throat. A dozen yellow eyes he has, a tongue the length of your arm. 'Not so long as I have breath in me head,' I says, 'Not so long as I can still draw blood. Get back under the earth,' I cry, 'and you take your stinking nag along with you!' Well, he didn't like that now, did he?
>
> **Ellen** No.
>
> **Dermot** He didn't like that.
>
> **Ellen** He didn't like that, no.
>
> **Dermot** Him all fallen from Heaven and I no better than ink without the pot, let alone the hand that drives it. Oh, the noise he made, Ellen. I swear he would've shook the Lord from off his cross had he sense enough to mark it, had I not been Saint of this rock. Had I not such a wealth of angels in me breast and not seen off his poison already.

Of all the plays I've written, *I'll Be the Devil* is one of my favourites. Inspired by *The Tempest*, it's a violent exploration of English occupation in Ireland during the eighteenth century – a sort of psychotic lovechild of *Barry Lyndon* [Kubrick, 1975] and *The Texas Chainsaw Massacre* [Hooper, 1974]. One of the play's harshest critics – of which there were many – described watching the production, brilliantly directed by Ramin Gray, as 'like being held hostage by a violent lunatic', which, ironically, was the effect I was going for. Although a historical piece, *I'll Be the Devil* is, in part, a response to the illegal invasion and occupation of Iraq, which was in full swing at the time of writing – and which, from my point of view, was best served by a play that deliberately caused distress or made you feel sick. The savage Tavern scene at the heart of the play, for example, borrowed heavily from first-hand accounts of torture at Guantanamo Bay.

But it is also clearly about what happened to me in 1994 – the demonic voice that occupied my head and colonized my thoughts, the depression and desperation, and the liberating force of the hallucination in the woods. That's the hidden play. You can't see it, nobody (including the director, cast or audience) needs to know anything about it, but the experience and memory of those events in the woods is right there in the bowels of the text. As the dialogue above demonstrates, elements of my own experience found literal expression in the Caliban-esque character of Dermot; indeed, later in the play, his father, the permanently rattled Lieutenant Coyle, accuses him of eating magic mushrooms. Having been brutalized and left to rot in a standing stock by Coyle and the other soldiers, Dermot deliberately conjures the devilish encounter as a means of restoring some kind of spiritual faith. He is desperate for Ellen, his little sister, to say she saw the Devil too, or at least *pretend* she saw it – as one person's faith is only speculative, but a shared faith (rather like the contract between actors and audience) becomes flesh. Though he may be powerless against the military occupation, by enlisting Ellen into his wild fantasy, he can, at the very least, defeat an imagined evil and declare himself '*Saint of this rock*' as he stands on the precipice of death. Thankfully I didn't have my eyes gouged out by soldiers, but I do believe the drugs triggered some deeper, buried trauma and, consequently, my imagination gave this trauma the voice and image of a demon. Like Dermot, once I'd conjured it, I was able to spit it out and move on with my life.

Although it seems such a long time ago now – another lifetime – that confused nineteen-year-old kid is only ever a few feet behind me, haunting my footsteps. As filmmaker Chris Marker puts it '*time heals everything but the wound*', and that is why I used (consciously or not) elements of *I'll Be the Devil* to wrestle with that perplexing chapter of my life. It wasn't my intention – I thought I was just having a crack at adapting *The Tempest* – but writing a play (or a poem or a song) is a messy and unpredictable process, and the personal stuff just spilled onto the page like that.

I think it was Dennis Kelly or Simon Stephens who said that whatever play you're going to write next it's already hidden deep inside you and you're just waiting for the right form or structure to give it life. Brilliantly personal plays, such as Ayub Kahn-Din's *East is East* [Birmingham Rep, 1996], Sarah Kane's *4.48 Psychosis* [Royal Court, 1999] or Eugene O'Neill's *Long Day's Journey into Night* [Broadway, 1956] are decidedly *unhidden* works, which probably didn't require much coaxing from their authors. But I would argue that every single play – including juke-box musicals, kid's shows, and the eclectic work of Kelly and Stephens – contains some personal, hidden play drawn from the writer's private life. The hidden play needn't have a profound meaning, or be a literal memory, it may simply be a feeling or a passion, a longing, or a political conviction, and – God forbid – it might even be joyful or optimistic. My debut play *Made of Stone* [Royal Court, 2000] was a nostalgic love letter to Sheffield, and, more recently, when (alongside composer Robert Hyman) I wrote the pantomime *Cinderella*

[2022] for Stratford East, the hidden play gradually revealed itself as an outpouring of love for my wife and teenage daughter. I've also written plays – like the surreal short comedy *Juicy Fruits* [Paines Plough, 2011], or my adaptation of Buchner's *Woyzeck* [Birmingham Rep, 2018], which I initially believed had nothing to do with my own life, only to realize – usually during previews – that, lo and behold, I'd been up to my old tricks, secretly writing about myself all along.

The prolific playwright Edward Bond (whose early works *Saved* [1965] and *Early Morning* [1968] were, for my generation, no less than totemic) claimed that *'an individual only exists through society; outside society he is a monster. To say that a writer writes about "himself" is as meaningless as to say there could be an expression without its language'*. I respect Bond enormously and suspect his provocation might be a hidden critique of theatre's focus on 'identity politics' in place of, say, the politics of capitalism or neoliberalism. That is only an assumption, of course, and, taken at face value, I don't think anyone would argue with Bond's assertion that our 'individuality' or 'personality' cannot be separated from the times we are living in. Politics, economics and a society's transient values are as fundamental to our psychological development as our DNA, but surely that shouldn't discourage the writer from plundering their subjective life experiences as if – without broader context – they were meaningless? It is always useful (at some point in the writing or redrafting process) to consider the character's relationship to the culture they're living in, and to explore how that co-dependent relationship informs their psychological choices. The plays of Tennessee Williams and Debbie Tucker Green are, for instance, populated with characters whose private troubles are indicative, or reflective, of a collective social injustice; but, at the same time, they are no doubt also driven by the authors' fantasies and dreams.

Over the past two decades I have read hundreds of plays by first-time playwrights. Some of these plays were a complete mess to begin with – shambolically structured, narratively incoherent, with dialogue marred by weak exposition. None of that mattered, however, because they were heartfelt, impossible to put down; irresistible vomit on the page that clearly *meant* something to the writer. Inevitably – after a period of collaboration and redrafting – these same spewings were programmed, published, and (justifiably) became critical and commercial hits. A successful play is less about how professional it looks on the page, or how it adheres to the so-called rules of dramatic action, but more about the stuff in the drains, the gaps between the lines, the hidden play. I always tell my students that if you're going to put yourself through the hours of solitude and back-breaking graft that's required to finish a script, then you better make sure your guts are in it.

'Never try and second-guess what a theatre wants,' I tell them. 'Just write the play you want to see. It can be dark and brutal, or it can be warm and fluffy. You don't have to be Caryl Churchill and reinvent the wheel. If it *resonates with you on some level, and you allow yourself to make mistakes along the way, then you might find you have a decent first draft in your hands.'*

Even as I write this, I've just returned from teaching an 'Introduction to Playwriting' group at the Marlowe Theatre in Canterbury. As part of the session, I introduced them to George Orwell's essay *Why I Write* [1946], in which he outlines the four reasons why he believes most writers write. One of his reasons is . . .

Sheer egoism. Desire to seem clever, to be talked about, to be remembered after death, to get your own back on grown-ups who snubbed you in childhood, etc., etc. It is humbug to pretend this is not a motive, and a strong one. . . . Serious writers, I should say, are on the whole more vain and self-centred than journalists, though less interested in money.

After reading the essay, I challenge the group to come up with their own list of reasons to add to Orwell's list. One of the writers, Lizzie, offers the phrasal verb 'to puzzle through' – which, I think, is brilliantly accurate. There are many reasons for writing a new play, and no writer should ever feel pressured to justify their idea into existence. But even when there's a clear plan of action – a detailed plotline and a set of complex characters with painstakingly prepared backstories – something is always just around the corner to fuck it all up. As you put your pen to paper, characters will suddenly misbehave, revealing secrets you knew nothing about. Settings will fall apart, you'll get stuck on page fifteen for weeks, bombs (metaphorical and literal) will detonate at the most inappropriate moments, and you might even find yourself writing about a demon in the woods when you were nineteen years old. That's your subconscious at work – the hidden play – so make it your ally and puzzle through. Put simply, if every person on the planet were simultaneously commissioned to adapt *The Tempest,* it may turn out to be an excruciatingly long night at the theatre, but – if we're true to our instincts – I'd lay money on each version being utterly unique.

2

Getting started

Here is a page from the notebook I sometimes use when helping playwriting students generate ideas for new plays.

IMAGE 1 *Butler's teaching notebook* © Leo Butler, 2024.

It may appear like the diary of a lunatic, but if you look a little closer you'll see a list of 111 questions (and some provocations) that I've amended and rewritten over fifteen years or so. Although it's a struggle to decipher, I'm very fond of this sheet of A4 paper – its history and corrections, its coffee stains and smudges of cigarette ash. If you flick to the Appendix, you'll find I've transcribed them for you.

The idea is to answer each question as honestly as you can, then take one or two of your answers and use them as raw material for a scene or speech. Some of the questions are easy, such as *'Describe a dream you've had recently'* or *'Who or what makes you laugh?'* – and some are more difficult, such as *'What do people say about you behind your back?'* or *'What's the best sex you've ever had?'*. No one's holding a gun to your head, so it's up to you what you choose to ignore, but sometimes what you ignore might prove to be the most useful.

As you work your way through the sludge, you might find yourself dredging up uncomfortable memories or you might remember something joyful or tender. It's creative therapy at its most basic. It may not be for everyone, but I know it's helped many writers find the starting point of a play or confirm some of the ideas they're already thinking about, or sometimes help them locate the 'hidden play'.

Once you've finished answering the questions, you'll probably find one or more of the memories (or triggered emotions) have stayed with you.

Here are five suggestions of how to turn those memories into a piece of dramatic writing.

1) **Freestyle.** Write without thought or censorship for a minimum of half an hour. Don't pause, don't consider, don't stop for breath. It's harder than you think. Once you've finished, read over what you've done. Most of it will be rubbish, but I guarantee you'll find at least one line – or word even – that you'll be pleased with, and can perhaps use as a line of dialogue or include somewhere in a future scene.

2) **Write a speech or monologue as yourself.** Think about the memory and write it down verbatim as it happened – in the past or present tense – either as a speech or a scene of dialogue. You might, for instance, imagine you're recounting the memory to a friend, a family member or a stranger. Sometimes (not always) describing the event (to a character or audience) in the present tense – as if it's happening *right now* – is more dramatic and entertaining. The dialogue might help you find a character's voice, their rhythms of speech or dialect. Similarly, you may use the scene as a backstory, to discover the history of your characters – and, who knows, it may help you find the story of the play itself.

3) **Write a speech or monologue as a fictional character.** Think about the memory and change one aspect of yourself – such as your age,

gender or the period of history when it occurred. Divorce the experience from your own. For example, I take this private memory from when I was a thirty-year-old man, and I adapt it into the experience of a ten-year-old girl during the French Revolution, or to a boxing club in 1950s Leeds. Think about <u>who your character is talking to</u>, and – this is very important – WHY they might be recounting the memory. Is the second character connected to the memory? Is it painful for them to tell the story, or is it enjoyable or cathartic? What does your character GAIN from telling the story? How do they use the memory or emotion as AMMUNITION to do or to get something from the other person?

4) **Write an autobiographical scene.** As with the second exercise, simply recreate the memory on the page, using the real names and (as far as you remember) the things that were said at the time. When you've finished, you might find you've got a knockout scene to build a play around, and you can always change the names later.

5) **Write a fictional scene.** Take the memory and change one fundamental thing. Alter the names or ages or genders of the characters. Relocate the event to a different place and time. Give the scene a physical activity to hang the dialogue around, such as a birthday party or homecoming or celebration. Disrupt the ritual with the problem. Why is it happening now? What's brought these characters together? What do they feel or think about each other? What needs to be *done*? How difficult will things get? How will the scene end? Will things be resolved or get worse?

There have been times when students have found the Q & A emotionally gruelling, and I don't want to upset or offend anyone for the sake of a writing exercise ... but, then again, if you can't be honest with yourself, how do you expect to be honest with your audience? Doesn't it make sense for dramatists – such as songwriters or poets – to excavate private aspects of their own lives (or to confront uncomfortable truths about the wider world) if we're to have vital theatre?

One of the most alarming features of recent years is how many first-time playwrights are anxious of offending the audience if they dare to explore polarizing themes or create unsympathetic characters. It's as though creating characters who don't share the same beliefs, or values, as us – whoever 'us' are meant to be – were some sort of thought crime. Several students have told me that if they were to write a character such as Shakespeare's Iago, or pen a play such as Sarah Kane's *Blasted* [Royal Court, 1995], they would be ostracized or 'cancelled' by their peers. Most intelligent audiences can, of course, distinguish between the author and their characters, but it is a genuine fear for some of these talented young writers, and I suspect it's partly a symptom of the social media revolution, with its penchant for mob rule.

I'm no theatre snob. I love watching shows such as Cole Porter's *Anything Goes* [1934] or Disney's *Frozen* [2017], but I also enjoy being challenged by more 'serious-minded' dramas of, say, Jon Fosse or Florian Zeller. A playwright, like anyone, doesn't have to be 'right' all the time. Whether you write a bat-shit-crazy musical such as Andrew Lloyd Webber's *Cats* [1981] or a bat-shit-crazy polemic such as Peter Handke's *Offending the Audience* [1966], the best any artist can do is ignore public taste and write for an audience of one. If playwrights avoid tackling difficult issues or refuse to explore darker or contradictory aspects of human nature, then aren't they diluting their creative potential and denying the audience a memorable experience?

In Act 2 Scene 3 of *Hamlet*, Shakespeare's eponymous hero claims that the purpose of playing is *'to hold as 'twere the mirror up to nature: to show virtue her feature, scorn her own image, and the very age and body of the time his form and pressure.'*

If theatre – like most art forms – is a means of holding a mirror up to our true nature, then start by holding the mirror up to yourself.

3

I know my place!

I grew up in Pitsmoor, which is a five-minute bus ride out of Sheffield City Centre – past the Wicker Arches, up Spital Hill and to the top of Burngreave Road, where my parents still live. With its rows of back-to-back terraces and council houses, Pitsmoor is one of the poorest areas of the city and, although being largely comprised of ordinary families quietly getting on with their lives, it has a bad reputation for crime and gang violence. For instance, if you visited the Catherine Arms at the top of Catherine Street anytime during the 80s and 90s, you'd find scores of dealers – mainly Rastas – blatantly selling ganja out of their BMWs. The undercover cops, parked metres away, were more interested in handouts or hand jobs from prostitutes than dealing with the hassle of a few minor 'intent to supply' charges, so – being a bit of a free-for-all – you'd head up Catherine Street to buy a £5 bag of weed. By the time you reach the pub, you're besieged by a crowd of dealers, arguing between themselves, trying every trick in the book to convince you to make the deal 'with me, not that other bumberseed'. For a spotty white teenager like me, it was 50/50 if you'd get scammed or not, and it wasn't uncommon to go home and find you'd been sold a bag of sawdust, or a lump of dogshit.

'Donkeymans' – the 'Blues' club on Rock Street – just two minutes from my house – was a much more reliable source. It wasn't a club as such, just someone's terraced house that had been turned into a kind of speakeasy. You'd tentatively knock on the back door and some surly looking bloke would let you though into the smoke-filled living room where there was a makeshift bar and a sound system playing reggae or lover's rock. If you wanted your £5 bag of weed, you'd head upstairs where a bunch of guys were playing poker or dominoes in one of the bedrooms. A hanger on would quickly ask you what you were after, money was exchanged and a couple of minutes later you'd be handed a decent bit of rocky to smoke downstairs while you had a self-conscious boogie or played a game of pool. All very civilized, and – being years before the likes of crack and heroin obliterated the area – there was usually a friendly atmosphere.

That's not to say that harder drugs weren't available, or that there weren't shootings or stabbings, because there were (and still are), with some of the culprits achieving a kind of mythological status dependent on their level of violence or choice of weapon. In my teenage years, I got to know some of these gangsters, either at 'Donkeymans' or acid-house parties, with some becoming friends or associates. During one particularly ill-judged chapter of our lives, me and my friend Huss – totally broke and inspired by Ray Liotta in *Goodfellas* [Scorsese, 1990] – convinced a drug supplier we knew to give us an ounce of speed and a sheet of acid tabs to sell. We quickly became 'the worst drug dealers in the world' when – being too lazy to sell it – we just necked the lot ourselves. Our supplier wasn't too happy, and we nearly got our legs broken by his cohort when they tracked us down in a pub in Crookes demanding the money we owed. But, although many of these guys were professional psychopaths – like the infamous Knowles Brothers or members of the BBC (Blades Business Crew) – there were also just as many small-time dealers who kept their heads low and their businesses steady; family men who took pride in the quality of the cannabis they were selling, and who sold it as a means of putting food on the table.

It's understandable that all the drugs, burglaries, muggings and prostitution would make outsiders feel intimidated, but, for those of us who lived (or still live) in Pitsmoor, there was also a genuine sense of community and people would look out for each other. I remember walking home from a nightclub in the early hours of the morning when I was about sixteen, and halfway up Spital Hill, a hooded crackhead throws me into a shop doorway, forcing me to empty my pockets, but I've got nothing on me except a bus pass and a fifty pence piece. He's irritated, waving around his crack pipe, spitting feathers and making threats, until he realizes I live on Burngreave Road and apologizes with a fist bump, saying 'oh, you're from round here? Safe man, safe!'.

Since the 1940s, Pitsmoor has been home to families from the West Indies, Nigeria, Pakistan, India, Somalia, Iran, Yemen, Eritrea, Sudan and, more recently, Eastern Europe. Decades of concentrated migration has made it an incredibly diverse area, and, rightly or wrongly – as kids growing up in the 70s and 80s – it seemed like we were all in the same economic soup. When I was three or four, my best friend Marcus lived two doors down from us and I was always round there, messing about, listening to records and playing pranks on his sisters. One day, his Jamaican-born mum pulled me aside and, somewhat aggressively, asked '*Don't you have any white friends to play with?*'. I was shocked that she didn't want us to be friends, but, after replying with a mumbled '*um, I'm not sure*', me and Marcus carried on playing anyway.

Although there were barely any skinheads or National Front groups in Pitsmoor – which is lucky for them as they would've had their heads kicked in – anyone who wasn't white would face daily aggression from the police, alongside slurs such as 'P*ki' and 'w*g' in the schoolyard. There were also varying degrees of animosity, or feigned tolerance, between West Indian and African families, as much as between Muslims and Hindus. In recent years, there's been increasing hostility between Romany and Pakistani families, which is inevitable when people from such polarized lifestyles are sandwiched together in an area that's taken such a beating. Tory austerity and a cost of living crisis have chipped away at much of the old community spirit. The churches and mosques remain, but it's sad to see so many boarded-up shops and pubs, or to see the parks untended and empty. For an area that didn't get much investment to start with, it's virtually non-existent now. Although there's less racism in the schoolyard (and more people like Marcus represented on TV), the lack of resources for young people have resulted in an increase of addiction and gang-related crime. Comparatively, back in the late 70s and 1980s, despite being in the throes of Thatcherism and her dismantling of local industry, there were a lot more community centres and play groups for us kids.

In the same way that Conor McPherson or Judy Upton might set their plays in, respectively, Dublin or Shoreham-by-Sea, I've always returned to Pitsmoor – its geography and people – as inspiration for my work. The excellent director Ian Rickson – who kickstarted my career by programming *Made of Stone* as part of the Royal Court's Young Writers Festival – once suggested I have a 'chemical connection' to Sheffield, going on to advise me to 'keep excavating that connection'. Mirroring Ian, I always encourage playwriting students to embrace the landscape of their youth, or wherever it is they call 'home', particularly when writing their debut plays. Even if you eschew naturalistic drama for something more surreal or expressionistic – there'll be something in the make-up of your community or the psychological complexities of the people you grew up with (whether that's in Glasgow or Harare or Lima) that – almost by default – bleeds into your work, lending it a degree of sincerity.

In my early twenties I'd been writing a bunch of imaginative, but wholly disingenuous, plays with titles such as *The End of the World Extravaganza* and *Dissection of a Rapist*, which, looking back, were formally ambitious, but God-awful in every other respect. It was only when I stopped trying to reinvent the wheel, and write honestly about home, and the kind of people I grew up with – including their accents and rhythms – that my line-by-line writing improved and people such as Ian Rickson started taking notice.

In Scene Two of my debut play *Made of Stone,* we meet two old school friends, Miles and Errol, who are playing pool at a pub and catching up with . .

Miles   Honest to God, Errol, yer wunt believe it.

Errol   Serious?

Miles   Fuckin' fanny everywhere.

Errol   What, down University like?

Miles   Union n'that. By the interchange.

Errol   Mandela Centre.

Miles That's the one. Proper shit'ole init? Went down there Friday, just f'buzz like. Me n'Stevie Cyclops, yeah? You know Cyclops init? Used to 'ang about Abbeyfield on 'is bike? Twitchy little fucker with the lazy eye.

Errol Right.

Miles Fuckin' works in WHSmiths now.

Errol No.

Miles See 'im all the time. Fuckin' psycho on the sly. Used to be a gas sniffer n'that.

Errol You went this student bar?

Miles Just blagged it init? Said we were art students.

It may not have the wow factor of *The Cherry Orchard* [Chekhov, 1903] or *Waiting for Godot* [Beckett, 1953], but it's a decent introduction to Miles and Errol, whose questionable friendship makes up a large chunk of the play. Its (phonetically precise) dialogue and specificity of place give it a degree of authenticity that was lacking in my previous efforts. The '*Interchange*', and the '*Mandela Centre*' were real places, and the characters – including off-stage Stevie Cyclops – were drawn from a bundle of different people I knew growing up. '*Used to be a gas sniffer n'that*' is a throwaway line, but it alludes to something very real that happened to a close school friend of mine. '*Used to hang about Abbeyfield on 'is bike*', meanwhile, has a direct personal connection as Abbeyfield Park was the view outside my bedroom window when I was growing up. Here it is in a photo (below) taken some time in the 80s.

IMAGE 2 *View of Abbeyfield Park from author's bedroom window c.1982. Photo courtesy of author's archive.*

Abbeyfield is not only the place where *'twitchy little fucker'* Stevie Cyclops rode his bike, but it's also where middle-aged Eddie disappears with Lucky the family dog in my 2004 marriage play *Lucky Dog*.

Eddie   Took 'er round park.

Sue   Oh.

Eddie   Round park f'ten minutes.

Sue   Guessed as much.

Eddie   Down Crabtree Pond. Up through woods. Over heliport n'back

Sue   You work that dog too hard.

'Crabtree Pond', the *'Woods'* and the *'Heliport'* are also real locations, and, as with Abbeyfield, make frequent appearances (whether name checked or not) in my plays. Despite Pitsmoor's rough exterior, it's also peppered with green spaces which, as a kid, were the backdrop for countless adventures and acts of stupidity, and later, way into adulthood, the location for more sedate moments of reflection.

At the time of writing this book, I've been living in London for more than three decades, way beyond the years I spent in Pitsmoor, but I've always been drawn to areas that are geographically (and demographically) similar. South East London, in particular (where I've lived for the past eighteen years) shares the same rich diversity, has bundles of parks and woods, and – as in my youth – you have to take a bus or train to 'go into town'. I'm not sure if that's coincidence, or whether it's part of the same behavioural pattern that keeps me returning to Pitsmoor in my work. Perhaps we're all, through different means, trying to recreate aspects of our youth, scratching at scabs, trying to make sense of who we are and what we're supposed to be.

Marcus and his sisters moved away – I can't remember where – but I quickly made a new best friend, Martin Murray (or 'Martin Murray-mints' as I called him), who shared my ridiculous sense of humour, and who lived in the block of flats at the bottom of our road. I hadn't started primary school, so I must've only been five or six, but I loved knocking about those flats, even if I had to sneak around to get there. I remember we made our way down there one summer's afternoon, when Matt – forced to adopt the role of 'responsible, older brother' – was instructed to keep an eye on us in the park while our parents were at work. Matt and I (pictured below) rarely had a serious fight or argument, but our three-year age gap was as deep a chasm as our interests – with Matt being far more interested in football or cricket than my daft role-playing games – and we'd usually leap at the first opportunity to play with our own friends.

IMAGE 3 *From left to right: Leo and Matthew Butler c.1980. Reproduced from the author's archive.*

This day was no exception. Matt quickly heads up to the top field to play headers and volleys with Nathan Utter and Stephen Harrison, leaving me and Martin Murray to leg it out the back gates, disappear down the road and into the flats where we could get into trouble in peace. We throw stones at the local skinhead who chases us through the concrete stairwells, finally dragging us out from under a parked van to give us a beating. We cajole a couple of the local girls to hang out in the lifts, hammering at the buttons until we're stuck between floors so we can play 'show you mine, show me yours'. I even manage to get a first girlfriend – Nicola – for about half an hour, which, despite going no further than holding hands on the waste ground behind the back of Fox Hill, was mind-blowing for a six-year-old boy who was still using a comfort blanket to get to sleep. Of course, neither me or Nicola had the foggiest what we were doing, except enjoying the thrill of being naughty – curious of being curious – and it wasn't until Madonna's arrival on *Top of the Pops,* a couple of years later, that it starts to dawn on me what all this boy-girl stuff is about.

It gets dark, and I return home to discover that poor Matt's got into terrible trouble for keeping his eye off me like that. My mum's furious, dragging me upstairs where – unmoved by my fitful tears and gargled apologies – I'm laid across her knee and given a proper spanking. Although I was forbidden to hang out with Martin for a while, I quickly realize that I should refine my misbehaviours if I'm going to avoid a sore bum again. Fortunately, she never spanked us again, or – at least – only when we deserved it, such as when Matt snapped the arms off my precious Incredible Hulk toy and, to get my revenge, I yanked one of the metal bars off his table football set (which I still feel guilty about).

For the most part, our parents gave us free reign to occupy ourselves however we pleased. Despite some dodgy encounters, we were pretty good at spotting trouble – whether it was the glue sniffer in Roe Woods, or the weirdo couple (with their half-naked, feral children) who lived on Christ Church Road. And there was always a large, excitable group of us – down the flats or kicking about in the park's playground; its dull-metal bars and thick wooden crossbeams a breeding ground for many a graze or broken bone. I remember once foregoing the metal stairs that took you to the top of the slide, choosing to clamber up the chute instead. As I reached the top, Matt came hurtling down feet-first and knocked me over the edge. Time slowed down as I dropped, reaching for the bars, cracking my head open on the concrete below, blood gushing everywhere. I can still picture Matt carrying me home like a babe-in-arms, bursting into the kitchen where our parents are settling down for Sunday lunch, then being rushed to the hospital in the backseat of our dad's Vauxhall Astra. Another time, Matt was himself rushed to the Northern General after he bashed his head on the thick wooden swing that had been flung at him by someone for a laugh. Unlike my minor graze, he had to have actual stitches, which everyone thought was dead impressive and a surefire way to 'pull birds' – even though 'pulling birds' wasn't exactly a priority. Back then, we were far more interested in riding our BMX bikes to the Wicker Arches, where we'd scale the walls to explore the tracks and deserted stationhouses of the Great Central Railway. Or sometimes we'd cycle down to Attercliffe, breaking into the disused steel factories to look for ghosts, and when it rained we'd stay home and watch *The New Shmoo* or *Bagpuss* on TV. Often we'd just muck about in our overgrown backyard, which we shared with our immediate neighbours.

Pitsmoor had been heavily bombed during World War Two, and at the far end of our backyard was an old dark tunnel that had served as an air-raid shelter. It was pitch-black and full of cobwebs, the perfect place to hide out and scare each other with stories of zombies or radioactive dust. The cold war was reaching crunch point at that time, and it's easy to forget how terrifying it all was. Not only were there genuine predictions of World War Three, but there was also Barry Hynes's devastating docu-drama *Threads*, which aired on BBC in 1984.

Threads imagined the nightmarish fallout of a nuclear bomb that's been dropped on Sheffield, obliterating the city, and sentencing the handful of survivors to a future of famine and birth defects. We were all traumatized by the show, and I remember quickly heading to the 'Sheffield Peace Centre', behind Sheaf Market in town, where I asked if I could join CND (the Campaign for Nuclear Disarmament). The pretty, punky-looking woman behind the counter was taken aback by this shy ten-year old kid with his bowl-haircut and King Kong t-shirt, but she dutifully obliged, handing me a membership card that I carried around in my schoolbag, showing it off to everyone. And when no one else was around, I'd creep into the air-raid shelter and draw up a list of people I intended to save from the nuclear blast; a list that would have included Martin Murray-mints if (like Marcus), he hadn't moved away a couple of years earlier, or if we hadn't fallen out just before he left.

My mum had finally cooled down from my 'vanishing act', and we were up to our old tricks, looking for trouble in the park where – one afternoon – I suddenly decide it'd be hilarious to snap a branch off one of the bigger trees. I twist, yank and kick the branch clean off the trunk, but, surprisingly, Martin doesn't find it funny at all. When I ask him why he's got a *'face-on all of a sudden'*, he starts talking about God and how everything – including *'that bloody branch you've just killed'* – is part of God's creation. I try to justify myself, telling Martin that *'it dunt matter, 'cause I don't believe in stupid God anyway'*, but this only makes things worse. *'Well, if you don't believe in God, we can't be friends anymore'* he declares, storming off, leaving me stranded with the broken branch in my hand. When I get home I find my parents watching *Grandstand* on the telly and I ask if they believe in God, which they answer with a resounding *'no'*. Still struggling to compute Martin's evangelical turn, I follow up with 'so what happens when you die?'. *'You get eaten by bugs'* comes the terse reply.

Not that my parents were particularly morbid. There'd never been much – or any – talk of God in our house, and it never dawned on me that any of my pals might be churchgoers – it just wasn't part of our world. Shortly after Martin and his family relocated to Derby, I remember finding a dead wasp in the backyard, spending hours making a coffin (out of whatever junk I could find), burying it in a tiny wasp-sized grave (adorned with flowering weeds) and praying for it to get to heaven before it got eaten by bugs.

My parents, Bill and Judy Butler, were aspirational ex-hippies, having grown up in the height of the psychedelic sixties and being part of that first generation to go into higher education. The house was full of books and music (and lots and lots of booze). They were still in their early twenties when Matt and I were born, and I remember there were many parties or late-night drinking sessions with their best friends, Penny and Justin Myles (and their young kids). In contrast with their feminist beliefs, but like most couples in the 70s, they retained a rather archaic dynamic with Judy doing all the housework, while Bill worked full-time at the timberyard. Even when Judy started working full-time, she still did all the housework – washing the pots, doing the laundry, taking care of me and Matt – always making sure Bill's dinner was on the table when he got home. To his defence, Dad did commit himself to a back-breaking job that he hated, and even if he had offered to cook dinner, Mum would never have let him anywhere near the oven anyway. Our house on Burngreave Road was large – three-stories with an attic at the top – but it was a dump when they first moved in, and Bill took it upon himself to renovate the lot by hand. On Sundays, the smell of roast dinner would float through the house, mingled with clouds of sawdust, accompanied by the relentless battering of hammers from whichever room he was gutting. Drowning out the racket, and switched to top volume, would be back-to-back compilations of Van Morrison, Dylan or Genesis playing from his tape-deck, which, quite frankly, used to drive me nuts.

It was only as I got older that I started to appreciate my parents' musical taste, and it was a thrill to discover that Mum had twice seen The Beatles at Sheffield City Hall, and Bob Dylan and The Band at the Gaumont Theatre in 1966. Equally impressive was my dad seeing and meeting blues-legend Howlin' Wolf at the Lafayette in Wolverhampton, and Led Zeppelin at the Bath Festival, and how they'd both sneaked into the City Hall to see Pink Floyd during their first 'Dark Side of the Moon' tour. Our parents may not have passed down religious beliefs, but Matt and I certainly inherited their love of rock 'n' roll, and the idealistic politics that go with it, both of which have bled into my work.

They were life-long Labour supporters, fiercely left-wing, supporters of everything that Thatcher's government opposed, from the miner's strikes to the anti-Apartheid movement and, especially during the AIDS crisis, gay rights. I cherish the memory of my mum (drunkenly) singing along to Tom Robinson's 'Sing if You're Glad to be Gay' on the *Old Grey Whistle Test* one night, or to being brought to tears by Robert Wyatt's haunting anti-Falklands anthem 'Shipbuilding'. Way before having the shit scared out of us by *Threads*, me and Matt were driven down to London to take part in the 1982 CND march where we joined 60,000 like-minded protestors marching past Downing Street chanting 'Maggie Maggie Maggie, Out Out Out!'.

Election nights were also a big family event, lasting way into the small hours of the night. Empty beer cans steadily mounted up the bin as Michael Foot or Neil Kinnock suffered yet another crushing defeat by the Tories. Many years later, I was living with friends in Forest Hill, South East London, when I pick up an unexpected call and hear Mum (drunkenly) singing 'Red Flag' down the phone at me. It was spring 1997, and Tony Blair had just won a landslide victory in the General Election. For a while, it genuinely felt like the well-spun optimism of New Labour might put an end to the inequality that had dogged communities like Pitsmoor for the previous two decades. But things are never quite as simple as that.

When people think of 'up North' during the 70s and 80s, they often imagine picket lines on cobbled streets, populated by noble, dust-smirched grafters (with untapped talents for ballet dancing or male stripping). The dismantling of regional industries did, of course, devastate multiple communities, but in Pitsmoor you would have been hard-pressed to find a placard or picket, let alone a cobble, anywhere. Despite an exponential rise in unemployment, barely anyone in our area would have set foot in a steelwork or coal mine. Most of the factories had already closed in the early 70s, and most working adults (many of them immigrants) would have been brickies or labourers or cleaners, or working in the service industry, or in hospitals or schools. Similarly, the reality for us kids, growing up in the 1980s, was a far cry from the terminally overcast life of Billy Caspar in Ken Loach's *Kes* [UK, 1969]. Whatever the situation at home – and many of my friends did live on the breadline – we were all raised as hyperactive consumers, steeped in pop culture that was, by a stroke of capitalist genius, accessible to all. The backdrop of our lives wasn't the coalface or the dole queue, but the fantastical dreamscapes of *Star Wars* [Lucas, 1977], *Ghostbusters* [Reitman, 1984] and Michael Jackson's *Thriller*. We were the first to discover the thrill of the Big Mac or Knickerbocker Glory, or to embrace 'shopping' on the High Street as a Saturday afternoon routine. You didn't have to be wadded to buy that pair of bleached-jeans or that preposterous 'Frankie Says Relax' t-shirt, and you could drown out the news of Chernobyl by playing *Jet Set Willy* or *Double Dragon* on your mate's Commodore 64.

Frustratingly, me and Matt never had a Commodore 64, or a ZX Spectrum, instead having to make do with a BBC Microcomputer with educational games like *Granny's Garden* or the imaginatively titled *Adventure*. But if we dared complain, Judy – our mum – would sharply remind us that when she was a kid all she got for Christmas was an orange in the stocking at the end of her bed.

She was born in 1948 and grew up in a small house behind a bike shop on Abbeydale Road. Her dad – our grandfather – John Gordon Barber (known to everyone as 'Gordon') used to train greyhounds for local races. Here he is with two of them, sometime in the 50s.

IMAGE 4 *John Gordon Barber and dogs in the 1950s. Photo reproduced from the author's archive.*

Despite his cheeky grin, Gordon was often described as 'a bit of a moaner, who had a lot to moan about'. He was married to Ada J Oldfield – our grandmother – and their first child, Ernest, died from meningitis at the age of eight. My mum said they never recovered from Ernest's sudden death, which muddied her own relationship with her dad somewhat.

Further strain was to come when Ada was unexpectedly diagnosed with cancer, passing away when Judy was still a toddler. Mum later said she never remembered anything about her, but it's difficult to know what was true or not as she was fiercely private and rarely disclosed anything about her past. It's obvious, however, that she'd been obliged to take over every aspect of the housework, which explains her reluctance to ever let my dad pick up the hoover or a saucepan. Here she is, dressed up for a special occasion on the doorstep of her house.

IMAGE 5 *Judy Butler (née Barber) c.1953/1954. Photo reproduced from the author's archive.*

By the sixties, Gordon had become a lorry driver, and, during school holidays, my mum had to accompany him on his daily rounds, squashed into the passenger seat as he delivered lorry loads of fibreglass around Derbyshire. They never had much money, hence the lack of presents on

Christmas Day, but it obviously instilled in her a sense of determination through hard work, as well as a gift for tight-lipped stoicism.

After leaving school, Judy briefly immersed herself at the Evangelical Church of St Thomas's in Crookes, but – as she later explained – she woke up one morning to realize she 'just didn't believe any of it'. In the mid-sixties she finally left home and joined a teacher-training college in Leeds where she not only discovered her vocation, but also the lifestyle and idealism of the hippy scene.

By 1969, at the age of 21, she was back in Sheffield, sharing a bedsit with her friend-of-a-friend-of-a-friend, Justin, who'd recently arrived from Dublin (with his obligatory acoustic guitar). Having started work at a nursery school close to Park Hill flats, she arrived home one evening to discover a scruffy, long-haired pal of Justin's sitting on the doorstep dressed in an old black overcoat and bowler hat.

IMAGE 6 *Terence 'Bill' Butler c.1974/1975. Photo reproduced from author's archive.*

Our dad, Terry Butler (known to everyone, bizarrely, as 'Bill'), was born in Willenhall in 1950, the middle brother of Alan and John, and they'd had a considerably more secure upbringing than the Barbers of Abbeydale Road.

His father – our grandad – Joseph Butler had fought as a conscript in Burma during the Second World War, eventually rising to the rank of lieutenant. A self-proclaimed workaholic, Joseph set up his own wood and metal pattern makers business after the war, which he managed until retirement at the ripe old age of seventy. In 1947 he married our grandmother, Evelyn Mary Harrison (with her impressive shock of bright-red hair), eventually uprooting their three sons to a semi-detached house on the outskirts of Wolverhampton.

Bill Butler has always been a huge Van Morrison fan, and that could have been part of the reason he moved to Northern Ireland to study at the University of Coleraine. However – in a mirror image of my drama-school experience – Bill soon lost interest and quit. He learnt to play the harmonica and decided to go busking on the streets of Ulster with his friend Brian Collery. Meanwhile, back in Wolverhampton, Joe and Evelyn were worried that Bill had gone missing and contacted the Salvation Army for help. They were too late, however, as Bill and Brian had already left Ulster for the West End of London, where they were, once again, gatecrashing parties, dossing about, soaking up the delights of late-sixties Soho.

Running out of money, they sailed back to Dublin where they stayed with Brian's friend, Justin, in his flat on Grafton Street. Bill was about to turn twenty and, with the seventies fast approaching, they needed a drastic plan of action. After getting involved with a couple of holidaying American girls, Bill and Brian decided to escort them back to California. Unfortunately, Bill was broke, so Brian went alone, never to be heard from again. In the meantime, Justin suddenly gets in touch from Sheffield and invites Bill to cross back over the Irish Sea, hitchhike down the M1, and stay with him and his flatmate, Judy, on Crookesmoor Road.

Judy returns home from work and finds Justin's scruffy, long-haired friend sitting on the doorstep in his long black overcoat and bowler hat. A few months later, she discovers she's pregnant. Bill finally gets in touch with Joe and Evelyn, who are delighted to become grandparents, helping them find a cheap house on Burngreave Road.

When Matt and I are toddlers, Gordon Barber lost a battle with emphysema and Evelyn Butler died of a sudden heart attack. However, growing up, we were frequent visitors to Grandad's house in Wolverhampton, particularly during Easter holidays or Christmas. Here we all are (pictured below), enjoying a day out in the countryside.

By the mid-seventies, Bill realizes he can't survive on benefits, finding work at a nut and bolt wholesalers, before eventually working his way into the timber trade. Judy also returns to part-time work at the children's ward of the Northern General Hospital, until she secures a teaching position at Rainbow Forge Nursery School where she stays until 2008.

It's now 2024 and I've just returned to London on the East Midlands train from Sheffield (via Chesterfield) where Bill and Judy – now in their mid-seventies – are still living in that large house overlooking Abbeyfield

IMAGE 7 *From left to right: Joseph Butler, Leo Butler, Matthew Butler, Terry Butler and Judy Butler on a day out in the countryside c.1975. Photo reproduced from author's archive.*

Park. A quiet life full of extraordinary ups and downs, their devotion to each other is beyond question.

As Ian Rickson suggested, I've plundered aspects of my youth throughout my career. Not just memories, but a political and ethical foundation that growing up in Pitsmoor instilled in me. Plays such as *Made of Stone*, *Redundant*, *Boy*, *Lucky Dog* and *Living* may be minor or forgettable for some, but they have deep meaning for me.

From the misadventures in the flats at the bottom of our road, to the dealers on Catherine Street, to the imagined terrors in the darkness of the air-raid shelter, these memories linger in the mind and reawaken on the page into something called art. And nothing has inspired this transfiguration more than the love song of my parents.

4

Tungsten carbide drills or what is a working-class playwright anyway?

The title of this book pays homage to the *Monty Python's Flying Circus* 'Working Class Playwright' sketch in which young coal miner Ken (*Eric Idle*) comes home to visit his mum (*Terry Jones*) and belligerent dad (*Graham Chapman*).

Mum How are you liking it down the mine, Ken?

Ken Oh it's not too bad, mum . . . we're using some new tungsten carbide drills for the preliminary coalface scouring operations.

Mum Oh that sounds nice, dear . . .

Dad Tungsten carbide drills! What the bloody hell's tungsten carbide drills?

Ken It's something they use in coalmining, father.

Dad *(mimicking)* 'It's something they use in coalmining, father.' You're all bloody fancy talk since you left London.

Ken Oh not that again.

Mum He's had a hard day dear . . . his new play opens at the National Theatre tomorrow.

Ken Oh that's good.

Dad Good! good? What do you know about it? What do you know about getting up at five o'clock in t'morning to fly to Paris . . . back at the Old Vic for drinks at twelve, sweating the day through press interviews, television interviews and getting back here at ten to wrestle with the problem of a homosexual nymphomaniac drug-addict involved in the ritual murder of a well-known Scottish footballer. That's a full working day, lad, and don't you forget it!

So, is 'working-class playwright' an oxymoron? The definition of working-class, according to the Oxford English dictionary, is . . .

Noun. The social group consisting of people who are employed for wages, especially in manual or industrial work: *the housing needs of the working-class.*

Adjective. relating to the characteristic of the working class: *a working-class community.*

Despite being a centuries-old industry, I'm not sure you can equate theatre to, say, the coal or shipping industries of which the definition alludes. And aside from the occasional wrist cramp, I'm equally unconvinced you can liken the labour of a playwright with the labour of a bin man, nurse or coal-mining Ken.

'Employed for wages' is also questionable when comparing a playwright's salary with the UK Living (or minimum) Wage.

As of 2024, the commission fee for a full-length play is roughly £7,984 for mid-scale venues, and £12,998 for theatres such as the National Theatre, RSC and Royal Court. The fee for a play under seventy minutes is £6,110, and for a play under thirty minutes it's £3,056.

The full amount of any of these sums is then divided into three separate payments, which, depending on a range of creative and administrative factors, are often received months or years apart.

On signature of commission, the playwright receives half or a third of the sum, which might seem like a decent amount to get started, but if the playwright takes six months or a year to write the damn thing, and doesn't have any extra income, then that money is soon going to run out.

Once the first draft is delivered, the theatre pays half of the total remaining sum – £4,345 for the top-tier commission, £1,878 for the mid-scale – and if the writer has representation, their literary agent will, contractually, take 10 per cent or 15 per cent of the fee.

The remaining unpaid sum of either £4,290, or £1,878 (before tax and agent's percentage) is only released once the theatre acquires the professional rights to the play and makes a commitment to producing, but there is no guarantee that will happen.

After delivery of the first draft, the writer will usually have to wait as the play is read, re-read and discussed, alongside a bunch of other plays, in various meetings over a period of weeks. If the play shows promise, but it's felt to not be quite ready yet, he or she will be given notes and asked to submit a new draft to an agreed timescale. The playwright won't receive any extra money for this work, which could take several weeks or months, and – as with the first draft – there's still no guarantee of a production.

Once the rewritten script is delivered, it may take another few weeks for the play to be read and, even if the theatre likes the new version, it's possible they still might ask for another set of rewrites before coming to a final 'final' decision. Sometimes the theatre decides they want to hear or 'see the play on its feet' and a director and actors are employed for a reading or workshop, and the writer is paid an attendance fee of (roughly) £80 a day.

The UK Living (or minimum) Wage as of 2024 and based on full-time employment of 7.5 hours per day, currently stands at £12 per hour. The full-length play commission of £12,998 (at the equivalent full-time rate) roughly works out at £6.66 per hour. The mid-rage commission equates to £4.09 per hour, while the play under seventy minutes is £3.13 per hour.

Given the figures, it's clearly impossible to survive on a single commission, particularly if there are large gaps between payments, without the risk of falling into poverty. As such, the idea of a jobbing playwright being financially better-off than *'the social group of people . . . in manual or industrial work'* is way off the mark. Even when a theatre decides to produce an un-commissioned play – i.e. one that lands with a thump on the artistic director's desk, and the writer receives the full sum in one single payment, the figure still falls short of an annual living wage. To earn the equivalent, a playwright needs to not only write two or three plays per year, but also have them accepted and produced within the same timeframe, which is, of course, completely unrealistic.

Playwriting can, of course, be lucrative and there have been times when I've treated myself to a pair of new trainers, a mole-skin notebook or maybe even a family holiday. But there have also been times when I've had no income whatsoever and been forced to bunk trains or walk across town to get to a rehearsal room or meeting. Without savings or a trust fund to fall back on, I've often relied on handouts from family, friends or associates. Over the years I've been lucky to receive help from charities such as the Peggy Ramsay Foundation and the Royal Literary Fund, but the constant financial wrangling is exhausting, and the shame can cut deep. As Wallace Shawn puts it in the wonderful film *My Dinner with Andre* [Louis Malle, USA, 1981] . . .

'When I was ten years old . . . all I thought about was music and art. Now I'm thirty-six, all I think about is money.'

Of course, it's unfair to blame the theatres, or their artistic teams, as there is constant negotiation with the Writers' Guild of Great Britain to hammer out better deals for writers, even when the creative industries are facing financial pressures of their own.

Politicians routinely peddle the idea that theatre is a luxury, an expendable burden to the taxpayer, but this contradicts the Arts Council's report that the industry generates more than £130 million for the Treasury each year.

Given such discrepancies, it seems fair to accuse governments – particularly far-right Tories – of fearing any vocation that encourages creative expression or individual thought, particularly from those who haven't attended public school.

Whatever the political reasons, many profitable (often regional) theatres have been forced to make redundancies, close their doors, or, when it comes to the plays, take fewer commercial risks. Without state subsidy, some venues have become reliant on sponsorship from individual donors or corporations. However, when some of these corporations are also profiteering from, say, arms sales or the burning of fossil fuels, then the theatres have little choice but to cut off that sponsorship too.

All these unenviable decisions eventually trickle down to the freelancers – the actors, directors, designers, stage managers, playwrights – and, as Wallace Shawn suggested, the desire shifts from creating great work to matters of financial survival, particularly if you come from a working-class background.

To make matters worse, the right-wing media often regard the arts with a derision that goes way beyond the light parody of the Monty Python sketch, with actors reviled as 'left-wing luvvies' sponging off the taxpayer, or ballet dancers who (as in the notorious post-pandemic advert) would be better off retraining in IT.

One of the solutions is, of course, to drastically reduce your outgoings, or as Woody Allen's character in *Manhattan* [USA, 1979] says . . .

'If I live like Mahatma Gandhi, I'll be fine.'

Another solution is to write a big West End or Broadway smash and survive off the royalties, which is not impossible, but never guaranteed (even with a well-oiled team of commercial talent).

Or consider writing screenplays for TV, radio and film. TV, especially, is much more lucrative and guarantees a bigger audience, but there's no straightforward way into that industry either, and the development process (like theatre) often means doing a lot of work for free.

Many successful playwrights – including Hanif Kureishi, Winsome Pinnock, Stephen Jeffreys, David Eldridge, Suhayla El-Bushra, Annie Baker, Simon Stephens, Michael Punter, Roy Williams, John Donnelly, Christopher Shinn, Tanika Gupta, Mark Ravenhill and myself – have supplemented their income by teaching at universities and drama schools, or within theatre buildings themselves. As far as I'm concerned, teaching and mentoring is as fulfilling as the writing itself.

I remember I'd just started running workshops for the Royal Court's Young Writers' Programme in September 2005, when nineteen-year-old Polly Stenham joined the group. Polly had never written a play before, but she was fearless in challenging the Royal Court's failure to represent the lives of its loyal middle-class audience in favour of a largely absent working class. It was a brave provocation, and when Polly submitted her debut *That Face* at the end of the course, its inspired portrait of a dysfunctional upper-middle class family went on to become a commercial and critical hit.

Overnight, the Royal Court stumbled into an identity crisis (which happens every ten years or so), questioning if it should continue pursuing working-class drama as it had done since George Devine, its first artistic director, established it as the home of social realism back in 1956.

The world has changed a fair bit since John Osborne and Arnold Wesker were first penning plays like *Look Back in Anger* and *Roots*, and the so-called kitchen-sink dramas of the 50s and 60s – regardless of their craft or emotional power – can sometimes seem as old-fashioned as L S Lowry's matchstick men trudging out of the factory gates.

Television drama, soap opera and countless gritty British films continue to embrace social-realism, whereas today's playwrights (particularly student playwrights) often consider the form to be outdated or too conventional and – inspired by the wild rides of Caryl Churchill and Debbie Tucker Green – do everything they can to avoid it.

Likewise, huge social changes, such as the collapse of local industry and the growth of the free-market economy, have re-directed many dramatists concerns from issues of class to the politics of identity. According to cultural theorist Mark Fisher:

'It's easier to imagine the end of the world than to imagine the end of capitalism.'

If we are living in a kind of neo-liberal prison, as Fisher suggests, then it's understandable why we find more plays exploring issues of identity, gender politics or climate change, as it's easier to foresee solutions to those problems through positive community action.

By comparison, those who are drawn to more traditional themes of class politics and economic inequality often produce pessimistic plays about fractured communities or alienated individuals spiralling into poverty or moral bankruptcy. As Polly Stenham suggested, the bleak outlook of these plays, however vital they may be, can be at odds with the tastes of middle-class audiences who buy the tickets and keep the theatres afloat.

One of my own bleak outlooks, *Boy*, produced in 2016, invited the audience to see the world through the eyes of 17-year-old Liam who has no money, no prospects and no discernible talent. Set in South East London, Liam attempts to fill the long empty hours of the day by looking for old school friends, failing to find work at the job centre or encountering hostile strangers as he wanders across the city on foot. Without function or agency, Liam turns to his GP for help, but the GP misinterprets Liam's dilemma as mental illness and prescribes a course of anti-depressants.

It wasn't an easy play to write, and it took a few years to find a home as it was rejected by several theatres – including the Royal Court where it was first commissioned, as well as several other major theatres. It may have been that they didn't think it was particularly well-written, which is fair enough, but a common criticism was that Liam wasn't sympathetic, interesting or dramatic enough – which, ironically, was the whole point.

It felt like the theatres were mirroring the attitudes of the characters who reject Liam in the play, and that if I'd decided to give Liam a knife, made him a heroin addict, a victim of child abuse or turned him into a *Billy Elliot* [Daldry, UK, 2000] figure waiting to be 'discovered', then the play might have had an easier life.

Young Woman I bet you've got a knife haven't you?

Pause.

Young Woman Do you carry it around with you then?

Liam Nah, I don't know, sometimes.

Young Woman That's cool.

Pause.

Young Woman I said that's cool, that's awesome.

Liam Thanks, yeah. Awesome.

Young Woman Yeah, I think I'm a bit scared of you actually.

Pause.

Young Woman I'm a bit scared of you I think, yeah. In a good way.

Boy finally found a home at the Almeida Theatre in Islington – largely thanks to the efforts of the play's audacious director, Sacha Wares – but when the theatre's sponsors read the play and decided they didn't want to invest in Liam either, it looked like the whole project was about to collapse.

Thankfully the Almeida's artistic director, Rupert Goold, heroically flew back to London from New York, where he was rehearsing another show, to find alternative funding. Within hours he'd met with Arsenal Football Club who agreed to sponsor the production in exchange for a series of playwriting workshops with their Community Foundation. Arsene Wenger, the club manager, wrote . . .

> 'Football can be a little bit the same as the theatre, because it has the power to bring happiness to young people and make them dream of what is possible. We are proud to be involved in this special project, and to be a positive force in our local community too.'

. . . which, even as a Sheffield United fan, was a special moment, and a refreshing contrast to the reactions we'd come to expect.

Rehearsing *Boy* at the Almeida was a fun and fulfilling experience and the play received rave reviews. However, there were some who questioned my working-class credentials – '*another middle-class writer trying to preach about the Endz*' – and others who accused us of peddling in 'poverty porn' as if the Almeida audience should be spared, or are incapable of, taking any responsibility for the thousands of kids like Liam.

Plays such as Stefan Massini's *Lehman Trilogy* [NT, 2018] or Lucy Prebble's *Enron* [Royal Court, 2009] explore the root causes of modern capitalism by placing powerful white men centre stage and the writers – regardless that they lack billionaire credentials – are justifiably lauded.

Plays that explore the symptoms of modern capitalism on the disempowered – even though audiences are closer, economically speaking, to characters like Liam – can be interrogated for simply existing, and sometimes by the people they're written about.

In the spring of 2001, while preparing for rehearsals of *Redundant*, directed by Dominic Cooke at the Royal Court, I decided to visit a crack house in Pitsmoor to gather some first-hand interviews to share with the actors for their research. The occupants were happy to talk about their experiences, until one young woman who, much like the play's protagonist, had fallen into addiction and prostitution suddenly became furious that someone like me could '*think I can come up from fucking London and write about me or my area when he knows fuck all about fuck all!*'.

It took me repeated efforts to explain that not only had I grown up in Pitsmoor, but I'd known her, her brothers and her ex-boyfriend since we were kids. But none of that mattered. The fact that I was a playwright was enough to convince her I was lying.

A few years later, I ran a series of workshops for Synergy Theatre Project, who specialize in working with prisoners or ex-offenders. I invited one of the participants, Luke, to join another course I was running at the Royal Court, as I thought he was a genuinely good writer.

During the course, Luke wrote a tough, uncompromising scene – set in a sauna and based on real-life experiences – about a group of men sharing violent anecdotes. I encouraged him to share the scene, but Luke didn't want to freak out the other members of the group, many of whom he imagined, rightly or wrongly, were polite middle-class university grads. As with the young woman at the crack house, I honoured Luke's decision, but his growing concern that neither the group nor the theatre were meant 'for people like me' meant he gradually stopped turning up to the sessions when we were still only halfway through the course.

Let's face it, regular theatregoing – especially in London – is a middle-class pursuit. Compared to a monthly Netflix subscription, a good book or a cinema ticket, theatre tickets are ridiculously expensive. Some may argue that you can spend the equivalent amount on a Premiership football game, but – whatever the cost or final score – you are, at the very least, guaranteed ninety minutes of thrills alongside likeminded fans. Likewise, if you only go to the theatre once a year, and save enough money to watch *Hamilton* or a Christmas pantomime, there is, generally at least, a guarantee of high production value and knockout songs.

The cost is equivalent to the expectations, and if you risk £60 or £90 or more on an unknown play like *Boy*, which leaves you bored or depressed, then it's unsurprising if you never set foot in a theatre again. And even if *Boy* leaves you inspired or galvanized, any new play requires *active spectatorship*, and a level of engagement that might be the last thing you need after a long day's work, especially when you've paid good money for it.

Theatres like the National Theatre or the Royal Court have been known to offer discounted tickets and employ 'outreach' departments to broaden or diversify the audiences, but such tactics can never completely dispel the perception of middle-class ownership.

The Almeida offered free tickets for *Boy* to groups of disadvantaged youngsters as part of the Arsenal partnership. I met with a few of these kids and some of them came to the show and had a great time. However, there were just as many who, like Luke, decided it 'just wasn't for them' and left before the play even started.

Was it something I said? Or was it the architecture, the bar? The clinking of wine glasses, or the £15 baked aubergine salad? Perhaps it was the tutting and huffing that followed them as they took their seats? Perhaps it was a combination of all these things, or maybe they just had something better to do?

Whatever their reasons, I escape the throng at the theatre bar and jump into an Uber to go home. The driver turns up the music, Lionel Richie's playing on Smooth FM, and I ask myself should I have pitched *Boy* or *Redundant* as single dramas for Channel 4 instead? Did theatres employ outreach departments for *A Taste of Honey* or *Live Like Pigs* back in 1958, or were audiences more diverse than they are now? Given the queues for the toilets and uncomfortable seats, should we be grateful for any audience at all? More than 100 years ago, Charlie Chaplin entertained working-class audiences in music halls across the country, but then he left for Hollywood and, arguably, took the audience with him. Are ordinary people only familiar with Arthur Miller and Bertolt Brecht because they were forced to study them at school? No, because many great working-class playwrights, like Willy Russell and James Graham, write hugely popular shows that transgress class boundaries.

And what the hell is a modern working-class play anyway? Is Michael Wynne's scouse family epic *The People are Friendly* [Royal Court, 2002] more 'working-class' than, say, Anna Jordan's *Yen* [Royal Exchange, 2015] or Alistair McDowall's *Pomona* [Orange Tree, 2014]? How do you compare Roy Williams's classic *Sing Yer Heart Out for the Lads* [NT, 2002] with Jasmine Lee Jones's meme-brimming *Seven Methods of Killing Kylie Jenner* [Royal Court, 2019]? Should we compare Peter Gill's *The York Realist* [Lowry, 2001] with Samson Hawkins's *Village Idiot* [Stratford East, 2023], or Alan Bennett's *A Cream Cracker under the Settee* [BBC, 1987] with Gary Owen's *Iphigenia in Splott* [Sherman Cymru, 2015]? What connects these terrific plays is not just that they are conjured from the playwrights' guts, but, like it or not, they each owe a debt to the kitchen sink. Didn't John Arden and Ann Jellicoe – just like Polly Stenham decades later – fight and kick and bite to prove that working-class drama is as valuable and multifaceted as anything by Noel Coward or Terrence Rattigan?

Ah well, what does any of it matter? I'm just trying to crack on with whatever idea takes my fancy at any given time, and I've never felt defined by, or even certain of, my social class.

When I was a kid, I felt self-conscious of our big house on Burngreave Road, with both parents in full-time work. Compared to some of my friends, I didn't even have a proper Sheffield accent, and I was frequently teased for 'sounding weird' or 'posh'. I suppose I was better off than the young woman at the crack house who accosted me for '*knowing fuck all about fuck all*'. But I also fancied a girl at my youth theatre and after visiting her family's enormous house in the posh part of town, Nether Edge, I went away feeling like a leper.

Similarly, years later, when I could finally call myself a 'professional playwright', it soon became clear that the theatre scene was riddled with ex-public-school kids, and, although sharing many of the same beliefs and aspirations, I never felt part of that club.

But you break your back to write something meaningful and tickets sell, or they don't. Wasn't it John Steinbeck who said, '*write for an audience of one*'? That's all very well, but one ticket isn't going to pay the rent.

Plays vanish as soon as they arrive. Theatre is impermanent, as are its politics. Give me Samuel Beckett, Steven Berkoff, Pina Bausch and Mercutio. Give me great actors. It's the moments of poetry, the bodies in space, which stay with you after the curtain falls.

As technology consumes our lives, theatre – regardless of who you are or where you come from – exists to remind us that we're all still human.

As the Uber turns off Highbury Corner, past the Garage Nightclub where my rock band, *Grass Hoppa*, once played a shambolic gig back in 1996, the driver turns and asks . . .

> '*So, what do you do for a living, mate?*'
>   '*Me? Oh, I'm a writer.*'
> '*Fuck, okay. What sort of thing do you write then?*'
>   '*Plays mainly. Theatre stuff.*'
> '*Can't say I go to the theatre much. Anything I might have seen?*'

5

Make it up as you go along!

When students ask me how long a full-length play is meant to be, I always – unhelpfully – answer, 'however long it needs to be'.

Samuel Beckett's *Not I* [Royal Court, 1973] is seven pages long, with a run-time of twelve minutes, and Caryl Churchill's *Far Away* [Royal Court, 2000] is thirty-five pages with a run-time of fifty minutes. Tony Kushner's *Angels in America: Parts One and Two* [NT, 1992], on the other hand, comes in at a whopping 190 pages and must be watched over two separate performances. How these three masterpieces were conjured onto the page is a mystery (perhaps even to the authors themselves), and their uniqueness has less to do with their length (or story or characters) but the writer's *character* and *style*. My advice to students is rather than worry about reaching the industry-standard length of sixty plus pages, start by thinking about the *spell* you're going to cast over the audience.

Beckett's *Not I* is a stream-of-consciousness monologue delivered by a mouth suspended in pitch darkness, but, looking between the cracks, there is enough hidden backstory to reconstruct the mouth into a full-bodied protagonist of a naturalistic play by the likes of Chekhov or Brian Friel. It's also possible to distil the epic, multi-plotted *Angels in America* into a jumbled ten-minute monologue in the style of *Not I* or Allen Ginsberg's *Howl* [1955]. Likewise, Churchill's *Far Away* could be rewritten as a multi-season TV series – in the spirit of, say, HBO's *The Handmaid's Tale* [2017] – given that, putting aside the play's mind-bending structure, it tells the linear story of a family caught up in an escalating world war. It's also easy to re-imagine *Macbeth* as a one-act drama with the real-time structure of David Eldridge's bewitching *Beginning* [NT, 2017] or David Gieselmann's satirical gore-fest *Mr Kolpert* [Royal Court, 2000]. Or, if you're really desperate, to propose an all-singing all-dancing version of *A Streetcar Named Desire* [Tennessee Williams, 1947], as demonstrated in the brilliant Simpsons' episode *A Streetcar Called Marge* [1992].

The reason Tennessee Williams didn't have Blanche Dubois bursting into song, or Beckett didn't write *Not I* as a three-act naturalistic drama, is – as obvious as it sounds – because they didn't want to. If I randomly take two of my own plays, *All You Need is LSD* [Birmingham Rep, 2018] and *Made of Stone*, they are so stylistically different that they could have been written by different people, and – on some level – they were. If I were to write either of those plays today, they would – for better or worse – be worlds apart from the originals as I'm worlds apart (in age, perspective and experience) from the bloke who wrote them in the first place.

Aside from a few practical hints and tips, playwriting cannot be taught in a classroom, because imagination never clocks in at the workshop door, and the process of mining who you are (and your relationship with the world) can be done anywhere. You're as likely to dream up a great new play when you're sat on the toilet or washing the dishes than if you were to pay a ton of money for a fancy playwriting course. If a teacher or mentor can do anything, it's to create an environment in which the student feels free to explore their creative instincts without censorship and, using plays like *Not I* and *Angels in America* as examples of radically contrasting techniques, allowing each writer the freedom to repeatedly fuck up until they find a story and style of their own.

In the spring of 2011, I was teaching a writers' group at the Royal Court, and I asked the writers to bring in rough ideas for plays that they wanted to work on.

One of the writers decided not to bring in any scenes and asked us to watch a documentary about beekeeping instead. Although he had no idea what the play was going to be, he knew it was going to have something to do with bees. Interestingly, the writer also explained that he'd been listening to the latest album by Manchester band *Elbow* and, especially, its eight-minute opening number *The Birds*. Something about the cyclical repetitions of the track, alongside its enigmatic lyric, seemed to be suggesting a tone and structure for the unwritten piece. Although none of his fellow group members, or myself, could offer any practical advice, it was important to give the writer the space and freedom to talk about his idea, even at this primitive stage, and to encourage him to keep pursuing them.

The writer's name was Nick Payne and, in just a matter of months, his new play *Constellations* premiered at the Royal Court to critical and commercial acclaim, after which it transferred to the West End, moving on to Broadway in 2015. It's a beautifully written play, dazzlingly structured, with plenty of references to beekeeping, and, like Polly Stenham's *That Face* before it, resonated with audiences on an almost molecular level. Neither Nick nor Polly needed to be taught how to 'become playwrights' as they had bundles of talent to begin with, but, given that writing is such a solitary vocation, spending one evening per week with twenty other writers to share ideas in their infancy, can be hugely motivational.

And, of course, it's misleading to measure a play's success on how many tickets it may or may not have sold. Alongside *That Face* and *Constellations* there have been a plethora of equally beautiful plays that were shunned by most critics and audiences, generating only a small number of fans. Mainstream success is often just a matter of alchemy or timing. Likewise, there are outstanding plays that – for one reason or another, often timing or luck or a theatre producer's taste – were never produced and continue to be gathering dust on a shelf or buried in the hard drive of an ageing PC somewhere. Just because it never saw the light of day, doesn't make the play less valuable, it's the process that matters, and, as *Constellations* proves, you don't need a 'big idea' to start writing. Sometimes all it takes is a bee.

Ideas bank

One of the exercises I've used to explore this process is the 'ideas bank'.

Each student thinks of two or three play ideas that they are happy to donate to one of their classmates.

The ideas are scribbled on scraps of paper, and with a healthy dollop of Blu Tack, they're stuck to the classroom wall – which itself is a bit of fun, especially for writers (who don't get out that much).

If it's a group of, say, twenty writers, the wall is soon covered with fifty or sixty play ideas, some of which are as abstract as **'a woman sits alone in the dark'** or **'I dream of Michael Jackson'**. Others are more specific, such as **'a modern adaptation of Red Riding Hood'** or **'set in the Peruvian rainforest, the true story of Werner Herzog's descent into madness while filming** *Aguirre: Wrath of God* **in 1971'**.

The deal is that you're not allowed to claim ownership of your own idea, even if someone else takes it off the wall and later sells it to Steven Spielberg for a six-figure sum. If you're not a member of a writers' group, then you could ask friends or family to scribble some ideas for you instead. Here's a space for them to donate their ideas to you.

IDEA ONE:

IDEA TWO:

IDEA THREE:

Choose one of the ideas that you like the sound of and write a scene or moment from the show.

The scene can be whatever you want. A monologue, a song, a moment of drama between characters. Start them talking, make them *do stuff* to each other.

The worst thing you can do is try and produce something as good as Tony Kushner or Caryl Churchill. The best thing you can do is write *badly*; get words on the page as quickly and as effortlessly as you can, even if 90 per cent of it is unusable. It isn't an exam, and no one gives a shit. As with any play, never attempt to please everyone – you're not a Big Mac. It's vital that you please no one but yourself, even if you write something outrageous and offensive, or, on the flipside, if what you write feels safe and conventional. Sod the naysayers, everything is valid.

And if you don't manage a full scene, and only write a few lines of dialogue or a scene description, that's totally acceptable too.

Once you've finished, read over it or read it aloud with someone else. You're just *experimenting*, so have a sense of humour about it.

Take the best bit of the scene – even if it's *one line of dialogue* – and use it as a starting point for a new scene.

Write a page or two.

Read over the new scene.

Take the best bits and use it as a starting point for a new scene.

Write a page or two.

Repeat until you've got something you quite like.

Although it might not be a masterpiece (yet), you might start to get a sense of the kind of play you're drawn to write and the type of writer you are.

No one needs an original idea. Originality is not the thing itself, but the writer's taste and perspective. Originality is your life experience, your choice of footwear and the books you enjoy reading. To say you 'have nothing original to write about' is to deny your basic humanness.

Fuck originality anyway. Just as every band you ever loved (*The Rolling Stones*) were influenced by, or mimicked, bands of yesteryear (*Chuck Berry*) and who, in turn, were mimicking their own long-forgotten heroes (*Robert Johnson*), any so-called original idea has probably been dreamt up several times before.

And if you've never written a scene before, or if you don't have a reference point for existing plays, such as *Angels in America* or *Far Away*, then think about the kinds of novels or movies or paintings you like. What is it about Nancy Meyers' *Clueless* [1995] or David Lynch's *Mulholland Drive* [2001] that excites you? Why are you attracted to John Constable's landscapes, or Tracey Emin's tent? Do you want to write the theatrical equivalent of Kate Bush's *Hounds of Love*, Marvin Gaye's *What's Going On* or the B-side of The Beatles' *Abbey Road*?

Whatever it is that floats your boat, there are reasons – hidden or obvious – you're drawn to certain pieces, and they're likely the same reasons you're compelled to make art of your own.

Titles

Choosing a title can help too.

I had the title of my first play, *Made of Stone*, for years, as I wanted to pay homage to the classic Stone Roses' song of the same name.

Likewise, I had the titles of *Lucky Dog* and *All You Need is LSD* way before I wrote a word of dialogue. *I'll Be the Devil* was originally called *One of these Days*, which I ripped-off from the pounding Pink Floyd instrumental, as it captured the play's mood and urgency. It was my wife who later suggested I change it to *I'll Be the Devil*, being punchier and more in keeping with the play's *Hammer House of Horror* vibe – and, of course, a big improvement on my effort.

Likewise, the original title of *Boy* was *Nothing Like Something Happens Anywhere* – a quote from a Philip Larkin poem – which helped me through early drafts as a reminder that I was exploring unremarkable lives with remarkable problems. Unfortunately, everyone who read the play *hated* the title, and, in a frantic brainstorm – days before the Almeida press release – it was the play's director, Sacha Wares, who suggested the snappier title *Boy*, for which I was happy to take the credit.

Why not experiment with some of your own titles here?

TITLE ONE:
TITLE TWO:
TITLE THREE:
TITLE FOUR:
TITLE FIVE:
TITLE SIX:

What kind of play do these titles suggest? Drama or comedy or musical? Do they point towards a particular character or setting or story or theme? What stage pictures or scenes do you imagine when you read the title back?

Posters

If you're thinking of titles, you might also imagine a poster, book cover or image to go with it.

Although it may feel like you're jumping the gun – especially if you haven't written a word of dialogue yet – you might find *visualizing* the play and its production to be a useful way of crystallizing your ideas.

Grab a pencil and draw an image for the poster. It doesn't matter how vague your idea is, and it doesn't have to be a 'good drawing'. At this stage, it's about capturing the flavour of the thing you want to bring to life.

I once suggested this exercise to a bunch of playwrights, including master excavator of melancholy, Brad Birch, who was working on one of his early plays, *Brute*. Brad took a sheet of A4 paper and filled it with bright, horrible red. Other students were drawing characters and places, so Brad wondered if his effort was slightly against the spirit of the exercise. However, he later told me that it helped him realize that '*the gesture of the play was entirely in the tone. I suddenly realised that, like its poster, I was writing a heavy-metal play with an overwhelming, single, oppressive force*'.

Don't restrict yourself to posters or book covers either. Once you're going to write something, you will immediately start imagining moments or scenes in your mind's eye, in daydreams or in sleep.

Borrowed images

When I taught at the Royal Court I'd take the writers on day trips. Sometimes we'd go to the Natural History Museum or the Holocaust Exhibition at the Imperial War Museum to challenge the scale of our plays' themes. We'd maybe go to the cinema or theatre, or the pub. And sometimes we'd go to the Tate Modern or the National Gallery. Why? To plan a robbery.

I remember visiting the National Gallery with my mum sometime in 1999 and being drawn to Albrecht Dürer's painting *St Jerome* [c.1495], which shows the penitent Saint beating his chest open with rocks. I'm not religious and there are way better paintings peppered across the Gallery walls. But

IMAGE 8 *St Jerome by Albrecht Dürer (1471–1528), oil on pearwood, c.1496. Image reproduced with permission from* © *Ian Dagnall Computing/Alamy Stock Photo.*

there was something about the *drama* of the image – and the strangely pensive lion watching on – that stayed with me.

Months later, I was in my bedroom in Plumstead, frantically staggering through the first draft of *Made of Stone* to submit for the Royal Court's Young Writers' Festival. With only three weeks until the deadline, I didn't have time to do much planning, so I wrote it blindly, working day and night, making it up as I went along.

My favourite plotline in *Made of Stone* involves young barman, Pete, who enlists a teenage runaway girl, Carol, to join him on a suicide mission so he can be reunited with his dead dad. At the play's climax, Pete and Carol drive out to Derbyshire, finding a secluded spot by a cairn – (or stack of stones) – where Pete and his dad used to go rambling when he was a kid, . . . hmmm, and then what?

Right, well . . . Pete tells Carol the story of how his dad used to have to drag him out of bed to go hiking . . . very good, and then what? Hmmm.

Ah yes, Saint Jerome! With the pensive Carol watching on, Pete suddenly grabs a rock from the cairn and starts beating his chest open. Thank you Albrecht Dürer!

The following year, soon after *Made of Stone* had been produced, I was wandering down Woolwich Arsenal High Street and I was struck by the number of teenage girls pushing prams. These young mums reminded me of a couple of ex-girlfriends back in Sheffield, and I decided that I would make a teenage mother the focus of my next play. Unlike *Made of Stone*, however, I wouldn't set it in Sheffield, and I would try to be more ambitious or experimental with the form.

Around the same time, I'd been re-reading Brecht's *Mother Courage* [1939] and was struck by some of the photos of the original Berliner Ensemble production, which shows the titular hero towing her cart (in circles on the bare stage) as she navigates her way through the Thirty Years War.

I decided to mimic *Mother Courage* by having my teenage character – Lucy – towing a pushchair in circles, on a bare stage. It would be a solo piece, with Lucy delivering a monologue (rather like Beckett's mouth in *Not I*), re-enacting or recounting the confrontations with other people – boyfriends, family members, social workers – as she navigates the various pitfalls through one year of her life.

Unfortunately, the half-arsed script I came up with was rubbish, and I quickly scrapped the idea, opting for the more realistic setting of Lucy's flat in Sheffield instead. Once I stopped trying to be Brecht and honoured the characters and the world I knew, I finished a rough draft of *Redundant* in days.

But although I'd ditched the Brechtian conceit, the imagery of *Mother Courage* did seep into the play in more subtle ways. Lucy rarely leaves her flat, but she's forced to navigate a dangerous, uncaring environment, repeating the same mistakes – towing her baggage – making selfish, often morally indefensible, choices over the space of a single year – which, like Brecht's heroine, leaves her exactly where she started.

IMAGE 9 *Ingeborg Arnoldi in 'Mutter Courage', 1968. Photographer: Fred Erismann. Public Domain.*

IMAGE 10 *Photo credit: Lyndsey Marshal (Lucy) and Eileen O'Brien (Jo) in 'Redundant' (directed by Dominic Cooke, Royal Court, 2001). Photo reproduced with kind permission from @ Tristram Kenton.*

So, even if you don't directly replicate a painting of Saint Jerome, there may be other reasons – as with *Mother Courage* and *Redundant* – that you're drawn to a particular image – from existing sources, or your own imagination – that can help clarify your story.

Conjured images

Two years after *Redundant*, I was trying to figure out what my new play *Lucky Dog* was going to be about.

I already had the title, and I knew it was going to feature a middle-aged couple called Eddie and Sue. However, I wasn't sure if they were going to be serial killers (in the vein of Fred and Rosemary West), or if they were going to be ageing rockers (in the vein of Keith Richards and Marianne Faithfull).

I tried a few versions of the play, but none of them ringed true. I'd attempt a few plot outlines, manage a few pages, then get lost in a fog of crappy dialogue and even crappier action.

One day I was thinking about the series of powerful Dog-Woman paintings by Portuguese artist Paula Rego, and I wondered if I could attempt something similar for the play. Armed with a sketch pad and pastels from Ryman stationers, I sketched this scrappy image of Sue turning into a dog and barking at Eddie.

IMAGE 11 *'Lucky Dog' sketchbook #1* © Leo Butler, 2024.

It's hardly Rego, but I knew it had the potential for a terrific climax. I liked the tension between the domestic and the surreal, so I continued drawing and conjured up a couple more images.

The first (above) illustrates the faceless couple sitting at a table eating Christmas dinner, surrounded by darkness, and the next (below) shows the same couple sunbathing on a beach, bathed in yellow light.

IMAGE 12 *'Lucky Dog' sketchbook #2* © *Leo Butler, 2024.*

IMAGE 13 *'Lucky Dog' sketchbook #3* © *Leo Butler, 2024.*

Although I'd enjoyed wrestling with the serial killer/ageing rocker plays, it wasn't until I scribbled these pics that a simple story about a middle-aged couple in crisis began to emerge.

The images became anchors to build the script around. Likewise, the mood of the pictures helped determine the mood of the piece – the negative space in the sketches translated to excruciating moments of silence in the dialogue.

As for the narrative, the routine of Christmas dinner added pressure to Eddie and Sue's loveless marriage. The beach scene pointed me towards the play's final resolution and – when placed straight after the dog transformation – suggested a far more interesting journey than anything in the serial killer idea.

I could now ask the right questions about their relationship. Who are they? What's the problem? What's driven the couple apart? What pushes Sue to bark like a dog? How do they end up at a beach? What keeps them together? How do you get from point A to point B? Are there any missing scenes or characters?

As important as it is for the playwright to think like actors, it's just as helpful to think like designers, image makers or choreographers.

The great filmmaker Stanley Kubrick is often quoted as saying that every story contains five key moments – or tent poles – that the film, or play, cannot exist without. It's a wonderful concept, and in films like *A Clockwork Orange* [1971]*, Eyes Wide Shut* [1999] *or 2001: A Space Odyssey* [1968] you can see the five tent poles clearly delineated into sequences.

When mentoring students – especially at the early stages of play development – I encourage them to conjure three or four or five 'tent pole' images as a starting point, even if they end up being scrapped or changed later.

If you're working on an idea, why not grab a pencil and sketch some ideas for scenes/moments of your own?

Procrastination

No matter how many images you draw; at some point you must start writing.

As any writer knows, a normal day's work can involve doing the laundry, staring into space, arranging your books into alphabetical order, searching the internet for holidays you can't afford, sending random emails, hoovering, mopping, emptying the bins, having a shower, tidying your desk, searching YouTube for videos of old Fleetwood Mac gigs, fixing that shelf, staring into space, grooming the cat, scrolling through social media, posting something on social media, deleting something on social media, commenting on other peoples' posts on social media, popping out for a walk, picking up milk, making that phone call you should have made a fortnight ago, replying to random emails, getting up to stretch your legs, attempting some half-arsed yoga or Tai Chi, staring into space, researching a minor character's job on the internet, reading that play that's a 'bit like yours', wilfully ignoring that play that's a 'bit like yours', making lists of your top twenty favourite films for no reason, staring into space, picking your nose, reassessing your life choices, buying more milk and quickly writing three lines of dialogue before calling it a day.

If you have a regular job or small kids, you might treat yourself to one evening per week, or even an entire Sunday, to finish the play. The plan is realistic – six hours, six pages – but when the day comes you get distracted by the internet, doze off for an hour, feel shit about yourself and come away with zilch.

Procrastination, at its best, is scouring the internet and stumbling upon an exciting real-life story that you can dramatize or dreaming up a brilliant new idea as you're hanging out the socks. Procrastination, at its worst, is battling that voice in your head that tells you you're a fraud. You're not clever or talented, you haven't had an interesting life and you've got nothing interesting to say.

Ironically, once you *accept* that you're a fraud, you might find that you can write something good. Once you stop trying to be good, you might even find writing enjoyable.

It's OK and normal to be distracted, so procrastinate with reckless abandon! It takes energy and willpower to write. A half hour's rapid writing is better than torturing yourself for the whole day.

And if you feel blocked or uninspired, put a bomb under the thing. Destroy the structure, change the story, kill the characters, smash the play to smithereens.

Walk away, recharge and start something new. Usually when you start something new, it's usually the same idea dressed in different clothes anyway.

And if you're still staring into space, stuck in a creative rut, just freestyle the fuck out of it.

Freestyling dialogue

As I already mentioned in **Chapter Two**, freestyling (or free writing) allows you to vomit ideas and characters onto the page, hopefully producing some workable material.

In 2019, I was commissioned by producer Ola Animashawun to write a play for the National Theatre's Connections Festival. '*Connections*' is a wonderful programme of work that invites schools and youth theatres from across the country to stage brand-new, large-cast plays by established writers who want to experiment with stories that will engage and challenge the kids. I was delighted when Ola asked me to take part, so I rolled up my sleeves and put my thinking cap on.

My first idea was to write a knockabout farce about Victorian-era chimney sweeps who kidnap the Elephant Man, which I quickly ditched in favour of a more earnest drama about drug trafficking on 'county lines', which turned out to be . . . well, a bit too earnest.

Determined to find a decent idea, I spent the day in my favourite café – Sorrento in West Norwood – and, armed with coffee and cigarettes, started to freestyle in my notebook. Here's how it started . . .

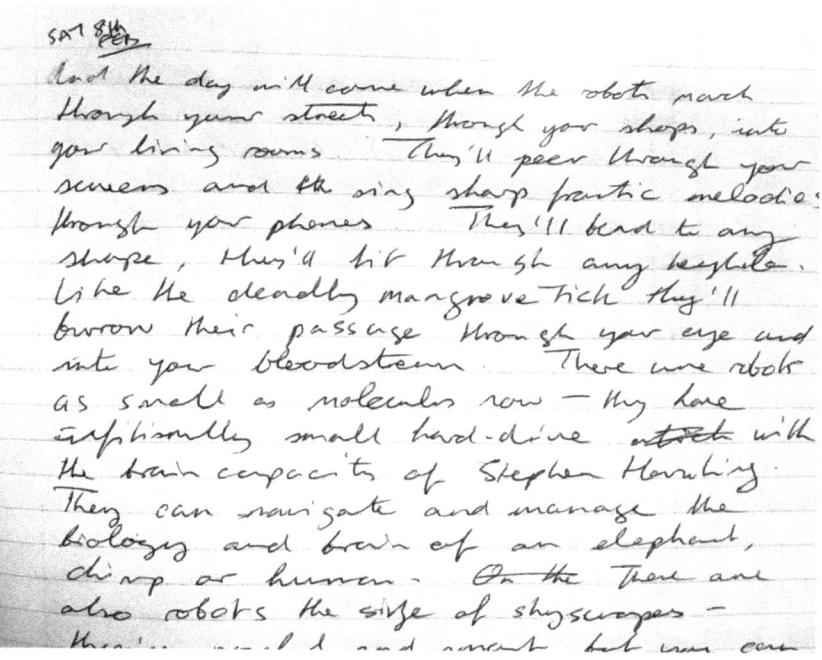

IMAGE 14 '*Innocent Creatures*' notebook #1 © Leo Butler, 2024.

Roughly transcribed, it reads *'Sat Feb 8th. And the day will come when the robots march through your streets, through your shops, into your living rooms. They'll peer through your screens and sing sharp frantic melodies through your phones. They'll bend to any shape, they'll fit through any keyhole. Like the deadly mangrove tick, they'll burrow their passage through your eye and into your bloodstream. There are robots the size of molecules . . .'*– and so it goes on for pages and pages; a mad stream of consciousness that concludes with the inner monologue of an octopus.

The following day – 9 February – I returned to Sorrento, and continued freestyling with . . .

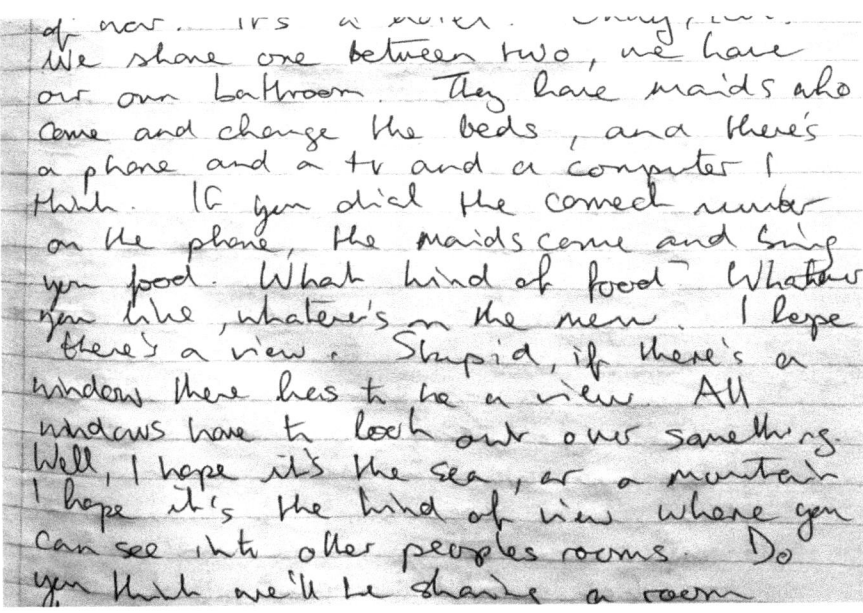

IMAGE 15 *'Innocent Creatures' notebook #2* © Leo Butler, 2024.

. . . which transcribes as *'They have maids who come and change the beds, and there's a phone and a tv and a computer I think. If you dial the correct number on the phone the maids come and bring you food. What kind of food? Whatever you like, whatever's on the menu. I hope there's a view. Stupid, if there's a window there has to be a view. All windows have to look out over something. Well, I hope it's the sea, or a mountain. I hope it's the kind of view where you can see into other peoples' rooms. Do you think we'll be sharing a room together?'*

Again, it continues for pages and pages, concluding with a dialogue about electronic tags and AI surveillance.

Suspecting I was onto something, I went home to type out the 'greatest hits' of the scrawl.

Connecting the various ramblings, I discover we're in a dystopian future where the world is governed (or infiltrated) by robots of various shapes and sizes.

Picking out shards of dialogue, it's clear that the voices belong to two children whose parents had been 'exterminated' for the good of the planet's ecosystem. They are now waiting to be rescued by helicopters and taken to a mysterious hotel. I decide to call them Enid and Mia; one of them has a knife, another one has a mechanized hamster. Why? *God knows. I'll have to figure that out later.*

I decide to place the children on a frozen, post-apocalyptic wasteland. There's a pack of elephant seals clambering over nearby Big Ben, and we can hear the distant screams of toddlers stranded on the ice.

Calling the play *Innocent Creatures,* I start at the beginning. The dialogue starts to flow out nicely (such as in this short excerpt, shortly after they've met) . . .

Enid   I once killed a moth and it turned out to be an android. Its hard drive went all over the wall, my Mum went mad.

Mia   You're funny.

Enid   Thanks. Do you think they'll have moths where we're going? Real ones, I mean.

Mia   Depends where we're going.

Enid   The email said 6.15. What time is it now?

Enid *shows* **Mia** *the email on her phone.*

Enid   Arrive by 6.15 it said, it says so here. Helicopters at 7. Check-in at the hotel by 8. Hey, I hope they put us in the same room! A big room with a view where you can see into other people's rooms. And if they don't, you know what I'm going to do? I'm going to ask them nicely.

Mia   Do you think Robots understand nice?

Enid   We could try and make them understand.

Mia   They're so much cleverer than us though. I'm not sure Robots know the difference between good or bad or anything. They're like brains on a stick.

Enid   If they weren't nice then they wouldn't send us an email.

Mia   Well, emails have minds of their own.

Enid   Everything has a mind of its own. That glacier has a mind of its own.

As the scene develops – by *improvising through dialogue* – I discover new insights about the world and the fears that are driving the characters. There's humour and friendliness at the start of the scene, but it's a sham. Over the course of twenty pages, Mia gradually reveals she has a hidden motive, and a more life-and-death situation emerges. It builds to a climax . . .

Enid   You're illegal, shut up.

Mia   You know I could cut out yours too if you'd like?

Enid   Cut mine out?

Mia   Your tracker, I can disable it. Stop you being lonely.

Enid   Who said I'm lonely? – You're cold and illegal, pull your scarf up.

Mia   My gran used to work at the hospital and she's good with a knife. Quick slice and it popped out like a fine-cut diamond it did. When the blu-tooth wore off I felt light as a feather, the Robots don't even know you exist. Stupid plastic chip beeping and sharing your location all the time. No-one knows you, you can go anywhere you want, you've got a cool scar. How about it, eh? I've seen things you wouldn't believe.

Mia *removes a knife from her belt and aims for* **Enid***'s neck (her microchip).*

Mia   You could stay and see things with me. We can go anywhere we want. We can teach the toddlers to dream without their data being screened.

Enid *turns and knocks* **Mia***'s knife out of her hand.*

Enid *(as she does so)*   I told you to pull your scarf up, stupid! Why'd you have to be so stupid?!

The sound of approaching helicopters.

Mia   Here, stamp on the ice with me, look.

Mia *starts stamping on the ice.*

Mia   Don't let them see you! Stamp with me, it's fun! Stamp your feet!

The ice starts to crack and **Enid** *runs away, heading to the helicopters.*

Mia   No, wait! Enid, don't!!

Massive sound of the helicopters, casting their shadow over **Mia**, *who crashes through the ice.*

End of scene.

With a rough draft of the opening scene in place, I think about Enid and Mia's backstories and the kind of journey I want to take them on. Under the surface, it operates like a classic romance. Their disagreements remind me of the broken branch/God argument I had with Martin Murray-mints when I was a kid.

I research the future of Artificial Intelligence in books and on the internet. I explore its role in saving the planet's ecosystem. *What if the logical way to save the planet from climate disaster is to eradicate humankind? And if the sun will explode and destroy the planet at some point anyway, why is life worth living?* Good questions for teenagers I thought.

I decide the play will span millions of years. Having spent many civilizations apart, a 'mechanized' Enid and a 'cloned' Mia are finally reunited at the end of time.

I call the play *Innocent Creatures* and play with some images and shapes.

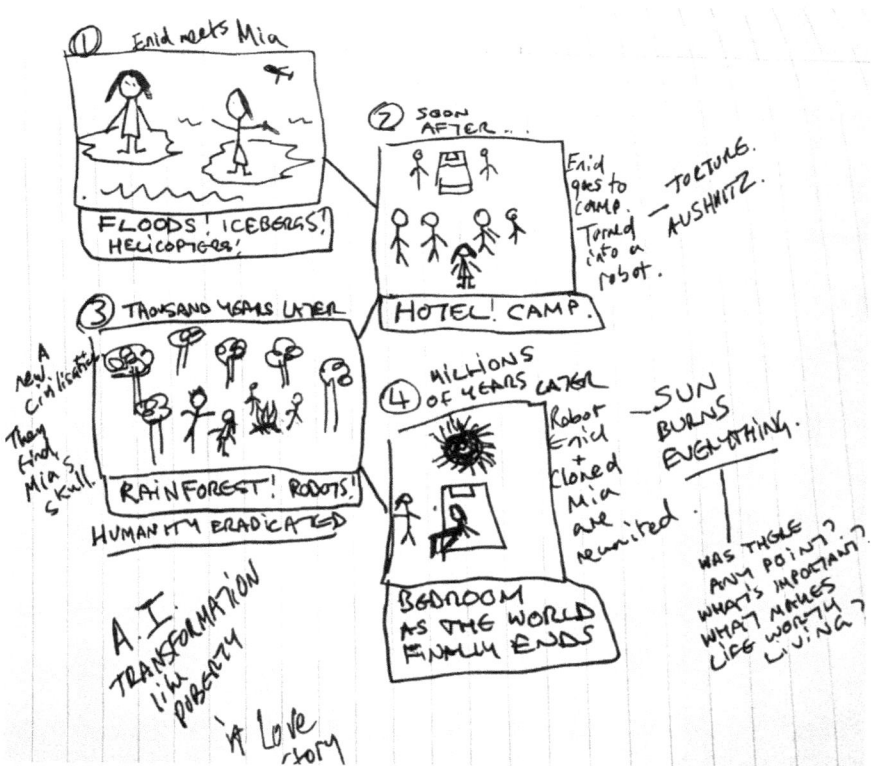

IMAGE 16 *'Innocent Creatures' notebook #3* © Leo Butler, 2024.

Each scene will have a different flavour and include plenty more characters, so there's lots of work to do. But I've got an architecture to hold it all together, which means I can attack each scene with the same freestyling abandon. I make mistakes and hit speedbumps along the way, which is part of the job.

Although it was one of the most *unconsciously* written scripts I've ever done, it turned out to be one of the most satisfying.

And if you're stuck

And if you don't like freestyling from scratch, here's a few lines of dialogue to get you started . . .

A: Hello.

B: Hello. How are you?

A: I'm fine. How are you?

B: I'm okay.

Could this be the dullest dialogue ever written?
Take a moment.
Imagine that **B** has been kidnapped and is tied to a chair in a windowless cell. **A** is the kidnapper and has just returned to the cell after a few days' absence, saying . . .

A: Hello.

B: Hello. How are you?

A: I'm fine. How are you?

B: I'm okay.

Is it still the dullest dialogue ever written?
Of course it isn't. With such a creepy, violent situation, sentences like 'I'm fine' or 'How are you?' suddenly have double meaning and are loaded with psychological and emotional intent.
Now, let's imagine a different situation . . .
A and **B** are on honeymoon, **BUT** character **B** has picked up **A**'s phone and seen a private message from his/her secret lover revealing a pregnancy.
A walks in from the shower, guessing something's wrong with **B**, and says . .

A: Hello.

B: Hello. How are you?

A: I'm fine. How are you?

B: I'm okay.

Again, the boring dialogue suddenly has fuel and subtext. It's weird that the newly married couple are greeting each other like that and, as such, we can *feel* something is amiss without either saying anything explicit. Each line of dialogue becomes a cover for the truth, an avoidance or a tactic to *do* or *get* something from the other person.

Now, imagine that **A** nervously walks into **B**'s office for a job interview, **BUT** character **A** has travelled back in time to warn **B** of some impending disaster.

We don't know it yet, but **B** and **A** are the same person!

A: Hello.

B: Hello. How are you?

A: I'm fine. How are you?

B: I'm okay.

Or imagine that **A** comes home to greet their mother, **BUT** character **A** has been missing for ten years and **B** (the mother) is either drunk or on drugs.

A: Hello.

B: Hello. How are you?

A: I'm fine. How are you?

B: I'm okay.

Two schoolkids meet in the playground, **BUT** character **A** knows that **B** has a big secret that no one's supposed to know about. Perhaps there's violence at home, or maybe **A** knows that **B** secretly fancies them.

A: Hello.

B: Hello. How are you?

A: I'm fine. How are you?

B: I'm okay.

Or imagine two unhappily married strangers have arranged to meet on an online dating app. **BUT** when they arrive at the restaurant, they realize they're already married.

A: Hello.

B: Hello. How are you?

A: I'm fine. How are you?

B: I'm okay.

Of course, the trick is to come up with the rest of the scene and to decide how long to keep the suspense or tension building to a climax.
Don't worry, reader, I have faith in you.
Good dialogue doesn't have to be clever, funny or full of poetry.
All you need is a couple of characters, a simple situation and a **BIG BUT.**
Once you have that, the stuff that comes out of their mouths is about navigation and tactics. It's a lot easier to write, and the audience will be hooked.
Grab a pencil, fill in the blanks and see where it takes you.

A: Hello.

B: Hello. How are you?

A: I'm fine. How are you?

B: I'm okay.

A:

B:

A:

B:

A:

B:

A:

B:

A:

B:

(Pause)

B:

A:

Who knows, you may have the beginning of a great new play. Good luck!

6

I can play the lion too!

Cackling with laughter, faces daubed with snot, they chase me up the stairs into the nearest bedroom and tackle me to the ground.

It's 1986, the final year of primary school. My best friend – who, I'm going to call CHARACTER C – has started hanging out with a bunch of punks who've been squatting in the house next door to his parents' place in Firvale (just five minutes down the road from Pitsmoor). In awe of the foul-mouthed twenty-somethings with their pierced nipples and homemade tattoos, CHARACTER C insists I come and meet them. The stick-thin, pink-haired alpha of the group – who calls himself Spike or Splodge or something – doesn't give a f*ck that we're kids and welcomes us into his entourage of bargain-basement Sid Vicious caricatures. He also has a sexy girlfriend with gravity-defying purple hair who – to an eleven-year-old boy who's finally growing pubes and getting erections – appears like manna from heaven with her smoky mascara and ripped lace tops.

Heroically piss-poor, the self-proclaimed psychos while away the days playing out a fantasy dreamed up by Malcolm McClaren in 1978, a soundtrack of Combat 84 crackling from their knackered dansette. CHARACTER C and I quickly adopt the role of their live studio audience, cheering them on in exchange for B & H cigs and bottles of Merrydown cider, which usually ends up puked all over the floor. One night we're there till long after midnight waiting for their dealer to bring a bunch of LSD tabs for us to sample, but Spike's girlfriend steps in and suggests that, even by their standards, it might not be the best idea in the world. Nevertheless, we keep turning up at their door after school and, for an intense couple of months, we feel like we're part of the band.

Then suddenly – out of boredom or competitiveness – CHARACTER C starts poking fun at me in front of the others, criticising my weight or punching me for preferring the Stranglers to the Sex Pistols – which, apart from their three big hits, I still do. I'm a friendly Beatles-loving kid, slightly chubby, often giggling in the corner of the room, and I'm rubbish at confrontation. The more I refuse to fight back, the worse the threats become. CHARACTER C's much closer to the group than I am, and they're happy to be riled, so it's only a matter of time before they're chasing me up the stairs to the upstairs bedroom.

I'm tackled to the ground and, armed with marker pens, they cover my arms and torso with swastikas. Struggling to break free, crying and shouting, they throw me into the wardrobe, blocking the door, and I'm trapped in the dark for the rest of the night. Finally forced to admit I'm a 'thick fat c*nt', they scrub the swastikas off my skin with fairy liquid and Brillo pads.

I never set foot in that squat again, but CHARACTER C sheepishly apologizes for what happened, and we decide to stay friends.

In September, we enrol at Firth Park Secondary School, where we're put into the same year group and class. Firth Park has some good teachers, but it's a rough over-populated place, so me and CHARACTER C stick together through the first term. Everything's fine until we're caught writing snarky comments about the form tutor in our school books and given detentions. CHARACTER C blames me for the incident, and soon – enlisting new classmates – the bullying and humiliation starts again. This goes on for about three years.

It isn't the physical violence that's damaging, but more the constant intimidation and threats. Being the 1980s, bullying is largely ignored by the teachers, with some believing it to be a natural part of growing up, or a means of character building (especially for boys). It becomes normal to dread getting the bus to school each morning, and to believe it's all my fault and, on some level, richly deserved. CHARACTER C was popular – even with teachers, my other friends or with girls I fancied – and, as a form of self-defence, I embrace my new role as a weirdo or freak. I start to eat more junk and gain a lot of weight – which gives CHARACTER C more ammunition – and by the third year I'm stealing booze from my parents' stash. Necking cans of lager or bottles of gin, I turn up to lessons drunk, as becoming the school 'alky' is preferable to being 'the fat, useless bastard who should be shot', and it commands a warped form of respect. At lunch breaks, I disappear into nearby Concorde Park, but I'm often tracked down and forced to hand over pocket money or made to repeat unspeakable things with a boot wedged on my head. By the fourth year of school, I've given up and start truanting every day. I spend a lot of time on the top decks of buses, travelling out of Sheffield into the countryside, my face buried in books or staring out of the window fantasizing about another life.

Even at my best I was never an A* student, but my report cards are now a horror show of Ds and Fs. Eventually, my parents are brought in for a meeting with the head of year, and I beg to be moved to a different class on the other side of school.

Firth Park Secondary was massive, with each year group split into two separate blocks, so the transition is easy. When the head of year asks why I want to be moved, I explain what CHARACTER C has been doing and he's finally brought in and reprimanded However, in the summer – just before joining my new class – our house on Burngreave Road is burgled while we're away on holiday, with everything, including my dad's prized record collection, stolen or trashed. Some years later, I discover – via a mutual friend – that CHARACTER C had admitted (or boasted) that it was him. But we'd left school by this time, and he was well off the radar, probably puking on the carpet in a squat of his own.

Although (to quote a famous song) my life has changed in oh so many ways, it's still painful to recount the experience, and I still feel pangs of shame for allowing it to happen. In darker moments, I've blamed my parents for not teaching me to stand up for myself, or I might (even in professional relationships) suddenly get paranoid of other peoples' motives. If there's an argument or confrontation, I sometimes want to disappear on the top deck of a bus or to disappear altogether (like the character Dave in my 2008 play *Faces in the Crowd*). When situations in adult life threaten to become echoes of the past, I'll struggle to pull myself together, reigning in childish reactions from my twelve-year-old self that I didn't have the maturity to deal with at the time. Likewise, my crazy experience with 'the demon in the woods' isn't entirely disconnected from what happened at school, and, although I sometimes wish they weren't, my plays – from *Boy* to *The Early Bird* to *Redundant* – are littered with references to those years.

But, as George Harrison sang, you can only ever 'be here now' and as much as I wished I'd kicked CHARACTER C's head in, I'd prefer to reflect on the positive aspects of my teenage years. Had it not been for the bullying, I may not have pursued my writing, or sought better friendships. And if I hadn't done that, I may not have fallen in love with my wife or started my own family.

At the age of fourteen, as much as I hated going to school, I was also bursting with excitement at the thought of rehearsing plays with my other (significantly older) friends at the weekends. In some ways, I was living a double life – the good, theatrical half fuelling my fantasies as I truanted on the top deck of the bus to escape the beatings.

This double-life began around the time that eleven-year-old me was being accosted by the punks, when, one afternoon, our primary school teacher introduced a mysterious-looking woman to our class. Her name was Meg Jepson, the director of the Sheffield Youth Theatre, and she'd come to invite any interested pupils to join her 1986 Summer School, culminating in a production of *A Midsummer Night's Dream*.

Having already shown an interest in acting, I happily met Meg for ten minutes after school. She was tall and thin, dressed in a wide billowing skirt; and with her spidery fingers and dark probing eyes, would be utterly terrifying if it wasn't for her wry sense of humour and ability to listen. Sitting in the headteacher's office, I told her how I'd played Willy Wonka and the Tin Man in our school plays, but I'd soon discover that Meg's interest was in classical texts like Shakespeare and the *Ramayana*, so my glittering CV was met with polite indifference. However, when I pulled a set of notebooks from my bag that were full of stupid stories and gruesomely comic sketches (that I'd also performed at school), Meg suddenly perked up.

Although it was unusual for a child of nine or ten to be writing and performing their own sketches, it felt perfectly normal to me. I'd been an attention-seeking sod for years, and I suspect that's why people like CHARACTER C sometimes wanted to beat me up. Here I am – about seven or eight years old, sitting at a typewriter.

IMAGE 17 *The author at typewriter c.1982/1983. Photo reproduced from author's archive.*

I could be writing a script, but it's possible I'm just dicking around – playing the part of a writer for the camera.

I think it was ska-band Madness that first gave me the bug for showing off. Bangers like *House of Fun*, *Shut Up* and *Cardiac Arrest* are as good as anything by The Kinks or The Clash in my opinion, and woefully underappreciated. But it was their music videos – in which the band play multiple roles with unabashed stupidity – that got me hooked. I remember writing to *Jim'll Fix It* to 'fix it for me' to join the band on stage, and I'd frequently coax Martin Murray-mints to join me at the bedroom window, holding tennis rackets, singing *Night Boat to Cairo* for the benefit of our neighbours.

At the same time, my mum ignited my lifelong obsession with The Beatles by bringing me LPs of *Sgt Pepper*, *Magical Mystery Tour* and *The White Album* from the library. The fab four's mind-bending creativity was much more exciting than anything on *Top of the Pops*, and – like Madness – opened a door to a fantastical, shape-shifting world that I wanted to be a part of.

During the summer holidays, our parents usually took us on caravan holidays to Blackpool or Great Yarmouth, which me and Matt always looked forward to. I remember Dad fixed up a tiny portable telly, powered by the car battery, so that we didn't get bored when they nipped to the pub of an evening. With nothing but a bag of soggy chips, we tuned into BBC Two and were suddenly confronted with Monty Python's first feature film *And Now for Something Completely Different* [MacNaughton, 1971]. Howling with laughter at sketches like *Hell's Grannies* or *How to Defend Yourself Against Fresh Fruit*, I was an instant convert, and – as with The Beatles and Madness – began collecting all their albums and books. When Dad bought our first Betamax player, I recorded all the films and TV shows whenever they were repeated on TV, learning all the sketches by heart.

Monty Python soon led me in the direction of sitcoms like *The Young Ones* [BBC, 1982–1984] and *Blackadder* [BBC, 1983–1989], and to the films of Woody Allen, Mel Brooks, The Marx Brothers and Charlie Chaplin.

Chaplin – who wrote and directed all his films, as well as performing, editing and composing the music – quickly became the benchmark of what a great artist should be. The simplicity of his storytelling combined with his working-class radicalism were, even to a snotty kid in the 1980s, as inspiring as they must have been to Federico Fellini or Satyajit Ray. Films like *The Kid* [1921], *The Circus* [1928], *City Lights* [1931] and *The Great Dictator* [1940] are as deeply moving as they are funny, and – with a masterful blend of gallows humour and pathos – champion those on the bottom rung of the social ladder. Years later, when I was working on *Boy*, I revisited Chaplin's *Modern Times* [1936], as the film's episodic story of a displaced misfit at odds with an industrialized world, mirrored Liam's odyssey through twenty-first-century London. During the play's rehearsal, I remember pointing the play's lead actor, Frankie Fox, in the direction of *Modern Times*, which was very helpful in the scene where Liam wordlessly struggles with a Sainsbury's self-checkout machine.

Kevin Brownlow and David Gill's documentary *Unknown Chaplin* [ITV, 1983], which delves into Chaplin's archives to explore his working methods, was equally inspiring. Chaplin didn't use a script, but, instead, built huge sets – such as an ice rink, an East End Street or a cargo ship – based on no more than a *hunch*. He would then improvise on these sets over a period of months or (in the case of *City Lights*) years, until the idea crystallized, and he could crack on with the film. The documentary reveals a treasure trove of footage showing Chaplin inventing and rehearsing ideas across hundreds of individual takes. He was a perfectionist, obsessed with logic, and would tear down sets, do away with characters or scrap entire storylines, until he was completely satisfied. It was amazing to discover how a short comedy like

The Immigrant [1917] – which, on the surface, seem so effortless – took months of mental strain and sacrifice to get right. Although I've never had my own studio or an ensemble of actors, I've always used Chaplin's trial-and-error process as a template for my own writing process, and when teaching.

Woody Allen, the heir to Chaplin, was equally instructive. It was a few years before I discovered films like *Annie Hall* [1976], *Zelig* [1983] and *Hannah and her Sisters* [1986], but those early, gag-tastic comedies like *Love and Death* [1975] and *Sleeper* [1973] – which I rented from *Video City* in Firth Park – gave me the first nudge that a good script was as important as good actors.

We were the TV generation, submerged in pop culture, and *Video City* (a short journey on the number 75 bus, next door to the KFC) was our mecca. The Betamax section was in the basement and each movie had a serial number. You'd choose the movie, press the intercom's buzzer and read out the correlating number to whoever was on the counter that day. Each videocassette was kept in a blank brown box, so the cashier had no idea what movie you were renting. Me and Matt quickly realized the flaw in their system and, over a period of months, gorged on a diet of X-rated movies, including *Dawn of the Dead* [1978], *Driller Killer* [1979], *The Exorcist* [1973], *Zombie Flesh Eaters* [1979] and the most prized possession of all, *The Texas Chainsaw Massacre*.

While other ten-year-old boys were consumed with Subbuteo, I'd be covering my bedroom walls with posters of *Psycho 2* [1983] and *The Evil Dead* [1981], then head downstairs to teach myself *Across the Universe* on Dad's rickety, second-hand piano. I'd wolf down a pot noodle while flicking through the screenplay of *Monty Python and the Holy Grail* [1975], then go back to my room to melt a couple of biros on the Calor-gas heater to see 'what they look like melted'. Bored, I pick up one of my notebooks and write a new script of *Dracula*, which I decide I'm going to record. Needing it to sound realistic, I catch the bus to the library and borrow an LP of *BBC Sound Effects: Death and Horror*, which includes everything from screams and stabbings to vampire bats and premature burial. My dad has an old reel-to-reel machine that I've learnt how to master, so I enlist Matt – who is now into far cooler stuff like Martin Amis and The Smiths – to help record the script. We perform all the parts with stupid voices, and, with the help of the Sound Effects album, pay close attention to the extended death scenes, which we're especially proud of. Once done, we play it back to anyone who'd listen – usually, our bemused parents.

Santa Claus also knew about my interest in movies as one year he left a second-hand Super 8 camera, with a projector and screen, under the tree. It was the best Christmas present I'd ever got – a toybox of celluloid, light and sprockets – and my five-minute pastiche of slasher flicks, *Horror at the Bloggs Motel*, soon went into production at my friend Ciaran's house in Lowedges. It was a delight to send the film off to be developed and receive an actual reel of film in the post, but as the projector was stored upstairs, in the cold dark attic, audiences for my horror masterpiece were slim.

Nearing the end of primary school, my usual partner-in-crime, Martin Murray, had moved away, but, fortunately, I'd made a new best friend called CHARACTER C who was intrigued by my unusual hobbies. We'd both enjoyed acting in the school plays, so when I showed him a script I'd written called *Happy Hospital* and suggested we perform it to our classmates during assembly, he was more than keen.

Happy Hospital had a gruesome (and very messy) premise and I've still no idea why the teachers agreed to let us do it. Me and CHARACTER C played 'mad' surgeons, dressed in scrubs, and we burst onto stage looking for an unwilling patient. We've 'planted' another friend, Kevin Footit, in the audience, and – to our classmates' delight – drag him onto a table covered with plastic sheets. We pretend to cut Kevin open with hedge cutters, and, using buckets of fake blood, discover a variety of ridiculous objects – plastic chicken legs, boxes of cornflakes and toy babies – wrapped up in his guts. Each item is more absurd (and gorier) than the last, showering blood everywhere, until finally, at the play's climax, we forget the patient altogether and kill each other instead. A contemporary classic.

When I told Meg Jepson about *Happy Hospital,* I suggested she meet my friend CHARACTER C as well, but he'd already left school, heading for the punks' squat instead, and I signed up for the summer school on my own.

Meg ran the Sheffield Youth Theatre from 1977 until 2008, and anyone who took part in one of her productions was guaranteed a unique – and possibly life-changing – experience. Having become a drama teacher in the mid-seventies, Meg had been encouraged – by fellow teacher Micheal Goater – to set up a youth theatre that was free and inclusive. She was passionate about creating high-quality theatre opportunities for working-class communities, with a focus on classical texts, especially Shakespeare. Peter Brook became the youth theatre's patron, and, for more than thirty years, Meg introduced advanced acting techniques, largely inspired by Japanese Noh Theatre, to hundreds of unsuspecting kids like me.

It was a shock that rehearsals of *A Midsummer's Night's Dream* were going to last all summer, but I knew there'd be trouble at home if I didn't give it a go.

Hopping off the bus on Langsett Road, I trudged up the steep incline to the top of Burnaby Crescent and, struggling for breath, finally arrived at the gates of Walkley House. Walkley House was an old nineteenth-century boarding school, which overlooked the city, and Meg had renamed it 'Drama Space'.

Through the gates, up the entrance stairs, you'd enter a large, sun-lit hall that served as the main practise space. At the edges of the hall were doorways leading into several unfurnished classrooms; two of which functioned as male/female changing rooms, while the others were used for singing sessions, fencing/fight practise and to work through individual scenes.

Whether at school holidays, or on Sundays during term time, rehearsals would start at 8.00 am and end at 5.00 pm. No one was allowed to leave the building, and at lunchtime we'd set up trestle tables where the whole company would eat. There were usually twenty or thirty kids in each production, and I was easily the youngest when I first started. Most were already in secondary school, and there were a half dozen 'senior' members in their late teens and early twenties. Two of these, Andrew Shepherd and Ian Champion, shared my love of comedy movies and – despite being five or six years older – took me under their wing, quickly becoming close friends. Andrew and Ian were talented actors and very funny, constantly doing impressions and slapstick routines, which they encouraged me to join in. Unlike CHARACTER C, they were decent people, and, in fact, so were all the youth theatre kids, as Meg fostered an environment without competitiveness or ego. She could be frustratingly strict, but she also had an unwavering belief in the creative potential of all her students, coupled with an infectious laugh that would echo round the hall.

We'd arrive and change into the youth theatre's homemade practise trousers – billowing, but roomy – and then spend the first hour cleaning the school. Sweeping the hall with long-handled brushes, cleaning under the pipes with rags, washing the windows with J-Cloths; no one was allowed to slack off and it was a thorough and exhausting job. Some parents were understandably alarmed by these strict chores, but the ritual of purifying the practise space – adopted from Noh theatre methods and practitioners like Stanislavski – was surprisingly calming, and a good leveller for jittery newcomers like me.

One of the senior members would then lead us through a physical warm up of sun salutations and yoga moves, all done with the utmost seriousness. Sometimes I'd get told off for giggling or making stupid jokes, as I was way out of my comfort zone. *Isn't a youth theatre meant to be fun? When are we going to start acting?*

The warm up would conclude with a meditation exercise. We'd lay on the floor, and Meg would ask us to picture a blackboard and, with a piece of imaginary chalk, ask us to write down everything that had happened to us the previous week. For me, with everything that was happening at school, this could be a challenge. Taking an imaginary cloth to the imaginary chalk, we'd wipe the events from the board as a kind of 'internal purification'. Then in silence, concentrating on our breathing, we'd gradually open our eyes and 'fall still'.

'Fall still' was Meg's mantra that followed every exercise or rehearsal as a means of keeping us focused – physically and mentally – before moving on to the next activity.

There were no chairs in the hall, so we all sat on the floor, and we'd finally start to read or discuss the text. Here's Meg leading a session at the front of the big hall . . .

IMAGE 18 *Photo credit: Meg Jepson teaching a Sheffield Youth Theatre class c.1986. Photo reproduced with kind permission from @ Sheffield City Archives.*

Unlike a lot of youth theatres, there were no sweary modern plays about the trials of teenage life. There were no pantomimes or musicals, and the plays – even Christmas shows – were rarely allowed a curtain call, often leaving the audience of bewildered parents applauding an empty set.

Meg was a purist, believing that the gesture of the whole play was more important that any single member of the company. In contrast to the aristocratic, Conservative peer – and *Downton Abbey* [2010] screenwriter – Julian Fellowes's assertion that audiences need a Shakespearean 'scholarship' to fully understand the plays, Meg believed that they belonged to everyone. She refused to cut, abridge or update. There was no dumbing down the language because we were ordinary state-school kids and, as such, didn't have the privately educated intellectual prowess of someone like Fellowes. On the contrary, she believed that we were more equipped than anyone to understand Shakespeare *because* we were kids, *because* of our working-class backgrounds.

I CAN PLAY THE LION TOO!

IMAGE 19 *Photo credit: Sheffield Youth Theatre production of 'The Tempest' (Merlin Theatre, Sheffield, 1987). Photo reproduced with kind permission from @ Sheffield City Archives.*

For the first two or three rehearsal weeks, we puzzled through the entire script together, scene by scene, moment by moment. We were forced to make sense of Shakespeare's verse by simply speaking it out loud and putting the scenes on their feet. If you didn't understand something, you might occasionally stop to look up the definition of a word, or examine a phrase, but, overall, Meg would encourage you to just keep repeating lines such as . . .

*'Things base and vile, holding no quantity,
Love can transpose to form and dignity.'*

. . . until suddenly – like a spell – it made complete sense. Rather than approaching the play from an academic perspective, we were directed to use movement and gesture to help root ourselves in the *emotion* or *intention* of each line. The casting was always gender fluid – regardless of age or experience – and so, in a single day, you might have the chance to play both Oberon <u>and</u> Titania, or Demetrius, or Cobweb or Flute the bellows mender.

Each character, large or fleeting, would be given equal regard, and if you were caught breaking character or *doing nothing*, you would be called out in front of the whole cast and made to start the scene all over again.

In both rehearsals and performance, no one was allowed to wander off or get distracted. During rehearsals, if you weren't in a scene, you stayed and supported your fellow actors by participating in discussions. And in performances, you were all expected to stay and watch from the wings.

Although it may sound sadistic, the sense of collective responsibility was galvanizing, and we became an ensemble in the truest sense of the word.

By the third or fourth week, the play was finally cast, and I was given the role of Snug the Joiner, who – in the play's anarchic sub-plot – joins the other tradesmen in rehearsing a disastrous play-within-a-play for the star-crossed nobles. It was frightening to be performing in front of a public audience, but there was a tangible camaraderie between us, and with the preposterously loveable Andrew Shepherd cast as Bully Bottom, rehearsals were always thick with laughter. We even got our picture in the *Sheffield Star,* as part of a feature on the youth theatre, which made us feel like showbiz royalty for about five minutes (even though they credited me as 'Leo Bullen').

IMAGE 20 *Photo credit: Sheffield Youth Theatre's 'A Midsummer's Night's Dream' in the* Sheffield Star *c.1986. Photo reproduced with kind permission from @ SWNS Ltd.*

The youth theatre didn't have a theatre of its own, so the plays toured to various venues in and around the city – including The Merlin and Library theatres, as well as the Crucible Studio – with audience numbers ranging from triple to single figures. Very often, productions were adapted for outdoor spaces, such as churches or the grounds of Manor Castle, and, in the case of *A Midsummer Night's Dream*, a secluded, tree-lined clearing of the Sheffield Botanical Gardens.

We performed to an audience of parents and *actual* theatregoers, in a string of afternoon and evening shows during the final days of the summer holidays. *A Midsummer Night's Dream* is a beautiful play – if not the greatest play ever written, then certainly the most joyous – and to play a small part in its cobweb-like plot of love potions, enchanted spirits and surreal transfigurations was one of the happiest times of my life.

As the sun set and the stars appeared, at the climax of the evening shows, each member of the cast would take a candle and line up on the edge of the gardens' winding paths, past the stone fountains and glass pavilions, to sing the audience home. Led by future West End musical talent Paul Hazel (who played Puck), the whole company belted out the song of the fairies – '*You spotted snakes with double-tongue*' – in a chorus of well-drilled rounds and double rounds. For the first time, I experienced theatre as alchemy; Shakespeare's 400-year-old text conjuring the Athenian Forest in that empty space between actors and audience.

The youth theatre, and Meg's unapologetically strict process, was an antidote to the misery of Firth Park School, and I don't know how I would have survived without it. Up until the age of sixteen, I took part in many SYT productions, playing numerous roles, including Trinculo in *The Tempest*, Friar Laurence in *Romeo and Juliet* and Shylock in *The Merchant of Venice*. When we took a break from Shakespeare, usually at Christmas, the company would adapt versions of John Bunyan's *The Pilgrim's Progress* [1678], the Grimm Brothers' *Briar Rose* [1812] or forgotten Japanese Folk Tales such as *Hoichi the Earless*.

No doubt remembering my notebooks full of gory sketches, Meg sometimes asked me to contribute to the adaptations. In *Briar Rose*, for instance, I was asked to write the speech (below) for the Fish who magically appears before Aurora's mother near the start of the play. And so, at the grand old age of twelve, my writing was performed before a paying audience for the first time.

Back at Firth Park Comprehensive, I badgered two of my drama classmates, Ryan and Paul, to sign up to the youth theatre and the three of us became thick as thieves. When the BBC approached Meg for a couple of kids to appear in an Al Hunter penned radio play, *The Carol Singers* [1987], both me and Paul were sent to London to play opposite northern acting legend Brian Glover in the wood-panelled studios of Broadcasting House. Meanwhile, Ryan and I convinced Meg to let us write and perform our own version of *The Pied Piper*, which we toured around infant schools during

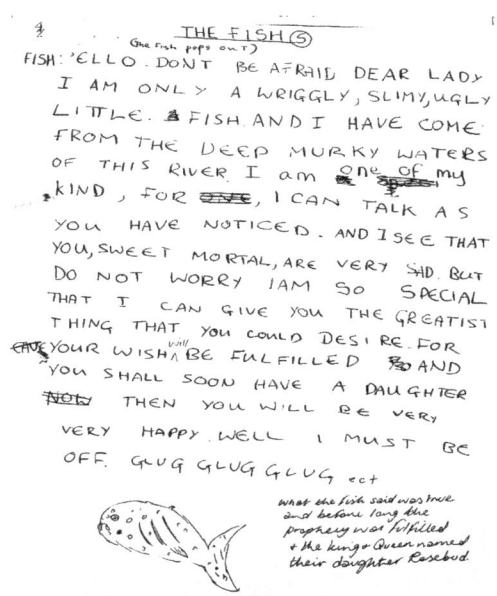

IMAGE 21 *Butler's Fish speech, Briar Rose, 1987* © Leo Butler, 2024.

term time, and, instead of doing homework, I continued writing daft stage comedies, such as *The Adventures of Foothead and Zobe*.

By the fifth year, CHARACTER C had long gone, but I continued to use my youth theatre training as a shield, perfecting a variety of roles to hide behind. I'd turn up to class dressed as Harpo Marx, cutting the handles off classmates' plastic bags with a pair of scissors I'd stashed in my schoolbag. When I wasn't being 'dead weird' with my homemade Ouija board, I'd become 'dead intelligent' showing off well-thumbed novels like Jean-Paul Sartre's *Age of Reason* that I'd pinched from my parents' bookshelf. Being a little bit in love with the dark-eyed girl in our drama class, we became Firth Park's own 'Burton & Taylor', performing emotional scenes from *Who's Afraid of Virginia Woolf* [Edward Albee, 1962] for our end of year exams, but I never had the courage to ask her out. Deep down, I was still that frightened little kid being chased up the stairs, and when not acting or writing, I'd continue disappearing into my fantasies on the bus. As much as they tried to stop me bunking off, my schoolteachers had largely given up . . . .

My long-suffering parents must have taken some relief from my commitment to the youth theatre, and that I'd finally escaped CHARACTER C, but as the end of secondary school approached, they were understandably concerned about my future.

Looking back, it's difficult to consolidate the two sides of my teenage life. While writing this chapter, I've frequently stopped to ask myself 'which one

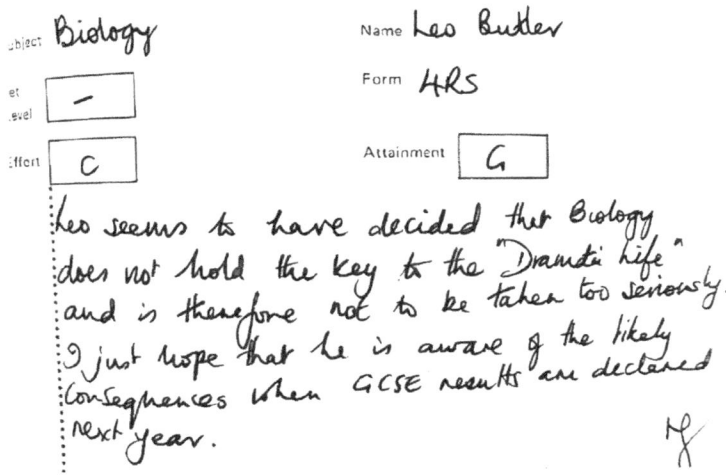

IMAGE 22 *Butler Biology Report, 1980s © Leo Butler, 2024.*

was more real? The discipline and focus of the youth theatre or the chaos and disorder of school? How did I manage to straddle these two worlds?'. And, crucially, what has any of this got to do with playwriting?

The youth theatre was my education, and I feel blessed that it gave me the ability to pick up any Shakespeare play and read it without difficulty. When teaching students, I have tried (in my own laid-back manner) to nurture focus and self-confidence in a way that Meg would approve. And in my own playwriting, I have always looked to Shakespeare, as much as I have The Beatles or Charlie Chaplin, as a benchmark of quality and a source of inspiration.

Shakespeare's plays aren't meant for the classroom, they're a universe to be inhabited. Like a hallucinogenic, they reveal the world as it really is and without judgement, levelling nobility and elevating the downtrodden to the same human face.

We encourage role play for small kids as a means of developing social skills and empathy for different people and cultures. Why stop after pre-school? Shakespeare is role play at its most advanced, a gift for people of all ages, whether they're trained actors or not. To step into the shoes of complex, morally questionable, characters, such as Prospero, Lady Macbeth or Lear, helps us grapple with the thorniest aspects of human nature, and our politics.

Pick any play from his complete works, and you'll find a universe of flawed characters written with objectivity. The playwright's own opinion or judgement is nowhere to be found and, instead, he offers that responsibility to the audience. *King Lear* and *Macbeth* are obvious examples, but even *A Midsummer Night's Dream* includes characters, such as Oberon or Puck, whose motives are questionable, with the quartet of lovers so brilliantly flawed they could quite as easily be running round naked in a Joe Orton farce. When Meg cast me as a fourteen-year-old Shylock, it was a challenge to connect the action and words of a character who gruesomely seeks a 'pound of flesh', but also delivers one of the greatest anti-racism speeches ever written.

Unlike religious texts, Shakespeare doesn't proselytize or impose a monistic viewpoint. Unlike a lot of modern drama, he doesn't reprimand or bark into the echo chamber. Like Brecht and Ibsen and Caryl Churchill, it is less the overall story, but the complex, often contradictory, choices of the characters that demand multiple interpretations, and that is why they stand the test of time.

I've always believed that the world would be a better place if we gave every world leader a fat dose of MDMA and airdropped them into a field with a playlist of classic trance rave. But if that isn't possible, then a summer school exploring *Henry IV: Part One* might be just as good. Shakespeare's plays are philosophy, poetry, politics and science *in action*, and perhaps they should be removed from the English curriculum and become a practice-based subject of their own.

Acting in those plays helped me muddle through the shit-storm of school by giving me a deeper understanding of what makes people tick. If my life were a play – as with Macbeth in *Macbeth* or Othello in *Othello* – it would be simplistic to play CHARACTER C as *villain*, or myself as merely *victim*. Good stories contain multiple truths, and CHARACTER C will no doubt have his own version of events that might contradict aspects of my own. Once I stepped back and tried to dissect why he behaved that way, the pain of those early years, the loneliness it caused, became bearable. If both our characters were played on stage with empathy, seen together they might illuminate, or add greater depth, to the events at the squat and at school.

Shakespeare's universe mirrors the human condition, and every character – from fairy queens to murderers – is written compassionately, with a strong motivation and a clear set of obstacles. Whether it's Richard III's murderous rampage to the throne, Edgar throwing his blind father from an imaginary cliff or Snug the Joiner's attempt to play the Lion's part without scaring the ladies; it's witnessing how the characters navigate their various psychological obstacles to get *what they want* that gives the plays real depth.

He doesn't need to shoehorn a political diatribe or provide a thesis; he just shows us how people try to improve their lives, whether we agree with them or not, while living under the constraints of a particular culture or hierarchy.

Regardless of the setting, each play usually begins with some kind of disorder, a social or psychological problem. Think of the riots that open *Romeo and* Juliet, Orsino's lovesickness at the start of *Twelfth Night* or King Lear dividing his empire between his three daughters. The characters want to 'end their suffering', but, because they're only human (and without the benefit of hindsight), they often make stupid or selfish choices that usually make things worse. Under pressure, facing mounting obstacles, they repeatedly fuck things up until things reach breaking point. Whether it's Juliet killing herself, Lear losing his mind (and his daughters) or the taming of Katherine, audiences delight in the characters doing the unthinkable, bearing witness to the *worst thing that could happen* in the given circumstances.

Most drama functions this way, and the simplicity of the pattern is a handy thing for the student playwright to know. Take any play – from David Hare's *The Absence of War* [1993], Wole Soyinka's *Death and the King's Horseman* [1975], or comedies like Mike Leigh's *Abigail's Party* [1977], or Stephen Adley Guirgis's *The Motherf*cker with the Hat* [2011] – and you'll no doubt uncover a variant of the arc.

Characters move from a state of disorder or anxiety, through desperation and crisis, to a final resolution that can be absolute like George Lucas's *Star Wars*, ambiguous like Antonioni's *L'Avventura* [Italy, 1960], transformative like Scorsese's *Raging Bull* [USA, 1980] or that brings things full circle with no change at all *(Waiting for Godot)*. Great television like *The Sopranos* [1999], *Succession* [2018] or *Breaking Bad* [2008] effortlessly employ a Shakespearean structure, and cinema – from Spielberg's *Jurassic Park* [1993] and Ingmar Bergman's *Cries and Whispers* [1972] to experimental works like Michael Haneke's *Seventh Continent* [1989] or Vera Chytilova's *Daisies* [1966] – play out, however obliquely, in much the same way.

Whenever I approach a character, I always try to excavate their flaws, or to ask: under the circumstances, if he or she is put under extreme pressure, what virtuous or repugnant action are they capable of? For instance, the lead character in *Lucky Dog* is put under so much pressure that she slaps a ten-year-old boy across the face, then prays that her grown-up son will get cancer so he'll come home. Liam, in *Boy*, is the antithesis of heroic, passively reacting to the world around him, mimicking everyone he encounters, until the penny drops and he realizes he barely exists at all. *I'll Be the Devil*'s leading lady, Maryanne, sells her daughter to an English Colonel to save herself from the hangman, helping him button up his uniform after he's raped and murdered the girl. As for virtue, in *Innocent Creatures*, one of the robots, Mia, travels the earth for millions of years to find her friend, Enid, so they can be reunited at the end of the world.

And, of course, it's not just a case of making good or bad things happen. It's working out the dilemmas or tactics that are possible within the parameters of the character's world. *Lucky Dog* is a domestic drama about a loveless couple in Sheffield spending their first Christmas without their kids, and so a giant extra-terrestrial slug is unlikely to appear. *Innocent Creatures* is set in a dystopian future where Artificial Intelligence is wiping out humanity for the good of the planet, so we're not (necessarily) going to focus on who's washing the dishes. The characters in both plays have equal amounts of emotional baggage, they're just navigating wildly different realities, and their tools or tactics to 'end their suffering' are specific to that culture.

All You Need is LSD is probably my most experimental play as it incorporates a Python-like structure with hundreds of locations and characters, as well as a female version of myself – Leonora – in the lead role. Beneath the anarchy, however, it still follows the same narrative pattern as the audience follow Leonora's struggle to finish a play called *All You Need is LSD* while under the influence of LSD. The play itself becomes the obstacle, with ideas and scenes folding in on themselves, then discarded, until things reach breaking point when Leonora gives up writing altogether, reading a bedtime story to her daughter instead.

When *Redundant* premiered at the Royal Court in September 2001, the frustration and craziness of the first few previews were allayed when I heard that Meg Jepson had travelled down from Sheffield to see the show for herself. *Redundant* couldn't be more different than *A Midsummer Night's Dream* or *The Tempest*, but Meg passed on a message of congratulations. Whereas the papers had taken issue with a lead character who turns to crack and beats her grandmother up, Meg had enjoyed the non-judgemental, objective presentation of a character in crisis. If objectivity is a skill, it was her training that taught me how to do that.

I don't think it was a conscious decision, but once school ended I stopped attending the youth theatre as well. Somewhat selfishly, I felt it had served its purpose and it was time to move on. In a circular turn of events, worthy of *Godot*, my closest friend, Ryan, and I had found another squat to hang out in while we figured out what to do next. Unlike the punks five years earlier, the house on London Road (just on the edge of the city centre, near Bramall Lane) was populated with a group of grungy misfits and amiable goths. For the next few weeks, we'd doss around on their sofa drinking tea and eating biscuits. With the *Angel Heart* [Parker, 1987] soundtrack on permanent rotation, we'd sit round the kitchen table and play fantasy board game *Talisman* for hours on end. Ryan's home life was violent and chaotic, so the mellow vibe of the squat was a welcome retreat, and, after a while, he decided to move in, but I always caught the bus home.

Glued to my portable telly, I'd stay up late watching art-house movies, or reruns of television plays like Dennis Potter's *Pennies from Heaven* [BBC, 1978], Alan Clarke's *Made in Britain* [BBC, 1982] or Mike Leigh's *Meantime* [Channel 4, 1983]. Not yet realizing the influence he'd have on my writing, Samuel Beckett also reared his head, when the screen versions of *Happy Days* and *Not I*, starring Billie Whitelaw, were shown on BBC Two shortly after the great man's death. I didn't understand why Winnie was buried to her neck in sand, or what the disembodied mouth was jabbering on about, or how the endless repetitions, with very little actually happening, could be so *mesmerizing*, but I fell in love with the plays for all those reasons. Beckett clearly didn't give a f*ck about public taste, and as such, regardless of the plays' stillness, he was very rock 'n' roll.

The early nineties were an exciting time for cinema. I remember I'd meet my mum after she finished work at the end of the week, and we'd go to Crystal Peaks Odeon to see everything from *Cinema Paradiso* [Tornatore, 1988], *Crimes and Misdemeanours* [Allen, 1989], *Goodfellas* [Scorsese, 1990] and *Do the Right Thing* [Lee, 1989]. Mum would catch the 75 back home, and I'd dash back to the squat to find the amiable goths beginning to drift apart, and Ryan quickly fading from view.

He was a talented lad, and when he played Mercutio in the SYT production of *Romeo and Juliet*, everyone – including Meg – thought he was destined to become a great actor. But soon after moving into the squat, he visited his ailing father in hospital and witnessed his death. Bereaved, he turned to gas sniffing, working his way through several cans a day. I tried some with him once, and it was horrific.

The last time I saw him, a matter of months after school finished, Ryan was living in the woods, covered in abscesses and talking gibberish. My parents, and the youth theatre, tried finding him a hostel, in the hope that some stability might bring him round. But the addiction wasn't conducive with stability, and he would smash up the furniture in his room and head back to the woods.

I thought about Ryan a lot when writing *Boy* some twenty years later, and I dedicated the published play to him. By a strange coincidence, during rehearsals at the Almeida, his photograph suddenly appeared on the *Sheffield Star*'s website, appealing for people to be on the lookout as he'd gone missing. The photo revealed a gaunt, hollowed-out middle-aged man, the remnants of a talented boy succumbed to a lifetime of mental illness. Fortunately, by the end of the play's run, he'd been safely found, and, for those of us who remember, his fifteen-year-old Mercutio is still the best I've ever seen.

Having managed to scrape four GCSEs, I enrolled onto a BTEC Performance Arts course at Norton College. It wasn't long since I'd left school, and I was already nervous about being in a classroom again, so when the head of year, Jo Beadle, advised me to do a Contemporary Dance GCSE as an extra qualification, my life flashed before my eyes. For the good of humanity, I'd never inflicted even the vaguest of dance moves in front of anyone before, and now, in a slim-fitting tracksuit I was trying my best to plie and pirouette in a room full of athletic eighteen-year-old girls. My efforts were applauded with sympathy, but everyone, including Jo Beadle, agreed that I should forego the GCSE, and concentrate on the BTEC instead.

It was a marvellous, practise-based course, with great teachers. Our motley crew became very close, and every day was a new adventure as we devised new work and rehearsed modern classics. Emboldened by my peers, I penned the absurd scripts for our adaptations of *The Iliad-ish* and *Robyn Hudd: The Pantomime*, in which I played the Sheriff of Nottingham (pictured below).

IMAGE 23 *Photo credit: From left, the author, Marc Fretwell, Matthew Burgess and Huss Garbiya in 'Robyn Hudd: The Pantomime', 1992. Photo reproduced from author's archive.*

My performance as Jimmy Porter in *Look Back in Anger* was a bit laboured, but I relished playing both Sir Douglas Haig in *Oh! What a Lovely War* [Littlewood, 1963], and the tragic hero of Vladimir Gubarev's Chernobyl drama *Sarcophagus* [1987]. But as much as I loved acting, plays like *Look Back in Anger* and *Sarcophagus* began to open the door to modern playwriting which had been, up until then, restricted to Dennis Potter and Beckett.

Since we were toddlers, Matt and I had been taken to see pantomimes and family shows, such as Ken Dodd and seaside favourites The Krankies. As we got a bit older, there were musicals at the Crucible Theatre, such as Bob Eaton's *Lennon* [1985] and Stephen Sondheim's *Gypsy* [1959], or homegrown productions like Joyce Holliday's *It's a Bit Lively Outside* [1987], directed by Stephen Daldry, that told the story of the Sheffield Blitz with an excess of pyrotechnics that scared the crap out of us. As a theatre lover herself, Mum would sometimes drag us to worthier dramas like *The Seagull* or *Of Mice and Men*, but, being teenagers, we were mostly interested in the sexy actresses and the snogging bits.

The most memorable show, before the BTEC, had been a small, studio production of Dario Fo's *Accidental Death of an Anarchist* [1970] that our primary school class were (bizarrely) taken to on a school trip. The plot was a bit confusing, but I remember being bowled over by the outrageous Marx Brothers style comedy, and when, at the play's climax, the actors suddenly broke the fourth wall to ad-lib expletives about Thatcher and the miner's strikes, my tiny mind exploded.

Under the tutelage of Jo Beadle, our BTEC group were introduced to writers like John Osborne, Harold Pinter and Caryl Churchill. Thinking I could do better than all of them, I decided to leave the likes of *The Adventures of Foothead and Zobe* behind and start writing serious stuff. In the second year, I tackled my first full-length play; a dystopian political thriller called *The Prime Controller* which, at more than 100-pages long, had a few interesting bits, but was largely rubbish. When I wasn't writing, I'd direct short plays like David Mamet's *Sexual Perversity in Chicago* [1974], which I drenched with red light and Van Morrison tunes. However good or bad these projects were, it was dawning on me that being behind the stage (or camera) was what I craved the most.

Me and my classmate, Huss, were inseparable during these years, and from the day we met – bursting into fits of laughter over the ineligible enrolment forms – we stuck side by side and encouraged each other to be the best we could. Huss was a few years older than the rest of us and, estranged from his family, with no previous acting experience, he also – like me – felt like an outsider. During the first term he didn't have anywhere to live, so, sharing a spliff between lessons, we agreed he'd be better off sleeping on my floor.

This was 1991, and hard-core techno was in the air. When we weren't at college, we'd tune into pirate radio stations and listen out for the location of the next illegal rave or warehouse party. Nightclubs like the Palais and Occasions became regular haunts, and there was an abundance of brilliant, wall-melting drugs to go round. We were a tight circle of racially diverse, no-nonsense pals who enjoyed bucket bongs and microdots by the dozen. Apart from our brief altercation with the psychotic dealers who threatened to break our legs (as mentioned in **Chapter Three**), it was a magical time, and, with my groovy gurning Bez shapes, I finally learned to dance. As irresponsible as it may sound, a bit of mind-altering illegality was way overdue after the miserable experience of Firth Park school, and I don't think I've ever laughed so much or felt so indestructible.

Rather than Shakespearean ditties, it was the flanging guitar riffs and heavenly Northern harmonies of The Stone Roses that kept us on our feet. Musically, I'd always been locked in the 1960s, but now – thanks to the Roses and Happy Mondays – there were suddenly bands who *belonged to us*, with songs that seemed to burst out of the paving stones, perfectly capturing the euphoria and self-determination we all felt.

After years of wanking, I even managed two or three girlfriends, albeit with varying degrees of success. I remember idiotically coaxing a sweet, red-haired girl to neck a few pro-plus tablets on our first date, making her vomit everywhere. Another fleeting dalliance, who liked a drink, would chase me round college yelling that I was the 'the greatest actor since Tom Cruise' – before trying to throw herself out of various windows.

With her braided hair and afro-funk fashion, my only 'serious' girlfriend (lasting a few turbulent weeks) became the inspiration for Lucy in *Redundant*.

She lived in her own council flat, and I'd frequently have to hide under the bed when her ex-drug dealer boyfriend – who assumed they were still an item – came knocking at the door. I think I offered some stability, but I wasn't exactly a saint, and the game was over after I staggered back to her flat, long after midnight on New Year's Eve 1992, only to have a homemade trifle flung at my head.

The drugs and partying fuelled my determination, and, in the final year of college, I decided to make a feature film called *Runners*. Loosely based on our run-in with the dealers (and borrowing heavily from *Goodfellas*), Huss and I wrote the screenplay, and I directed it myself. Stealing a camcorder from the college's media department and employing our mates as actors and crew, we raced around the city filming on location, and even set up a makeshift rave for one of the key scenes. The film is full of druggie humour and genuine suspense, with a disturbing climax when the fish-out-of-water hero is driven into Derbyshire to have his legs slashed. Using two video machines hooked up with cables for the edit, we completed *Runners* in a fortnight, and arranged its premiere at a drug-rehabilitation unit, which the patients loved. With its sloppy camerawork and questionable dialogue, it wasn't exactly Tarkovsky, but *Runners* had a lot of spirit, and I'm still proud of the ballsy way we got it made.

IMAGE 24 *Poster for 'Runners' (Strictly No Budget Productions, 1992). Image reproduced from author's archive.*

I'm lucky to have written some well-regarded plays for great venues, but some of my proudest achievements, like *Runners*, have never been seen (or heard) outside of family and friends. For instance, psychedelic-rock album, *The Collective Psychosis of the 21st Century* [2017], that I co-wrote and recorded with my friend (and awesome guitarist), Dan Persad, is right up there with *Boy* and *Lucky Dog* as far as I'm concerned. And there are a bunch of ridiculous films – with titles like *The Cat Who Loved a Bath, The Cat Who Loved a Bath Part 2* and *Horrors of the Forest* – that I made with my daughter, Bea, and her cousin Clara when they were little, and which I wouldn't trade for any number of Royal Court shows. Here's me and Bea, with stupid wigs, capturing a 'majestic condor' in our sketch-comedy film, *The Magic Chocolate Box* . . .

IMAGE 25 *The author and Bea Butler in home movie 'The Magic Chocolate Box'.* © *BeaPictures 2016. All Rights Reserved.*

Like the kid making slasher films on his Super 8, or Bully Bottom in *A Midsummer Night's Dream*, I've always wanted to have a go at *everything*, regardless of the results. It's the fun and collaboration that matters, and for every CHARACTER C there's always a Meg Jepson waiting in the wings.

By the summer of 1993, the BTEC was over. I applied for a place at the National Film School, but my parents couldn't afford the fees, so I decided to give Rose Bruford Drama School a go; it was just a *roll of the dice* that I chose the playwriting course in place of acting or directing.

The night before heading to London my mum made a valiant attempt to wish me luck, but, regrettably, I was far too stoned to speak – which, pretty much, summed up the rest of the decade. When I could have spent my early twenties learning how to write a decent play, I opted for bucket bongs and demons instead.

7

How to write a play

Laurel and Hardy's 1932 Oscar-winning short *The Music Box* is the best play Samuel Beckett never wrote. It's a passion play with laughs, *The Odyssey* in a fraction of the time and it contains the key ingredients of every play you'll ever read or write.

IMAGE 26 *'The Music Box' directed by James Parrott* © Hal Roach Studios 1932. All Rights Reserved.

If you haven't seen the film, why not order the DVD or search for it online? Here's an outline of the plot . . .

The plot

Stan and Ollie try to deliver a piano to a house at the top of a ridiculously steep flight of stairs.

In a nutshell, that's it.

The greatest comedy duo of all time, Laurel and Hardy's chemistry and comic timing were off the charts. They weren't explicitly political like Chaplin, but their loveable portrayal of blue-collar workers overcoming the odds at the time of the Great Depression was arguably as potent a statement as anything in *Modern Times*. It's unsurprising they were so popular during that decade, and why their unpretentious, working-class humour still delights to this day.

It's notable that, of all the forty-five classic shorts made for the Hal Roach Company in the 1930s – The *Music Box* is the only one that doesn't feature Leroy Shield's jazzy background score, leaving only Stan and Ollie's grunts and groans, some occasional dialogue, and various crashes and bangs. The image of towing a piano – worthy of Ionesco or Albrecht Dürer – provides the bulk of the film's action and for me suggests an absurd metaphor of the human condition. You wonder if Brecht was inspired by *The Music Box* when imagining *Mother Courage,* and it's well-documented that Beckett didn't conjure *Waiting for Godot*'s two bowler-hatted tramps out of thin air.

To use *The Music Box* as a guide – or template – for how to write a stage play may seem a bit odd, but its simplicity is preferable to using *Oedipus Rex* [Sophocles, 429 BC] or *Hedda Gabler* [Ibsen, 1891], and breaking down the basic elements can help when developing your own.

The setup: Disorder, piano and staircase

I already mentioned how Shakespeare begins his plays with a world – or culture – in a state of disorder, with characters like Hamlet and Lear struggling to repair their lives (whether they make regrettable decisions or not).

The Music Box may not have the epic scope of those plays, but it follows the same basic rules – established (below) in the opening title cards . . .

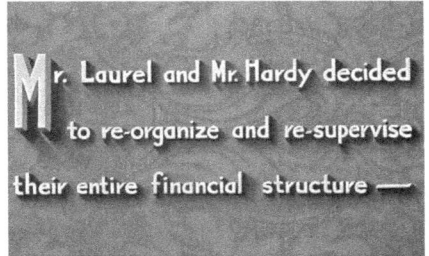

IMAGE 27 *'The Music Box'* directed by James Parrott © Hal Roach Studios 1932. All Rights Reserved.

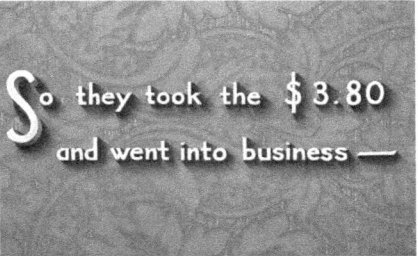

IMAGE 28 *'The Music Box'* directed by James Parrott © Hal Roach Studios 1932. All Rights Reserved.

It's a neat start, much like *Romeo and Juliet's* opening prologue . . .

Two households, both alike in dignity,
In fair Verona, where we lay our scene,
From ancient grudge break to new mutiny,
Where civil blood makes civil hands unclean.

Both suggest something is wrong, and a need for change. *Romeo and Juliet* introduces civil strife and prepares us for tragedy. *The Music Box* introduces financial hardship and prepares us for comedy. None of Laurel and Hardy's films should be taken too seriously, but the decision to 're-organize and re-supervise' will undoubtedly have resonated with working-class Americans of the day.

Following the intertitles, there's a short scene – or inciting incident – in which a wealthy lady orders the piano to be delivered for her husband's birthday. A screen wipe then introduces our distinctly unwealthy heroes, pulling the piano on a horse and cart. They are immediately confronted with the staircase.

IMAGE 29 *'The Music Box'* directed by James Parrott © Hal Roach Studios 1932. All Rights Reserved.

IMAGE 30 *'The Music Box'* directed by James Parrott © Hal Roach Studios 1932. All Rights Reserved.

IMAGE 31 *'The Music Box'* directed by James Parrott © Hal Roach Studios 1932. All Rights Reserved.

In little under two minutes, we're given the nuts and bolts of the story. Disorder and the need for change (financial instability), a choice or inciting incident (start their own business/a delivery job) and a central obstacle (the staircase).

The Music Box is not alone in employing a swift setup of these ingredients.

Star Wars, for instance, uses a (lengthier) prologue to describe the civil strife in a galaxy far, far away.

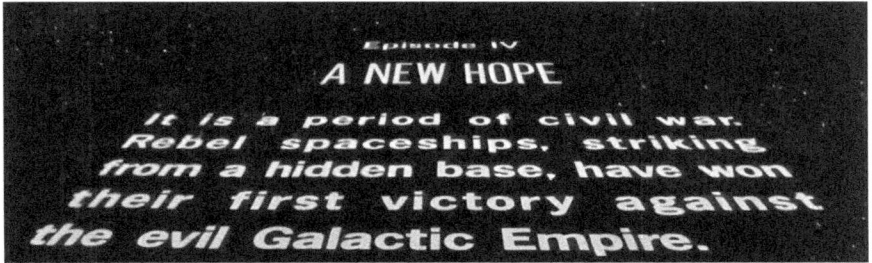

IMAGE 32 *'Star Wars: A New Hope' directed by George Lucas @ Lucasfilm/Disney 1977. All Rights Reserved.*

We are then introduced to Stan and Ollie-like heroes, R2-D2 and C-3PO, who are given 'secret plans' – the piano – by Princess Leia, before being confronted with the menacing, cloaked staircase, Darth Vadar.

IMAGE 33 *'Star Wars: A New Hope' directed by George Lucas @ Lucasfilm/Disney 1977. All Rights Reserved.*

The droids find their way to unsuspecting farm boy Luke Skywalker, who discovers that he has his own burdensome piano of 'destiny' to heave; one which is inexorably linked to Leia's secret plans. Halfway up the stairs – during *The Empire Strikes Back* [1980] – Luke and Leia's piano crashes down when they discover that Darth Vadar is their father, which leads – inevitably – to the operatic finale of *The Return of the Jedi* [1983]. Over the course of three movies, the piano gets heavier, the staircase gets steeper and that's what gives George Lucas's trilogy its enduring appeal.

In Beckett's *Happy Days* [Royal Court, 1962], the lights come up on Winnie who is trapped to her waist in a mound of sand, with nothing to do and nowhere to go. It's a visceral image, but the comparison is oblique. The sand is neither the piano nor staircase, rather the disordered culture – *Star Wars'* civil war, or Stan and Ollie's financial hardship – which Winnie is trying to navigate. The inciting incident is 'a new day', the piano is Winnie's eternal optimism and the staircase is the inevitability of death. Unlike *Star Wars*, there are no heroic space pilots, just an existential portrait of human folly, with Winnie declaring it's 'another happy day' as the sand swallows her up.

IMAGE 34 *'Happy Days', featuring Billie Whitelaw (Winnie), directed by Anthony Page* © *BBC 1973. All Rights Reserved.*

In all these examples, the piano is almost always an object of value, often a burden. It is usually connected to both the character's deeper needs and the existing (disordered) culture. When people talk about a drama having '**high stakes**', they are talking about the value of the piano and the need to protect it. Winnie's optimism has value, as does Luke Skywalker's destiny. In *Romeo and Juliet*, the piano is true love, in Scorsese's *Raging Bull* it is Jake LaMotta's need for validation, and in Valerie Fanis and Jonathan Dayton's superb *Little Miss Sunshine* [2006], it is eight-year-old Olive's dreams of winning a vacuous beauty pageant.

The staircase is the central obstacle, and it takes many forms. In *Romeo and Juliet*, the staircase is the existing prejudice and mounting violence between the two households, in *Raging Bull* it is Jake LaMotta's internal paranoia and self-loathing, and in *Little Miss Sunshine* it is the rising tensions within the dysfunctional family, threatening to destroy Olive's dreams, as they drive across America in their piano-like van.

IMAGE 35 *'Raging Bull', featuring Robert DeNiro (Jake La Motta), directed by Martin Scorsese © United Artists. All Rights Reserved.*

IMAGE 36 *'Little Miss Sunshine' directed by Valerie Fanis and Jonathan Dayton © Big Beach/Bona Fide Productions. All Rights Reserved.*

Both piano and staircase are connected to the disordered culture – riots on the streets of Verona, the poverty and violence in the backstreets of Little Italy, and the deluded aspirations of Olive's low-income family.

Every drama is different in tone and gesture, and how you present your various pianos and stairs will depend on the type of ride you want the audience to have.

In *Lucky Dog*, I attempted a Beckett-like image to open the play, with a middle-aged couple sitting in uncomfortable silence eating Christmas dinner.

IMAGE 37 *Linda Bassett (Sue) and Alan Williams (Eddie) in 'Lucky Dog' (directed by James Macdonald, Royal Court, 2004). Photo reproduced with the kind permission of @ Tristram Kenton.*

The silence (and absent son) creates a discord that belies the colourful fairy lights. Christmas Day is the inciting incident, and its plethora of rituals, including crackers and presents, become the staircase, with the burden (or value) of a loveless marriage being the piano they're forced to heave.

Jez Butterworth's *Jerusalem* (Royal Court, 2009) can also be compared to *The Music Box* as it cleverly sets up a backstory and obstacle within the first few minutes. Rooster Byron's immediate eviction from his caravan allows Butterworth to get on with the real job of dazzling the audience with his line-by-line comedy as he excavates the characters under pressure. The existing territorial tensions are the disordered culture, the forced eviction on St George's Day is the inciting incident and the piano is the sense of ownership – of both the caravan, and their divisive sense of Englishness. The staircase, meanwhile, translates as the surrounding characters, whose loyalty to Rooster are tested as the bulldozers approach.

Ingmar Bergman's masterpiece, *Persona* [1966], is comparable to *The Music Box* as it centres on a double act (who may or may not be the same person). Nurse Alma (Bibi Andersson) is caring for a famed actress, Elisabet (Liv Ullmann), who has unexpectedly suffered an on-stage mental breakdown and is refusing to speak.

IMAGE 38 *'Persona' directed by Ingmar Bergman* © SF Studios (Sweden) 1968. All Rights Reserved.

The disordered culture is the mystery surrounding Elisabet's illness, alongside the fractured form of the film itself.

Nurse Alma's piano is her desire to succeed (bound up with her persona), and Elisabet is the staircase on which she must climb.

Elisabet, on the other hand, heaves her existential trauma (bound up with her persona), up the staircase of Alma's questionable care.

As the plot progresses, Bergman deliberately muddies our perceptions – much like David Lynch's *Mulholland Drive* [2001] – blurring the identities of the two women via disturbing montage, sublime visual trickery and repetition of speech. By the film's climax it's as if we – the audience – are the ones heaving our cognizance up the Escher-like staircase of multiple truths.

Finally, Stanley Kubrick's *2001: A Space Odyssey* [1968] employs humankind as its protagonist. The disorder occurs at the dawn of time when a giant monolith suddenly appears. The monolith incites our wild ancestors to think beyond their immediate surroundings and, in a magnificent scene, use weapons for the first time. Within minutes, Kubrick dramatizes our first evolutionary step to becoming conscious (or civilized) beings, and for most filmmakers that would be enough.

IMAGE 39 *'2001: A Space Odyssey'* directed by Stanley Kubrick © Kubrick Productions/Metro-Goldwyn-Meyer 1968. All Rights Reserved.

Kubrick, however, was not 'most filmmakers', and *2001* takes us on a journey over centuries, with our piano-like consciousness periodically triggered by the reappearance of monoliths. The staircase, meanwhile, translates as the universe, stretching out into infinity until perceptions of time and space collapse.

The characters

Stan and Ollie may not be as complex as Hamlet or Othello – or, indeed, Kubrick's chimps – but neither are they just 'the fat one' and 'the thin one'. Audiences in 1932 will have already watched a bunch of their movies, so – as with *The Simpsons* or *Friends* [NBC, 1994–2004] – they enter *The Music Box* with a comforting familiarity drawn from a whole body of work.

As if bumbling from the footnotes of a Tennessee Williams play, Ollie feigns to be a member of high society, but his affected Southern drawl and general shabbiness are dead giveaways. He aspires for a lifestyle that is beyond his capabilities, but he never feels it's undeserved.

Stan rarely tries to be anything other than he is – an ordinary, absent-minded (and very clumsy), working man. He occasionally shares pearls of wisdom that startle everyone – including himself. When he comes up with a good idea or plan, he rarely complains when Ollie takes the credit. Instead, he lives through Ollie's aspirations, and will do almost anything, to make his friend happy.

Although Ollie doesn't hesitate to admonish Stan, it is usually Ollie who is to blame for their misfortune, bearing the brunt of the painful (often surreal) slapstick. There are also wonderful reversals when Stan retaliates or proves that he's capable of going it alone, exposing Ollie's dependence.

They bicker and fight like siblings, but because the whole world – even animals and objects – seem to conspire against them, they demonstrate genuine solidarity when dealing with tricky situations or thugs. Stan sobs when Ollie's upset, and Ollie cries out for Stan when he's in trouble. Gems like *Way Out West* [1937] and *The Music Box* include moments of physical harmony – in dance or song – or reveal quieter, even tender, moments when they're at their most vulnerable.

Some suggest that the duo's relationship is akin to a married couple, especially when we see them sharing a bed in films like *Laughing Gravy* [1930] or parenting mini versions of themselves in *Brats* [1930]. However, there's little suggestion of a romantic or sexual relationship, and it may be just as interesting to view their relationship as an example of close male friendship, with its capacity for intimacy and love.

The Laurel and Hardy Appreciation Society, *Sons of the Desert*, has groups of aficionados across the world. Each group – or 'tent' – meets once a month to watch films and drink beer, as well as travelling to international conventions.

IMAGE 40 *The Sheffield Sons of the Desert 'Brats Tent'* c.1988 Photo kindly reproduced with permission from @ Sheffield City Archives.

As a teenager, I joined the aptly-named *Brats* 'tent' at the Princess Royal pub in Sheffield – which is run to this day by local legend John Burton. I'm somewhere at the back of this picture from the group's first meeting in 1988, where we were joined by Bill Cubin (curator of the Laurel and Hardy Museum in Ulverston), and Stan Laurel's second cousin, Nancy Wardell.

As you can tell, there were very few women at the *Sons of the Desert* meetings, and I suspect that, unlike *Stranger Things* [Netflix, 2016] or *Star Trek* [Paramount, 1968} societies, the demographics reflect the relationship at the heart of the films.

IMAGE 41 *'The Live Ghost' directed by Charley Rogers* © *Hal Roach Studios 1934. All Rights Reserved.*

You can only really dig into the complexities of a character by exploring their relationships. Even lonely or alienated characters in dramas like David Mamet's *Edmond* [1982], Agnès Varda's *Vagabond* [1985], or Wim Wenders' *Wrong Move* [1975], can only be unpicked, or be perceived as lonely, through their attempted interactions with others.

One-person shows, such as Debbie Tucker Green's *Random* [2008] or Phoebe Waller-Bridge's *Fleabag* [2013], are dependent on the character's relationship to the offstage world, and the success of so-called 'lecture theatre' like David Hare's *Via Dolorosa* [1998] or Chris Thorpe's *Talking About the Fire* [2023] is dependent on the speaker's rapport with the crowd.

Throughout all of Laurel and Hardy's filmography, like the Macbeths in *Macbeth*, we learn next to nothing about their backstory, how they were raised, what school they attended, if they prefer cabbage to lettuce or what their favourite colours are. It is through their action and behaviour, responding to present tense situations, that we learn what they think and how they feel about each other. The rest is just decoration. In plays like Conor McPherson's *The Weir* [1997] or Edward Albee's *Who's Afraid of Virginia Woolf*, the past is employed as a psychological tactic and, as such, has a direct storytelling function.

When *Lucky Dog* was in rehearsals at the Royal Court, the lead actress, Linda Bassett, asked *'So what do these characters do for a living?'*. Despite having spent months writing this intimate, chamber piece about a complex, decades-old relationship, I literally *had no idea* how either character made their money. I knew they had jobs and could probably throw some suggestions about the *type* of employment it might be, but the detail made very little difference to the story on stage. The most important thing was – given the play's setup – what these characters feared and desired, why they felt this way, what they needed from each other to repair their damaged lives and how – within the limits of their culture – they were going to do it.

The needs and tensions between characters are what push any story forward. Lady Macbeth desires power and needs to reinforce her husband's failing strength, Blanche DuBois desperately clings onto a fantasized version of herself that she needs the unconvinced Kowalski's to accept, Elliot in *ET: The Extra-Terrestrial* [Spielberg, 1982] needs a father figure, so he adopts the dying alien to teach himself how to grow up. Back in 1932, Stan and Ollie need to reorganize their financial structure and are reliant on each other's intelligence to get the job done.

There are some wonderful writers who like to know as much about their characters as possible and will write extensive backstories before writing a word of dialogue. As I've mentioned before, I'm more of an improviser than a planner, preferring to work out the basic setup that's going to get the story moving. Once I've got the architecture, I let the characters discover themselves when writing the scenes, even if that means taking wrong turns or hitting speedbumps.

However, if you feel you need more information to get started, I recommend using the Q & A Exercise in the **Appendix**, answering the questions as your lead characters rather than yourself. Don't think too hard about the answers, just write the first thing that comes into your head.

If that's too rigorous or boring, imagine your lead character taking a good, hard look at themselves in a bathroom mirror. Then take a pencil and answer these questions . . .

WHAT'S MY CULTURE?

WHAT'S MY PIANO?

WHAT'S MY STAIRCASE?

Ultimately, there is no right or wrong way to invent characters. Through practise (and trial and error), you'll find an enjoyable process that works for you.

Repeated efforts and complications

Whatever the individual writer's process, there is one fundamental rule: fling shit at your characters.

Fling shit at your characters and you might have a play. Fling it at your characters repeatedly, and the audience will be engaged.

The shit can be physical, internal, psychological, emotional or everything all at once.

Things should not get better; things should only get worse.

If things do get better, it is only temporary. For instance, having heaved the piano halfway up the stairs, Stan and Ollie are accosted by an indignant top-hatted professor (played with over-the-top brilliance by Billy Gilbert) who orders them to move the piano to let him get by.

IMAGE 42 *'The Music Box' directed by James Parrott © Hal Roach Studios 1932. All Rights Reserved.*

An irritated Stan knocks the professor's hat off and it lands on the road below, crushed by a passing steamroller. It's another victory for the boys – a moment of solidarity – but one that will come back to haunt them.

Finally reaching the top of the stairs, they approach the house, but the piano – almost deliberately – hurtles back down. Ollie grabs hold of the box, and he's dragged down with it.

IMAGES 43–45 *'The Music Box' directed by James Parrott © Hal Roach Studios 1932. All Rights Reserved.*

They carry the piano all the way back up, and, once more, we think they've succeeded.

However, a postman tells them they could have just driven it up via a different road. Realizing their mistake, Stan and Ollie carry the piano all the way back down and drive it all the way back up.

They reach the house again and, unfortunately, there's nobody home.

They use a pulley to drag the piano through the window, above a stone fountain. The painful pratfalls escalate as Stan drops the pully on Ollie's head, who crashes through the front door.

IMAGES 46–48 *'The Music Box' directed by James Parrott © Hal Roach Studios 1932. All Rights Reserved.*

The bickering continues, including some very funny mix ups with their bowler hats, until they land with a splash in the stone fountain, drenching them both.

IMAGE 49 *'The Music Box' directed by James Parrott © Hal Roach Studios 1932. All Rights Reserved.*

Finally, they carry the piano into the living room and unpack it from its box. The box has filled with water, and the living room is flooded. They topple, get electrocuted, step on six-inch nails, fall from ladders and destroy everything in sight.

IMAGES 50–52 *'The Music Box'* directed by James Parrott © Hal Roach Studios 1932. All Rights Reserved.

Meanwhile, in a short cut-away scene – the professor complains to a policeman about the altercation with the hat. Back at the house, Stan and Ollie perform a little dance as they tidy up, but – thanks to the cut-away – we know there's danger approaching.

IMAGES 53–54 *'The Music Box'* directed by James Parrott © Hal Roach Studios 1932. All Rights Reserved.

Everything is in place for the film's climax. The simplicity of the setup, combined with an understanding of character and the overall tone, has allowed the filmmakers to have fun with the mounting obstacles, as well as preparing us for an inevitable confrontation at the film's closing finale.

The simplicity of *The Music Box* is not dissimilar to Peter Jackson's adaptation of Tolkien's *The Lord of the Rings* [2001–2003], which delights in raining down shit on Frodo Baggins as he heaves the One Ring to the fires of Mount Doom.

Interestingly, for all the Balrogs, Nazguls and Orcs, by far the biggest (and most engaging) obstacle is the web of lies that the wily creature Gollum uses to sabotage Frodo's friendship with fellow Hobbit, Sam. It's no surprise that Tolkien (and Jackson) saved this deeply emotional obstacle for the final instalment of the trilogy, as for all the visual flair, it's our connection

IMAGE 55 *'The Lord of the Rings: The Return of the King' directed by Peter Jackson @ New Line Cinema 2003. All Rights Reserved.*

to the characters – whether it's Tolkien's hobbits, Bergman's nurse/patient or Beckett's tramps – that resonates.

Master of emotional engagement, Anton Chekhov, opens *The Seagull* [1896] with the lines . . .

Medvedenko Why do you always wear black?
Masha I'm in mourning for my life, I'm unhappy.

This short exchange may not give us the whole picture, but it does introduce disorder and a slither of desire that's going to propel the story forward. Masha's unhappiness is in contrast with the preceding stage directions, which describe the opulent gardens of a private estate. Buried in the stage directions, much like Stan and Ollie's grunts and groans, is an offstage *'sound of workmen'*, which subliminally adds to the sense of disruption akin to *Romeo and Juliet's* 'civil strife'.

IMAGE 56 *A posed photograph of Anton Chekhov reading 'The Seagull' to the Moscow Art Theatre company, 1898. Public Domain image.*

Written in 1895, and embracing a radical form of naturalism, Chekhov disposes with melodrama (or monoliths or lightsabres) and, instead, introduces a plethora of personal conflicts through subtext and psychological tactics. *The Seagull* features an array of amusingly unhappy characters, heaving their discontent up a Mount Doom of deluded love triangles, professional failure and ill health. The obstacles are a direct result of the characters' misplaced desire and their repeated efforts for love and success, even when it's obvious the pianos are going to fall apart. For instance, experimental writer Konstantin declares his love for aspiring actress, Nina, but she is in love with another – more successful – writer, Trigorin, and she starts a new life with him in Moscow. Inevitably, her marriage and career end in disaster, and she returns to the estate a broken woman. It has been two years since Konstanin last saw her, and yet he continues (maddeningly) to plead for her hand. Nina repeats her resolve to become a famous actress – mirroring Winnie's deluded optimism in *Happy Days* – so that when she announces she's about to run away again, the audience are as confounded as they are with Frodo's rejection of Sam, or as electrified as they are by Luke's final duel with Vadar. It comes as no surprise that – much like Stan and Ollie's failure to 'reorganize their financial structure' because of their ongoing stupidity – Konstantin shoots himself because of his ongoing mental illness. Just as *The Music Box* 'plants' the angry professor halfway up the stairs, Chekhov 'plants' the gun (and the poor lad's attempted suicide) way back in the first half of *The Seagull*. With any good drama, it's less about inventing random dramatic events, but understanding the characters within a specific culture, planting the traps and keeping them firmly on the stairs.

Avoiding conflict

Mark Ravenhill once observed that it's less about writing characters *in conflict*, and more about writing characters doing everything to *avoid conflict*. Great advice from a great playwright.

The more Stan and Ollie *avoid* accepting that their methods of towing the piano are ridiculous, the more we enjoy their failures.

We enjoy the suspense of Luke and Han Solo entering the Death Star trying to *avoid* conflict with Stormtroopers, and we feel satisfaction when they're finally caught.

In *The Seagull,* we bear witness to the characters' unwillingness to face facts, to *avoid* the painful truth of their condition, and we are moved to tears when they do.

Winnie does everything she can to *avoid* admitting she is being buried in the sand, and Beckett forces us to contemplate our own lives.

If Beckett opened *Happy Days* with Winnie exclaiming, 'Oh shit, I'm trapped', or Luke Skywalker headed straight into battle without hesitation, or if Konstanin was to declare 'You know what, Nina? There are plenty more fish in the sea', then – like Stan and Ollie quitting at first base – there wouldn't be any drama, humour or insight.

I often advise writing students to hold off having the characters reveal their true feelings or deeper fears for as long as possible. Much better to allow your characters to try and solve their problems by making flawed choices until they sink under the sand, or realize they've been tricked by Gollum, or until they're crushed under the weight of their own lovesick delusion. In Kafka's *The Metamorphosis* [1915], the giant cockroach does everything it can to get out of bed, go to work and continue his normal life. It is only at the very end, when he realizes he isn't wanted anymore, that he crawls back to his room to die of starvation.

As with all these examples, you will find it far more rewarding to make the characters work hard to avoid admitting failure or going straight into battle. If you don't believe me, try writing a scene in which a couple are breaking up.

Write one version in which the couple steam into the scene and *tell* each other exactly what they feel.

Write a second version in which you *show* the breakup by having the characters doing everything they can to *avoid* even mentioning they're breaking up.

I'm always happy to be proved wrong, but I suspect you'll sustain a longer, more interesting scene with the latter.

Reversals and twists

There are plenty of 'how to' books that cleverly outline the difference between reversals and twists, so I'm not going to get bogged down in all that. All you need to know is that in every scene of every play, there will be plenty of twists and turns, victories and defeats, and – occasionally – even ground-shifting revelations.

The Music Box ends with a huge twist when the wealthy lady tells the raging professor that she bought the piano for his birthday. We feel maximum pleasure when the professor suddenly declares that he 'loves pianos' after all, and – like the twists of *The Usual Suspects* [Singer, 1995] or *Fight Club* [Fincher, 1999], or the earthquakes of '*Macduff was not of woman born*' – audiences rarely tire of new information, even after repeated views.

Some plays employ a *deux ex machina* – or an unexpected plot device – to solve a complicated story or to give it a happy ending. Euripides saves child-killing *Medea* [431 BC] with a dragon-drawn chariot sent by the Gods, and in *Blazing Saddles* [1974], centuries later, Mel Brooks has his feuding cowboys break out of the movie and into a neighbouring cinema to see 'how the movie ends'.

In *The Weir*, playwright Conor McPherson saves the twist – and, indeed, his piano and staircase – until the very end of the play. It opens with the vivid, turf-smoked setting of a small Irish pub being battered by rain. If you add that the bar taps aren't working, forcing the locals to drink bottles instead of pints, then our expectations for trouble are further aroused. The group of local men take their usual seats around the bar, and, as they banter, it's soon discovered that there's a newcomer in town – a young woman, Valerie, from Dublin. The bulk of McPherson's beautiful play consists of the older men trying to entertain Valerie with local ghost stories.

IMAGE 57 *Photo credit: From left, Kieran Ahern, Brendan Coyle, Jim Norton and Julia Ford in Conor McPherson's 'The Weir' (directed by Ian Rickson, Royal Court Theatre, 1997). Photo reproduced with kind permission from @ Tristram Kenton.*

Much like Jez Butterworth's comedy, the trick of the plotting is to give space for McPherson's talent for storytelling to shine through. Comparing it to *The Music Box*, you might be forgiven for thinking that the ghost stories are the piano, and Valerie is the staircase, as the men take it in turns – a bit like Monty Python's *Four Yorkshiremen* – to flirt or dazzle (or scare her away). But McPherson saves the play's real setup for the major twist – in the play's final pages – when Valerie tells her own devastating ghost story involving the death of her child. In a stroke of dramaturgical cunning, we discover that Valerie is heaving her grief up the staircase of an uncertain future. The twist gives depth to everything we've seen before, and is a demonstration of a writer in complete control of their craft.

Most plays or films don't rely on an earth-shattering twist, but they do usually conclude with the characters (maybe even their whole culture) altered or transformed in some way. Every Shakespeare play – from *The*

Comedy of Errors to *Hamlet* to *The Winter's Tale* – involves lead characters being punctured, renewed or killed, with the present (disordered) culture replaced by some kind of new world order.

But sometimes characters don't change at all. Klaus Kinski's deranged conquistador in Herzog's *Aguirre: Wrath of God* [1972] just gets more deranged, as does the Iraq-war veteran heaving his PTSD up the staircase of homeland complacency in Simon Stephens' savage *Motortown* [Royal Court, 2006]. In such cases, the writer deliberately subverts our expectations of change, forcing us to question the themes – our received moral judgement – instead.

In *The Music Box*, Stan and Ollie's personalities don't change much either, but they do endure plenty of physical suffering, and their prized piano – along with their financial scheme – is eventually destroyed.

Whether you're writing steadfast Aguirre, *The Godfather*'s mutating Michael Corleone, or Woody Allen's chameleon-like *Zelig*, what's guaranteed is that every small scene (or sequence) you write will be littered with mini reversals and twists.

Winners and losers

The basic structure of any scene is (a variation of) this:

There's a central character heaving a piano up a staircase.

They win, they lose, they win again, they lose, they win, they lose again, they win (or lose).

The basic structure of any play is (a variation of) this:

There's a central character heaving a piano up a staircase.

In Scene One they win. In Scene Two they lose.

In Scene Three they win again. In Scene Four they lose.

In Scene Five they win for a bit, then lose again, then win for a bit, then lose (or win).

At the end of the play, they lose (or win).

It's *Match of the Day* or chess. As long as you lay out the pieces – understand the world, its characters and what they're heaving – the rest is just a game of moves, countermoves, winners and losers.

Nearing the top of the staircase, the boys help a young Nanny with her pushchair, and the piano accidentally rolls back down to the street. It's a surprise when the nanny shrieks with laughter, and it's a shock when Stan retaliates and kicks her up the bum. Finally, we're delighted when the nanny smashes the baby's milk bottle over Ollie's head.

IMAGE 58 *'The Music Box'* directed by James Parrott © Hal Roach Studios 1932. All Rights Reserved.

It maybe just a vintage bit of slapstick, but the tit-for-tat violence is comparable to any scene of dialogue from any contemporary play.

I already mentioned, in **Chapter Five**, how I tried to keep Enid and Mia engaged in psychological combat during the first scene of *Innocent Creatures*, and – although no one smashes a milk bottle or gets kicked up the bum – the same tit-for-tat one-upmanship applies.

Rebecca Gilman's brilliantly dark New York comedy, *Boy Gets Girl* [Royal Court, 2001], begins with two strangers sitting down for a blind date in a restaurant, brought together by a mutual friend.

Audiences are detectives, and the fact that Theresa and Tony are even on a blind date suggests some kind of backstory that we'll enjoy trying to figure out as the scene cracks on. Theresa, the play's protagonist, may already be heaving her piano – an inability to reconcile her professional life with meaningful relationships – but Gilman holds off from revealing the story's main obstacle (or staircase) until twenty or thirty pages in. In the meantime, we're left to enjoy a funny opening scene with two characters engaged in an awkward sparring contest that is comparable to that with the Young Mother, but with nuanced New York dialogue.

Theresa   Oh, man, I'm older than you.

Tony   You're robbing the cradle.

Theresa   Yeah.

Tony   I had a guy tell me once, that men who go out with older women really want to have sex with their mothers. But I don't think that's true. Do you think that's true?

(Beat)

Theresa I wouldn't know. But I think I'm only about three years older than you are, so . . . *(Beat)* Was that . . .? Was that a joke? *(Small Beat)*

Tony *(lying)* Yeah.

Theresa Good, because you scared me there for a second.

Tony See? I too have a dry sense of humour.

Theresa I do see. You might actually out-do me, dryness-wise.

Tony I think we have a lot in common.

Theresa Well, we'll find that out, won't we?

Tony We will. *(Pause.* **Theresa** *finishes her beer)* Do you want another one?

Theresa Um, actually, I do have some work I need to do tonight.

It's great dialogue – each line a psychological manoeuvre – with Theresa trying to maintain status and *avoid conflict* even as the mini twists build to the revelation that Tony is a stalker.

Bending the rules

When teaching, I've often found students waste a lot of time trying to come up with examples of work that don't follow traditional patterns, rather than focusing on the patterns themselves. *What about monologues? What about site-specific work or performance poetry?*

Whatever man, you tell me.

It's natural to want to avoid any so-called rules, and I've spent hours trying out alternative narratives and structures for projects, such as sex-collage *Sixty-Nine* [Edinburgh Pleasance, 2012] or psychedelic *All You Need is LSD*. Sometimes it works, sometimes it doesn't, but it's naive to dismiss centuries-old techniques as some sort of dusty-old conservatism.

If an actor is playing Gregor in *Metamorphosis*, you would expect them to be in the best of physical health when attempting to contort their limbs into the shape of a giant cockroach. Similarly, if a writer wants to bend or break the rules, you expect them to know the existing rules of narrative first.

Subversive films like Abbas Kiarostami's *Close-Up* [1990], or Chantal Akerman's *News from Home* [1977], might seem to exist on their own terms, but they too are motored by characters pushing pianos up staircases, facing mounting obstacles, tensions and reversals. Plays that dispose of a linear narrative in favour of episodic – thematically linked – scenes, such as Martin Crimp's *Attempts on Her Life* [Royal Court, 1997], David Eldridge's *Under the Blue Sky* [Royal Court, 2000] or Anne Washburn's *Mr Burns* [Almeida, 2014], are, likewise, brimming with desires, obstacles and stinky shit-pies.

Breaking the fourth wall

In all their shorts and features, Oliver Hardy repeatedly looks through the lens, sharing his exasperation or pain.

IMAGE 59 *'The Music Box' directed by James Parrott © Hal Roach Studios 1932. All Rights Reserved.*

It unites us with the characters, as if we're complicit in the action, or a sniggering third party. *Can you believe what's happened? Can you see what I must endure?*

Bertolt Brecht and Dario Fo use the same technique of looking through the lens to provoke political activism, while musicals like *Hamilton* [2015] or *The Rocky Horror Show* [1973] reach out beyond the footlights to recruit us in their revolutions. In the marvellously gut-wrenching *Funny Games* [1997], Michael Haneke lambasts the audience for their enjoyment (and enabling) of violent imagery by allowing one of the film's torturers to break the fourth wall and wink at us.

IMAGE 60 *'Funny Games'* directed by Michael Haneke @ Wega Film 1997. All Rights Reserved.

And in *Persona*, Bergman slaps us round the chops by having the film catch fire and disintegrate, reminding us that we're in a cinema, watching a version of reality, not reality itself.

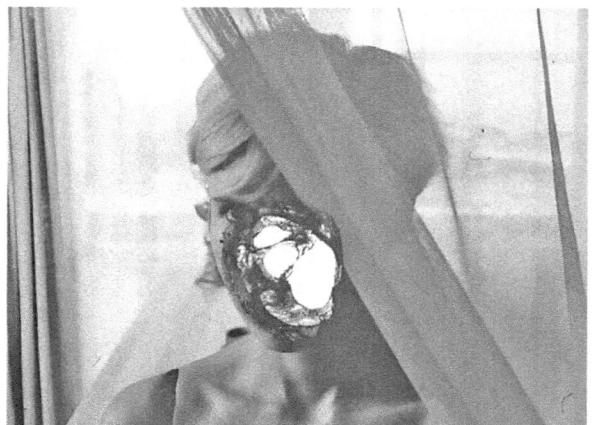

IMAGE 61 *'Persona'* directed by Ingmar Bergman © SF Studios (Sweden) 1968. All Rights Reserved.

In theatre there are countless examples of monologues or soliloquys that aim to delight or enlighten, or, like Tim Crouch's *The Author* [Royal Court, 2009], grab us by the bollocks and force us to question our responsibility as spectators.

In the participatory tradition of stand-up or cabaret, Jackie Sibblies Drury's *Fairview* [Young Vic, 2019] went so far as challenging theatre's representation of black characters by replacing them with white actors halfway through the show.

At the play's climax, Drury then puts the audience on trial, shattering the fourth wall, looking us straight in the eye and unrhetorically asking *Do I have to keep talking to white people?*

But even if you don't smash down the facade like Drury or Crouch, any play that utilizes **suspense** and **dramatic irony** invites the audience to participate in a game in which they *think* they're always two steps ahead of the game. Whether their expectations are satisfied, or if the rug's pulled from under their feet, is up to the style and temperament of each writer.

Suspense and dramatic irony

As armchair experts, we enjoy watching football players who deploy tactics that we came up with first. When things go wrong, we scream at the television, berating the manager for his mistakes. When things go well, we nod our heads with a 'yes, that's exactly what I would have done'.

Good drama operates in much the same way, creating a live dialogue between audience and players.

Near the start of *The Music Box*, the boys decide to lower the piano from the cart onto Ollie's back so they can start shifting it up the stairs. It's a farcical manoeuvre made funnier when the horse intentionally trots forward, forcing the piano to topple and crush Ollie instead.

IMAGES 62–66 *'The Music Box' directed by James Parrott © Hal Roach Studios 1932. All Rights Reserved.*

Later, they're about to repeat the same mistake, with an identical shot of the scheming horse, and we laugh because we know what's coming. However, Ollie quickly wises up and indignantly untie its stirrups.

IMAGES 67–71 *'The Music Box'* directed by James Parrott © Hal Roach Studios 1932. All Rights Reserved.

It's one of my favourite bits of the movie and a nice reminder of how to use expectation and suspense for comic or dramatic effect.

Always be aware of your audience, let them take pleasure in the game.

The formidable Alfred Hitchcock famously allows the audience to see everything before the character does. The great scare in *Psycho* [1960] is seeing the shadow approaching an unsuspecting Janet Leigh from behind the shower curtain. And if that wasn't enough, knowing the audience are still recovering from the grisly murder, Hitchcock again raises the temperature when Martin Balsam's (slightly less unsuspecting) detective creeps up the stairs of the Bates Motel.

IMAGES 72–73 *'Psycho'* directed by Alfred Hitchcock © Shamley Productions 1960. All Rights Reserved.

As with the horse gag, the audience become active spectators, screaming at Balsam from a disconcerting, overhead shot, moments before he gets slashed.

We knew it was coming.

In theatre, mad-cap farces like Joe Orton's *What the Butler Saw* [Queen's Theatre, 1969] or Clive Coleman and Richard Bean's *Young Marx* [Bridge Theatre, 2017], create nail-biting suspense with characters hiding under beds or preposterously smuggled into cupboards. Operating from another planet, Manchester playwright Alistair McDowall keeps us on the edge of our seats in *Pomona* and *X* [Royal Court, 2016] by embracing shocks and suspense inspired by flicks like *Alien* [1979] or *Don't Look Now* [1973].

Famously, Chekhov introduces a loaded gun early in *The Seagull* so we spend the rest of the play anticipating when it's going to be fired, and the whole of Georg Büchner's *Woyzeck* is anchored on when and how, and on who, the antihero is going to use his knife.

Suspense, of course, doesn't have to be bound up with scares or gags.

The script of my 2008 play, *Faces in the Crowd,* allowed the audience to see into each room of a one-bedroom flat during a volatile reunion of ex-lovers. The production's set, fabulously conceived by director Clare Lizzimore and designer Rae Smith, put the seating *above* the flat, so that we could peer into each room like creepy voyeurs. When Dave (played by Con O'Neill) disappears into the bathroom to take a gob full of Viagra, Joanne (played by Amanda Drew), suddenly strips off in the adjoining room and climbs into bed. By seeing what they're up to behind each other's backs, the audience know more than both, so there's instant **dramatic irony,** and we'll be full of giddy suspense for the moment when they're back in the same room.

Production trickery aside, there's usually always some level of irony or suspense drawn from the dialogue and setup of any half-decent play.

King Lear banishes his only loving daughter, Cordelia, in favour of her self-serving sisters, Goneril and Regan, so we scream at him for being stupid. Knowing more than he does, we *anticipate* and *enjoy* the suspense leading up to Goneril and Regan's cruel rejection of their father and look away when the foolish old man is lashed by the storm. Like a botched penalty shootout, the result was inevitable.

Fling shit at your characters by setting traps for them. Even if the traps are set by their own ignorance or avoidance of the truth.

In *Boy Gets Girl,* the audience realize that Tony is not all he seems way before Theresa does (or can admit). Our enjoyment is her avoidance – and gradual realization – of the threat he poses, even (or especially) when it's too late for her to do anything about it.

The surreal setups of Samuel Beckett's plays also, arguably, prepare us for the moment when the lead characters realize the fruitlessness of their actions. The ticking time bombs in *Rockabye* [1981] or *Krapp's Last Tape* [1958] are comparable to *Psycho*, but whether Beckett allows them to explode is another thing entirely.

Audiences are detectives and will try to be ahead of the game whatever you do, so try to be in control of their expectations even if they don't comply, or – like Luis Bunuel or David Lynch – you're going to ignore them completely.

I sometimes find it useful to include moments when we see one of the characters alone on stage. *What does so-and-so do in private, behind the other characters backs?* In the opening scene of *Redundant*, seventeen-year-old Lucy privately rummages through Darren's bag to discover he's brought a toothbrush to her flat. The discovery reveals new information about both characters – Lucy's not as indifferent as she wants to appear, and bashful Darren is planning on sleeping with her – which changes the direction of the scene. In *Lucky Dog*, I enjoyed letting the audience see Sue repeatedly checking her left breast for lumps when alone at the dinner table. The hope was to provide further insight into the character's anxiety, adding voiceless irony to the scenes where she's putting on a cheery front for others.

Likewise, if you reveal a protagonist modifying their behaviour with different sets of characters, then you're also letting the audience become one step ahead of the game. Think of how Mike Leigh's Beverly in *Abigail's Party* differentiates her behaviour and manners among various guests, or the shifting power dynamics between characters in the work of Terrence Rattigan or Harold Pinter.

Like James Stewart peering through his binoculars in *Rear Window* [Hitchcock, 1954], reveal your neighbours' secrets or murder weapons, and the audience may soon become obsessed.

The worst thing that can happen (the climax)

The worst thing that happens in *The Music Box* is when the angry professor returns home and takes an axe to the piano.

IMAGE 74 *'The Music Box' directed by James Parrott © Hal Roach Studios 1932. All Rights Reserved.*

Similarly, the worst thing in *King Lear* is when, shortly after being reunited, Cordelia is killed, with Lear himself, moments later, suffering a fatal heart attack. Othello murders his beloved Desdemona, Gertrude drinks the poison intended for the King, and, in *Oedipus Rex*, our hero realizes he's shagged his mother despite all his best efforts to abstain. Lucy Prebble's excellent debut, *The Sugar Syndrome* [Royal Court, 2003], may not have the silliness of *The Music Box* or the fait accompli of Greek tragedy, but when eleven-year-old Dani discovers her grown-up crush is a paedophile, the climax is no less devastating.

Unless you're Monty Python, it's a cheat to have a ten-ton weight dropping on the character's head. Unless it's a play about illness, try to avoid your characters becoming ill for the sake of a good ending. The *worst thing* must happen in relation to the truth and limitations of the world, its characters and its setup.

Spike Lee's *Do the Right Thing* is a classic example of this. It's the 'hottest day of the year' in Brooklyn, which exacerbates existing disorder, or 'civil strife'. Mookie, played by Lee, heaves his piano – a regular wage to support his family – up the staircase of increasing racial hostility, as clashes between the oppressed community and his white, racist employer come to breaking point.

At the film's climax, Mookie's friend – Radio Raheem – is murdered by the NYPD, and Mookie is forced to do the *worst thing possible* by throwing a garbage can through his employer's window, starting a riot.

IMAGES 75–77 'Do the Right Thing' directed by Spike Lee © 40 Acres and a Mule Filmworks 1989. All Rights Reserved.

By not providing easy solutions, the audience are gifted the question: given the circumstances, was Mookie doing the right thing or the worst thing? And, like Ollie staring through the lens in exasperation, Lee masterfully breaks the fourth wall to implicate us all.

Whenever I start work on a new play, I always have half an eye on the climax or endpoint.

Sitting down to write *The Early Bird* in 2005, I knew the play would end with a gigantic speech in which the grieving mother imagines (and vocalizes) the *very worst thing* that could have happened to her missing daughter. Likewise, I always anticipated that *All You Need is LSD* would build to a final dramatization of Aldous Huxley's LSD-assisted death.

The climax is the <u>essence</u> of the story, or the play <u>distilled</u>. If your lead character is an onion, then the climax is when all the layers have been peeled off, exposing something primal or vulnerable.

It's Jack Nicholson wielding his axe in *The Shining* [Kubrick, 1980], Celia Johnson's desperate farewell to Trevor Howard in *Brief Encounter* [Lean, 1945] or Jean-Pierre Léaud escaping the juvenile facility in Truffaut's *The Four Hundred Blows* [1959]. American plays – from Hansberry's *A Raisin in the Sun* [1959] to Neil Simon's *The Odd Couple* [1965] – classically work their way towards a 'massive argument', which, like a Spaghetti Western-style showdown, feels applicable to that culture. British characters are, arguably, more likely to implode or lash out, as with Virginia Woolf's *Mrs Dalloway* [1925], or the sozzled friends in Jim Cartwright's *Road* [1986], venting their rage to the strains of Otis Redding.

If you were to present your play as one essential image, what would it be?

As with the painting of Saint Jerome that helped me find the climax of *Made of Stone*, contemplating the end of the play can help you work out the start.

A good exercise – which I nicked from Simon Stephens and Lucy Prebble, who probably nicked it from Stephen Jeffreys – is to imagine either *the very worst thing that could happen to the character* or *the very worst thing the character is capable of.*

Once you've come up with something, write it out at the top of a new page.

Don't worry, you can always change your mind.

Once done, work down the page asking yourself *why that worst thing might happen.*

It might be physical or internal, but it should have some kind of cause-and-effect logic.

Look at your new answer and ask *why that might happen.*

Write down your answer.

Ask yourself *why that might happen* again – and again and again – until, eventually, you have a long list of possible events or insights that could help get under the skin of your character or might even help plotting the story.

THE WORST THING _____

WHY MIGHT THAT HAPPEN? _____

WHY? _____
WHY? _____
WHY? _____
WHY? _____
WHY? _____
WHY? _____
WHY? _____
WHY? _____
WHY? _____
WHY? _____
WHY? _____
WHY? _____
WHY? _____
WHY? _____
WHY? _____

It's up to you where you decide to place the climax. And, ultimately, how you end the play depends on the gift or insight you're giving to the audience before they set off home.

The curtain falls on Caryl Churchill's *Far Away* only when the whole world – including gravity and silence – is finally at war. By contrast, the baby-stoning climax of Edward Bond's *Saved* and lustful entanglements of *A Midsummer Night's Dream* occur several scenes before the final resolution.

The resolution

The resolution is, of course, the fallout from the climax – which is the fallout from the initial setup.

The Music Box resolves itself with the sudden arrival of the professor's wife (Hazel Howell) who reveals that the destroyed instrument was intended as a birthday gift. The professor suddenly declares he 'loves pianos' and offers to pay Stan and Ollie for their work. It's a triumph over adversity.

IMAGE 78 'The Music Box' directed by James Parrott © Hal Roach Studios 1932. All Rights Reserved.

IMAGE 79 'The Music Box' directed by James Parrott © Hal Roach Studios 1932. All Rights Reserved.

However, when the boys ask the professor to sign for the delivery, the fountain pen backfires, squirting ink all over his face. Enraged, the professor changes his tune again, chasing Stan and Ollie out of the house.

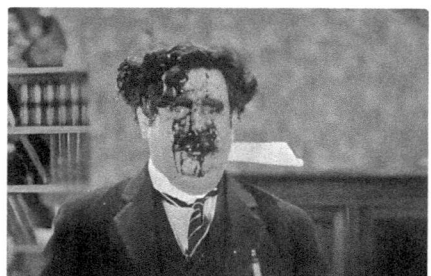 

IMAGE 80 'The Music Box' directed by James Parrott © Hal Roach Studios 1932. All Rights Reserved.

IMAGE 81 'The Music Box' directed by James Parrott © Hal Roach Studios 1932. All Rights Reserved.

You win, you lose, you win, you lose and the movie ends.

The fountain pen gag is cheap, but not out of character in Laurel and Hardy's universe. It's a deliberate means of leaving the audience laughing.

Plays and films do, of course, regularly present stories where the *best thing* finally happens, as with Nora Ephron's *When Harry Met Sally* [1989], Jackson's *Lord of the Rings* or Shakespeare's extended wedding celebration in *A Midsummer Night's Dream.*

They also frequently end with devastation, such as the ritual slaughter in Pasolini's *Salò* [1975], or the rain dripping through the war-torn floorboards of Kane's *Blasted.*

There's comedy and horror with the husband's heart attack at the end of Mike Leigh's *Abigail's Party,* while *Not I*'s chattering mouth simply fades away.

Edward Bond's *Saved* is one of the most disturbing plays ever written, but it ends with a moment of quiet perseverance; a man mending a broken chair.

One of my favourite plays is Annie Baker's *The Flick*, produced at the National Theatre in 2016, and set entirely in a one-screen cinema in Massachusetts with a cast of three young ushers. The play takes its time, embracing the power of silence, as Baker punctuates the action with extended scenes of characters sweeping the aisles between screenings. With lashings of humour and Chekhovian subtext, Baker chronicles the erosion of the friendships as the cinema moves from celluloid to digital, threatening their livelihoods. There's an inciting incident of new cinephile usher, Avery, joining the team, heaving his lofty aspirations up the staircase of small-town opportunities and questionable friendships.

As Avery becomes more comfortable in his job, tensions between the co-workers build, and we slowly learn painful details about their pasts and uncomfortable truths about their present circumstances. Over its three-hour running time, the characters unpeel like onions and our understanding of the world deepens, leading to heart-breaking betrayal, which exposes small-town racism and an erosion of social values. The fakery of cinema is mirrored in the fakery of their friendships, and *The Flick* concludes – as it started – with a moment of bittersweet silence as the empty cinema is plunged into darkness.

Like Laurel and Hardy, Annie Baker understands the rules and limitations of the culture and, with astounding confidence, lets the drama unfold (and resolve) from the everyday needs of her characters.

When it comes to my own resolutions, I've twice had characters facing uncertain futures while looking out of windows – in *Redundant* and *Faces in the Crowd* – as well as brief moments of optimism, round a dinner table or on a dream-like beach, in *Made of Stone* and *Lucky Dog*. It was fun to end my wacky version of *Cinderella* with a socialist celebration, while both *I'll Be the Devil* and *Boy* conclude with a deliberate gut punch. None of these choices were created in a vacuum.

The resolution traces back to the reason why you're writing the damn thing in the first place. Why spend hours or weeks or years slaving over a script? What's the fairground ride you're selling tickets for? What kind of audience are you aiming for? Do you have an age restriction? Are you writing for a particular class or gender? By writing this story, what is it you're trying to figure out about your own life? What do you need to get off your chest? Does the journey and its conclusion suggest something about all our lives? Given the tough circumstances on display, is it possible for people to transform or change? Who or what is responsible for the problems your characters face? What is it that keeps people together? Is there hope for the future? Should the audience feel guilty or complicit, or do you want them to learn from example? Or, like Stan and Ollie, do you just want to make people laugh?

8

The multi-locational life and times of (insert name here) and other structures

You're commissioned to write a play about some aspect of your life.

You think your life's been uneventful, but then you go back and answer the questions in **Chapter Two**.

You call the play *The Life and Times of* .... and you decide to tell your life story in chronological order, and it looks something like this . . .

IMAGE 82 *Storyboard #1 © Leo Butler, 2024.*

Several multi-locational scenes, from birth to death – with big jumps between years.

Good start.

But hang on a minute. It may be that seven scenes don't do justice to your fascinating life. Let's say you're sixty-two years old. Here are sixty-two scenes for each year of your life.

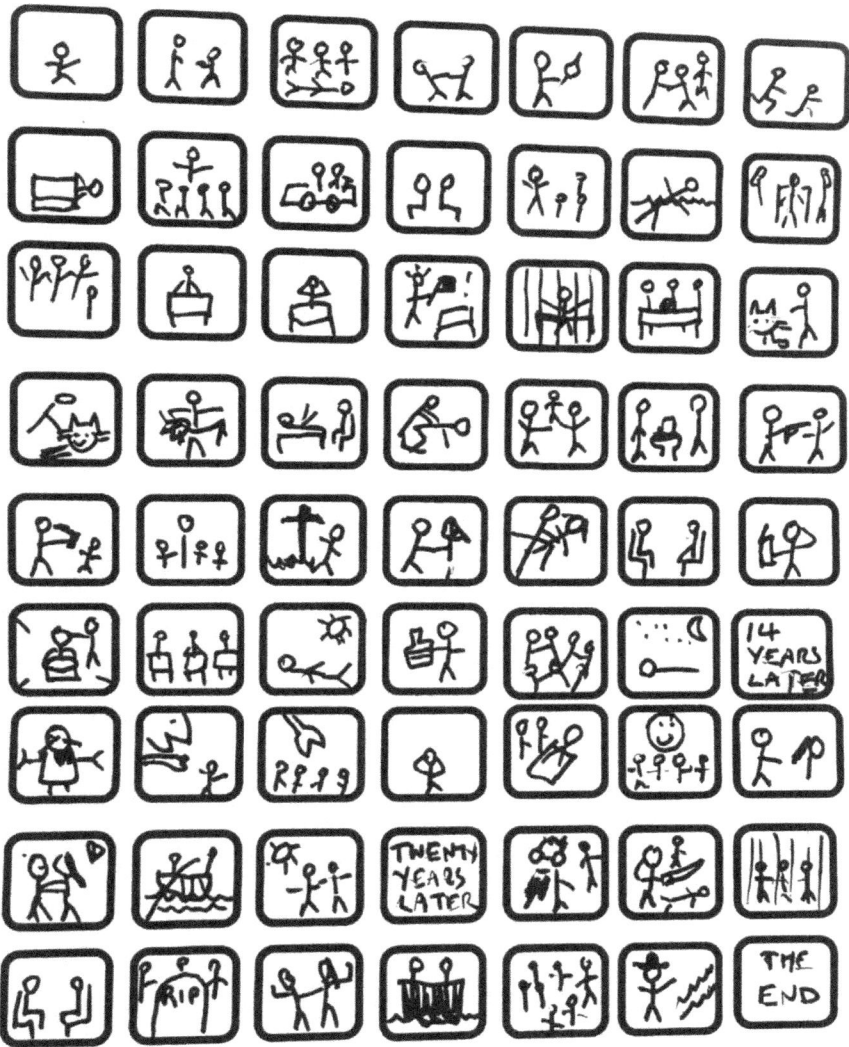

IMAGE 83 *Storyboard #2* © Leo Butler, 2024.

Sixty-two scenes in ninety minutes or more. Exciting.
Expensive sets for each location, and hundreds of supporting characters.
You pitch your idea to a theatre. They call security and throw you out the door.
You compromise and say you still want to dramatize all sixty-two years, but . . .

IMAGE 84 *Storyboard #3 © Leo Butler, 2024.*

... just like a clever German production, the *ensemble* will be on stage throughout, each actor playing a multitude of roles. It will have a bare stage with the odd object – such as a ladder or a table that can transform into other objects, characters or animals.

Lots of movement, dance and live music. Video projections. Non-linear action, so the story goes backwards and forwards. You might use a narrator, or Greek-style chorus, to connect all the scenes. Several actors playing different versions of the main character. Unashamedly live.

The theatre tells you, sadly, they can only afford one actor.

You decide to do this instead . . .

IMAGE 85 *Storyboard #4 © Leo Butler, 2024.*

A one-person show, or monologue. You'll tell the exact same story by . . . well, just telling it.

Unfortunately, the theatre tells you, '*We don't do monologue plays anymore.*'

'*What if we offered you two hot young actors off the telly instead?*' You agree.

Can I still have sixty-two scenes? '*No*', they say. '*You can only have one setting. And there can't be an interval or scene breaks. It must play out in real-time.*'

So, you go back to your notebook and think about the chapter of your life you really want to write about.

You decide to write about **that** relationship and **that** breakup.

You decide to set it in a bedroom because it's intimacy's greatest arena. And it may look like this . . .

IMAGE 86 *Storyboard #5* © *Leo Butler, 2024.*

Real-time without any breaks, the final ninety minutes of a long-term relationship. *Who <u>doesn't</u> want to see that??*

You change key facts about the characters – such as their gender or age – to divorce it from the real-life events on which it's based. Liberate the imagination, protect yourself from lawyers.

The single setting in real time is like a bear pit or boxing ring. There's going to be lots of arguments, recriminations and award-winning tears.

Even though you know you're exploring a familiar breakup, you still need to think about who your characters are and what they're doing.

You re-read **Chapter 7** of this book, and it's very useful.

As you freestyle your way into the play, you discover – without the luxury of time, or multi-locations – that it's a challenge to communicate all the information about who your characters are and where they come from.

You can always include a big speech . . .

IMAGE 87 *Storyboard #6 © Leo Butler, 2024.*

. . . or they can say nothing at all.

IMAGE 88 *Storyboard #7 © Leo Butler, 2024.*

Silence speaks volumes. Let the audience fill in the blanks.

The trick is to work out: **what the audience need to know to understand the story.** But frustratingly: **you might only discover the story by experimenting with the structure or shape of the thing.**

You start writing and it's all going rather well, but then the theatre tells you that the two telly actors aren't available.

Try a bigger cast instead.

This might be good news. Perhaps a two hander wasn't working out anyway.

Keep it in the bedroom, keep it in real time. Introduce lots of supporting characters with their own needs and obstacles whose presence communicates something about the wider world beyond the central relationship. Clever.

And it looks a little something like this . . .

IMAGE 89 *Storyboard #8* © *Leo Butler, 2024.*

You show your script to the theatre, and they hate it. Deep down, you hate it too.

Time to rethink.

You like having more than two characters, but you don't want to be constrained by a real-time structure. It's a pain in the arse.

You want to *show* the beginning, middle and end of the relationship over the course of months or years, but you still like the bedroom setting.

You divide the action into three separate events, weeks or months apart . . .

IMAGE 90 *Storyboard #9* © *Leo Butler, 2024.*

The luxury of time allows you more freedom, more room for character and plot development. Even the setting – the bedroom – has an interesting physical journey that reflects the character's emotional journey. Nice work, genius, two thumbs up.

Then the theatre suggests you scrap the single setting. *'We've just had a big Arts Council grant. Why not have more locations and lots of characters?'*

Oh shit . . .

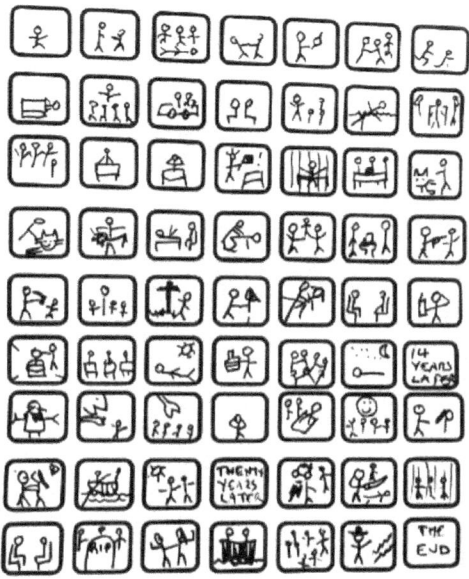

IMAGE 91 *Storyboard #10* © *Leo Butler, 2024.*

. . . you're back where you started. Um . . .

IMAGE 92 *Storyboard #11* © *Leo Butler, 2024.*

Or you could try this again . . .

IMAGE 93 *Storyboard #12 © Leo Butler, 2024.*

Fuck it. Be more adventurous . . .

IMAGE 94 *Storyboard #13 © Leo Butler, 2024.*

The play begins with a mysterious monolith at the dawn of time. It then makes a huge jump to the protagonist arriving at the bedroom. Then we have the breakup scene, after which we jump to the death of the boyfriend many years later. Finally, we're jumping years ahead when aliens invade the earth.
Is that the story I want to tell?
Or, perhaps, you decide to tell the story backwards.
Or naturalistic scenes are punctuated with dream scenes. Or songs.
Or you slot that monologue back in somewhere.
Or maybe you'll scrap the idea entirely and start something new.
Take your hunch and try fitting it into a range of shapes.
Find the setting, timeline and order that reveals the play you most want to see.
Fingers on the keyboard, and . . .

9

Ch-ch-ch-ch-changes!

Me and Rhyd are having a beer in the Royal Court Theatre bar when a young actress walks by.

    ME: Man, she is fit as fuck, and she's got a voice like honey.

    RHYD: Then you should chat to her after the show, man, serious. Her and her mate, we can bring them back to ours.

    ME: Fuck that, she is way too good for me.

It was October 2000 and my debut play, *Made of Stone*, was being staged in the Theatre Upstairs as part of the Royal Court's Young Writers' Festival. I was also homeless and dossing on the floor of Rhyd's one-bedroom flat in Queen's Road Peckham. As well as being the lead singer of our rock band, *Grass Hoppa*, Rhyd had trained as an actor at Rose Bruford and, by sheer chance, had been cast in another festival play, Arzhang Pezhman's *Local*, that was playing in rep with mine.

Both plays were rehearsed at the Court's rehearsal rooms, so the casts and crews would regularly mingle. Arzhang's excellent play was set in an Iranian corner shop and included an inspired scene when the shop owner explains the history of Zoroastrianism using chocolate bars. Rhyd played a rival shopkeeper's son, and his sister was played by a dazzling actress – who I'll call 'N' – with big brown eyes and long dark hair.

'Man, she is fit as fuck, and she's got a voice like honey.'

Like a Fellini belladonna, 'N' would sidle over during lunch breaks, and with a hushed, sexy 'hi', ask smart, insightful questions about my play. Pulse racing, I would instantly break into a sweat, mumbling incoherently like a great, galumphing lunk.

'Then you should ask her to come out after the show, man, serious. Her and her mate, we can bring them back to ours.'

'Fuck that, she is way too good for me'.

There was no way I was bringing her to our unkempt shithole on the Clifton Estate. Not only would she have never spoken to me again, but we might never have got married eighteen months later, or raised our teenage daughter, or still be growing older and sillier together to this day. Even as I write this chapter, 'N' continues to sidle over with sharp, insightful questions, while I try – in vain – to sound cleverer than I am.
Say hi to the readers, 'N'.
'Hi'.
For all the success or acclaim, the most rewarding part of working in theatre is the friends and relationships you make along the way. It's a close-knit culture and the degrees of separation are small, even among admin staff and stage crew. Many careers are fleeting, or chewed up and spat out, while some achieve longevity to the bewilderment of others. That said, you can't begrudge another person's success because we all know how difficult it is to make headway in this oversubscribed, underfunded circus. Unlike the luvvie stereotype that's peddled for comedy, most theatre folk are affable and self-deprecating, with genuinely good intentions. The Royal Court Theatre team of the early noughties were no exception as they not only springboarded my career, but also (unwittingly) brought me and 'N' together during those lunch breaks of our two plays.
It took a good while to get there though. The years between leaving Rose Bruford in 1994 and penning my debut in the spring of 2000 might have been chock-a-block with crazy adventures, but they were also a monumental waste of time.
I'd left Sheffield on a high, brimming with confidence after making *Runners* and writing *The Prime Controller*, and, in hindsight, I should have used the school's resources to keep developing my skills. Roy Williams was also on the Writers' Course (in the year above me), and he wasted no time in writing his debut, *The No Boy's Cricket Club* [1996], which was picked up by Theatre Royal Stratford East soon after he left. In contrast, the kid who wanted to do *everything* became lost and aimless, choosing pot-induced lethargy and a servility to the routines of others who were just as stoned as me. There were arrests and drug raids, nights in prison cells and naked sweat lodges in the countryside with self-proclaimed 'medicine men'. We scaled the fence of Glastonbury Festival in 1995 with no supplies or money, blagging our way into strangers' tents to scoff their food. At home there was rarely a night's peace as the front door was always open. At best, we'd welcome dealers or fellow stoners to listen to the KLF's *Chill Out* album while getting shitfaced on the sofa. At worst it was the sociopathic, Khat-chewing mystic who fed us chicken hearts before ritually exorcizing the fleas from the sofa. There were girlfriends and

breakups. Other peoples' girlfriends and breakups. Breakups of the same girlfriends with other peoples' boyfriends. Pregnancies and terminations. There were harmless drugs, harder drugs and not-so-secret addictions. Socially acceptable cans of Stella Artois vied for space on the living room floor with bowls of miracle fungus, Kombucha. Rare periods of abstinence or quests for spiritual enlightenment were punctuated with fortnightly trips to the dole office. Some people graduated, some didn't. Instead of getting real jobs, we'd spend hours playing *Abe's Odyssey* on the PlayStation, and there were endless conversations about conspiracies and the illuminati that lasted well into the night. As the years passed, tensions increased when some of the actors started getting agents or parts in movies, while some were lucky to audition at all. We'd started as equals, but became competitors, leading to a Chekhovian pressure cooker of arguments, betrayals and mental breakdowns. Although we remained close friends and, as individuals, were decent people, the toxic gang mentality – strung out over five years – brought out the worst in all of us, and it was a relief when we went our separate ways.

There were, of course, moments of genuine friendship and irreplaceable lived experience. Failing to hitchhike to Penzance with my good friend, and future movie producer, Denzil Monk, was a blast, as was taking to the streets to film short slapstick comedies with director Dave Lovatt simply for the fun of it. Likewise, travelling solo across Europe with an *Interrail* pass in the summer of 1994 will always be a cherished memory. Admittedly, there were some challenges, such as running out of money in the backstreets of Paris or being hauled off the train by the Austrian Border Police and their sniffer dogs, but I relished the solitude, learning how to navigate strange places and meeting equally strange people around campfires along the way. Like escaping school on buses or improvising a new play on a hunch, there's a strange serenity to moving forwards without a plan. I'd often sleep on overnight train carriages or set up my tent on the mountains of Chamonix, where I spent my twentieth birthday with a group of friendly climbers and their wine.

On returning to London, I picked up my guitar and wrote a couple of verses for a new song – *'On the road to Chamonix, two fat ladies on my knee'*, etc. – which I played to Rhyd's younger brother, Dan. Being a musical prodigy, Dan managed to combine my verses with a belting chorus he'd already written, and we soon had a groovy new song, *Risin' Still,* which we played to the rest of the band.

We were called *Grass Hoppa*, with Rhyd on vocals, me and Dan on guitars, and our octopus-like drummer, Jim Smith. We all wrote the songs, which had a funky rock 'n' roll groove influenced by Hendrix, and when we rehearsed in the studio we were tight. However, when we gigged at venues around Camden or New Cross we could (occasionally) be a little less tight.

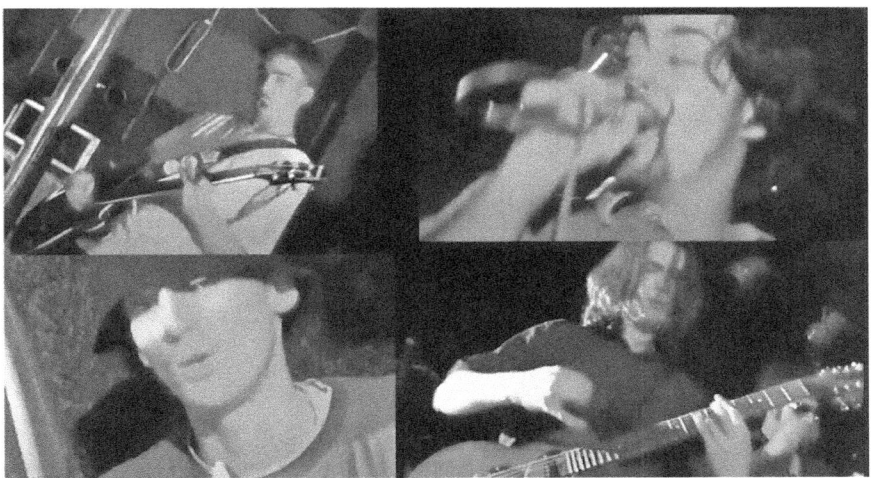

IMAGE 95 *Clockwise from top left: Dan Persad, Rhydian Persad, Leo Butler and Jim Smith are Grass Hoppa c.1998. Photo reproduced from author's archive.*

Having no van to bring our equipment, we'd persuade the support bands to let us use their kit and, as there were always a few hours to kill after the soundcheck, we'd take to the bar to kill time. Stumbling on stage at ten or eleven o'clock at night, we'd blast through our set with a plethora of broken strings, blood-splattered fretboards and ear-splitting feedback. It was a beautiful thing.

There's no better feeling than playing live music on stage; the connection between the band and the audience to create, in Dan's words, 'something positive', is as real as any piece of theatre. Ultimately, it didn't matter if we got a record deal or any of that bollocks; the pleasure was in the playing, and, all these years later, we still get together when we can.

I've loved messing around with music since I was a kid. I'm not the world's greatest player, but I can knock out a decent tune. Unlike writing a play, there's a wonderful *immediacy* to composing a song and putting it on tape, and, in 2011, Dan and I wrote *Alison! A Rock Opera* for that reason.

Across eighteen uninterrupted songs, *Alison!* tells the story of a young woman whose life is turned upside down after a breakup with her boyfriend. Following a botched suicide attempt, Alison has a series of musical encounters – with crooning bailiffs, mad doctors and Jagger-like priests – until she's finally reunited with her homeless and repentant ex. It may not have had the most nuanced plot, but the combination of high-street politics with high-energy rock seemed to connect with working-class audiences.

The finished show, directed by Nick Bagnall, toured to various venues over the next couple of years, including the Royal Court and Islington's King's Head. It remained a family affair, with Rhyd joining the likes of Clare

Cathcart, Lucy Edge and Roger Evans in the cast, with the other prodigious Persad brothers, Nathan and Joseph, on drums and bass. Our sold-out series of shows at The Spread-Eagle Theatre in East Croydon went entirely unnoticed by everyone who wasn't there, but it remains a career highlight, and we may even bring it back some day.

IMAGE 96 *Poster for 'Alison! A Rock Opera' at the New Cross Inn, 2013. Image reproduced from the author's archive.*

I was still gigging with *Grass Hoppa* when *Made of Stone* was selected for the Young Writers' Festival in 2000, but once the theatre picked up my second play, *Redundant,* I made the tough decision to quit (temporarily at least). Thankfully, there was no bad blood as Rhyd and Dan knew I'd been trying to get my plays on all through the nineties, and without much success.

After leaving Rose Bruford, I thought I'd change the world by writing a series of half-arsed drafts of ill-conceived plays called *Treading Water, The End of the World Extravaganza, Dissection of a Rapist* and *Starship Gaia.*

Starship Gaia – a comedy about a bickering couple hunting for UFOs in the woods – was probably the strongest of the bunch, and *Dissection of a Rapist* – despite its contentious title – was an ambitious Kafka-esque attempt to physicalize the mind of a psychopath. However, each of these plays were lacking authenticity and a basic understanding of structure – partly because I was flailing around in my own life so much. When I visited the Nottingham Playhouse to see Huss perform in a production of *The Loneliness of the Long-Distance Runner* [1959], I was lucky to meet the book's author, Alan Sillitoe. After a bit of Dutch courage, I asked him for a bit of writing advice. Sillitoe, dapper in his grey suit, took one look at this scruffy, long-haired space cadet and said, 'lad, don't do drugs'.

As I write this, I'm about to turn fifty and still feel mortified about some of the choices I made back then. When I teach young writers, I instruct them not to fuck around like I did and be more like sixteen-year-old Anya Reiss who turned up to one of my Royal Court writing groups and penned two shit-hot plays, *Spur of the Moment* [2010] and *The Acid Test* [2011], before she'd turned twenty. What I most admired about Anya was her ability to listen and take notes when it mattered, combined with a 'fuck you and your mother' attitude to anyone (including critics) who dared question the merits of her work. In short, teenage Anya was her own biggest fan, whereas twenty-year-old me couldn't decide who I was or why I was writing anyway.

Nevertheless, I was constantly drafting and rewriting projects, sporadically sending them out. The bible for aspiring writers was *The Writers' and Artists' Yearbook* – a fat directory that you could proudly place on your bookshelf to *look professional,* and which included the names and addresses of every literary agent and new writing theatre across the UK. I probably spent as much time scouring that book for in roads as I spent writing the plays to send, and there was always the problem of postage.

The internet wasn't even a word until 1998, and by the time of *Redundant* – three years later – there was still no such thing as emails or PDFs. As a kid I'd scribble my early efforts in notebooks or my parents' second-hand typewriter. By the time I moved to London, my dad got me a word processor, which – like voodoo – allowed you to make corrections on its tiny electric screen. Finally, by the end of the decade, I was the proud owner of a clunky PC, complete with *Word '97*, and a slow-as-arseholes printer.

Unlike today when you can air drop a script to anyone in the world from your *mobile fucking phone*, sending out a script in the nineties was a test of mettle and endurance. You'd begin by glaring at the printer as it slowly spewed out a single copy of script, page by bastard page. So long as the paper didn't jam or run out of ink, you'd then charge to the nearest post office – clutching the script like a newborn – to have it photocopied for 10p a sheet. Next came the challenge of binding the script in a smart WHSmith folder; hole punching the pages with pinpoint accuracy, carefully weaving the pages together with lengths of tasselled string. Once done, you delicately ease the script into a large brown envelope, making sure to include a covering letter, which you painstakingly correct so it doesn't sound too arrogant or grovelling. Double check you've got the right address on the front of the envelope, sellotape the flaps for good measure. Hopefully it isn't pension day, and you're not stood in the post office queue the rest of the morning. Then finally hand the script to the cashier with an extra five or six quid to have it sent by special delivery. And always ask for the receipt.

You'd strut back home feeling like Hercules, settling down with a nice cup of tea and a cig.

Then came the waiting. Then came the waiting.

More waiting. More tea and cigs.

Waiting.

Every day listening out for the phone or the letterbox to give you the good news.

Days turn to weeks, and weeks to months, until you forget about waiting altogether.

Then, out of nowhere, you receive something like this . . .

PICTURES LT

9th November 1995

Leo Butler

101 Blackheath Road, Greenwich

Dear Leo Butler
Many thanks for letting us see WASTED.

It looks like a lively project, but unfortunately not one with which we are able to become involved.

I wish you luck with it in the future.

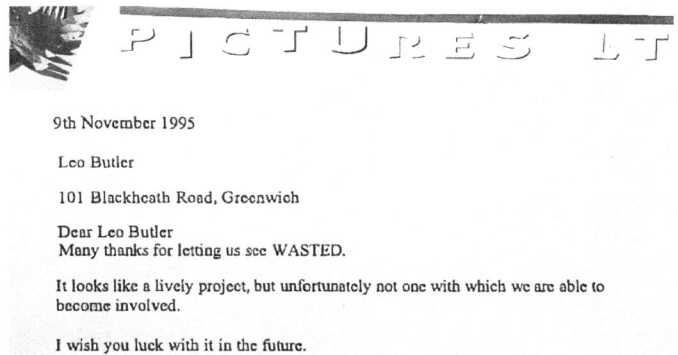

IMAGE 97 *Rejection letter #1 @ Leo Butler, 2024.*

Or this . . .

Dear Leo Butler

Thank you for your letter.

I am afraid we are not looking to take on new clients at present. We are a small agency and have recently taken on two new writers so will not be expanding our list for some while.

Good luck in your search for representation.

Yours sincerely

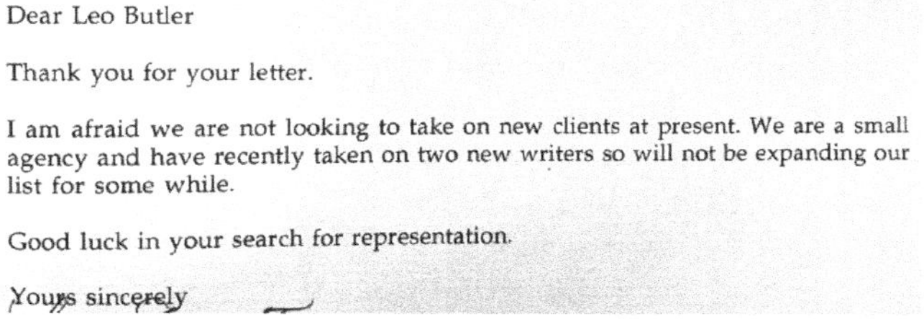

IMAGE 98 *Rejection letter #2 @ Leo Butler, 2024.*

Scouring *The Writers' and Artists' Yearbook*, you'd find more competitions or schemes to hurry back to the post office for.

A few more months of waiting, then . . .

> Dear Leo
>
> **BRIEF ENCOUNTERS: KIDS**
>
> Thank you for your submission for BRIEF ENCOUNTERS. It was read with great interest but has not been shortlisted for production.
>
> I am sorry you've had to wait so long for a response and thank you again for your interest in this scheme.
>
> With best wishes

IMAGE 99 *Rejection letter #3 @ Leo Butler, 2024.*

Or . . .

> Dear Leo
>
> Thank you for submitting your script to LWTP's New Writers Award 1998.
>
> Unfortunately, after a great deal of consideration and a careful reading process, your script has not been selected for the next round.

IMAGE 100 *Rejection letter #4 @ Leo Butler, 2024.*

Theatres were generally more detailed with their feedback . . .

> Thank you for sending us the above play. Apologies for the delay in responding to you.
>
> Sadly after all this time I can't offer to produce this piece. Whilst our reader thought the play quite topical, in the end we felt that there was perhaps a little bit too much repetition and it needed sharper characterisation and dramatic drive. In the end it wasn't something that we thought would sit easily with the programme of work we have planned. I wish you luck in finding a home for it elsewhere.
>
> Sorry to disappoint you on this occasion but we receive around a thousand scripts a year and can only take on one or two of these.

IMAGE 101 *Rejection letter #5 @ Leo Butler, 2024.*

Or . . .

> I enjoyed elements of the play and though that some of thescenes had excellent ialogue and strong dramatic action between the characters. However the overall structure lacks coherance. Scenes come out of nowhere rather than following on in an organic way, which weakens the drama and the premise. The characters need to be given stronger motivations for why they are all together in the first place. I also had a problem with the characters as you seem to be asking the audience to laugh at them and care about them at the same time, which doesn't work. We would be interested however in reading more of your work.
>
> Thank you for your interest in the company and good luck with placing your play.

IMAGE 102 *Rejection letter #6 @ Leo Butler, 2024.*

When the Royal Court announced its 1998 Young Writers' Festival, I sent two of my repeatedly rejected plays in two separate envelopes, receiving a single knockback for both.

> *Dissection of a Rapist* There is some good writing in this piece, the assault scene between the girl and the three men is skilfully handled, Gary and Miles have good dialogue throughout and the dilemma of your lead character is gripping. The character of the Mother, however, does tend to be a little stereotyped. The actors device at the end of the play is a bit too contrived and obvious and the last scene with Priapus and the young man too didactic. You need to focus and to control your imagination so that it serves the play and the theme (why the blood in the cake?) and don't overload the audience. You have a very good eye for the stage picture and an ambitious and impudent theatrical sense.
>
> *Treading Water* As with *Dissection of a Rapist* you have a very good sense of theatre with good structure, dialogue and generally well defined characters. I wasn't too sure about the song at the end - what are you trying to do with it?
>
> We would like to thank-you again for entering your play in the Festival and to encourage you to keep up with your writing. We enclose information on the Royal Court Young People's Theatre and if you would like any further information, please contact us on 0171 565 5017. We wish you good luck in your future writing.

IMAGE 103 *Rejection letter #7 @ Leo Butler, 2024.*

Only years later did I accept it was accurate and encouraging feedback. At the time, I thought they were fucking idiots.

By a stroke of luck, the future *This is England* [2006] actor, Stephen Graham, had also been in our year at Rose Bruford. Back in 1994 – having cut his chops as a child actor at the Everyman Theatre – Stephen generously put me in touch with that other proud scouser, Willy Russell.

Educating Rita [1980], *Blood Brothers* [1981] and *Our Day Out* [1983] are some of the finest (and funniest) working-class plays ever written, and it can't be overstated how important those plays were to my generation growing up. They may not have the 'in-yer-face' swagger of bleaker Northern fare, but – like a Paul McCartney melody – they feel like they've been around forever.

As such, I was terrified when I first sent a sample of my work for him to read, which he had no obligation to do, and delighted when he wrote back with honest, detailed notes, asking me to stay in touch.

I quickly wrote back, and, to my astonishment, so did he . . .

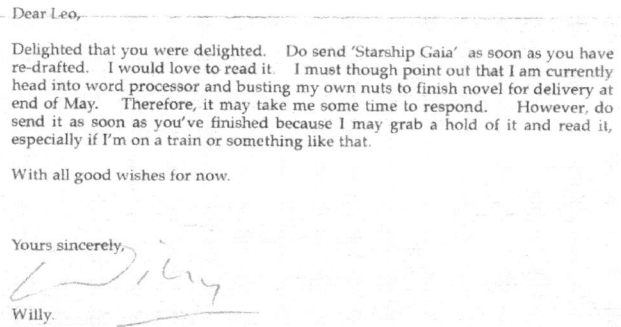

IMAGE 104 *Excerpt of Willy Russell correspondence #1. @ Leo Butler, 2024.*

From our first correspondence in 1994, Willy and I regularly stayed in touch for more than five years, and his endorsement was one of the few things that kept me going.

> As with 'Dissection of a Rapist', there is absolutely no mistaking the quality of the writing and I am more than happy to recommend such good writing (indeed I have already, on a number of occasions, mentioned your work as being an example of fine and exciting writing).

We became accustomed to sending letters back and forth, and if I sometimes challenged his criticisms, he would respond like a peer.

> I'm not remotely surprised that you were 'slightly' disappointed by my criticism. It's a cruel fact but whether a play turns out to be successful or not, the chances are that exactly the same energy, commitment, passion and long, long hours of work go into the making of it. To then meet with any kind of unfavourable reaction is, I well know, bitterly disappointing.

Other times, he would give me a kick up the arse . . .

> What sort of theatre do you want to write for? Where do you see your plays being presented? Do you have a sense of your audience? Are you thinking in terms of a small studio theatre, the main stage at The National or Shaftesbury Avenue? These questions might seem somewhat crude but they are, I think,

vital. What I get from your work is an intuitive sense that, if you could somehow take a certain leap, you could address a large, broad audience. I may be wildly wrong in this and it might even be destructive for me to say it. However, one must take the chance.

They were great, overdue provocations, but I still couldn't make any headway and, approaching the millennium, I barely left my bedroom let alone visited any theatres.

Apart from one or two part-time jobs, I stayed on the dole for years, reliant on my fortnightly £75 cheque and other benefits. It wasn't that I refused to work, I was just convinced that a great artist needed all the time in the world to make great art. Ironically, it wasn't until I finally got a real job that I wrote anything worth reading.

In the summer of 1998, I was moping around in front of daytime TV when my good friend and flatmate, Simon Notton, inadvertently changed my life. A thoroughbred South-East Londoner, Simon's sweary, mischievous sense of humour, and happy-go-lucky attitude were infectious. His workplace happened to be the Royal Court Theatre, where he was working as head barman, and he suggested I try for a job to '*get out of the fucking house, man!*'. Within days, he put me in touch with the front of house manager who offered me ushering work, which turned out to be the best job in the world.

Ripping tickets and showing people to their seats was dead easy, and as most of my colleagues were also aspiring creatives who liked a drink or two, the social life was a blast. After being stuck at home for so long, it was great to be out in the West End every night and, as Simon Notton promised: '*Mate, you'll earn some cash and get to see all these mental fucking plays for free.*'

At that time, the Court's Sloane Square site was being renovated, so short runs of 'mental fucking plays', like Richard Bean's *Toast* [1999] and Werner Schwab's *Holy Mothers* [1999], were staged at the New Ambassadors Theatre, while down at the Duke of York's Theatre on St Martin's Lane, in a run that lasted more than two years, was Conor McPherson's *The Weir*.

As an usher, I must have watched *The Weir* about 100 times, and its testament to Ian Rickson's production that – even when nursing a hangover or having a sneaky nap at the back of the stalls – I never got bored. On the contrary, it was an education in dramaturgy – better than any playwriting class – and gradually came to inform my own work.

I remember marvelling how magician McPherson used slight-of-hand dialogue to end one unit of action and casually begin another without anyone noticing the joins. He gives us the impression we're having a laid-back evening in the pub, but every detail – from the pub's broken bar taps to the jokes about German tourists – has a deliberate (often metaphorical) connection to the themes.

As in Shakespeare, we're given the bare minimum of backstory, but we feel an intimate connection to the characters by how they interact, under pressure, in the present moment. Their contrasting rhythms of speech, unashamedly packed with colloquialisms from County Leitrim, tell us more about who these people are than any list of biographical facts.

As there were several cast changes during the play's run, it was fascinating how each new actor's tone and intonation, without changing a word of text, could flip your opinion of a character on its head. Likewise, audiences would come away with different interpretations of what the play's really about, which is far more interesting than being heckled or told what to think. Having wasted a lot of time wracking my brain for a big idea, I suddenly realized you didn't need one.

Be truthful, tell a simple story. Create space (or mystery) around the characters so that the actors can bring their own creativity to the job, and let the audience make up their minds.

Like most playwrights, I'd always revered the Royal Court. Since Osborne's *Look Back in Anger* in 1956, it was arguably the world's most influential theatre. Under George Devine it had staged some of the first productions of Beckett, Ionesco and Brecht, then under William Gaskill it had introduced the likes of Bond, Orton and Pinter. The seventies ushered in kaleidoscopic seasons of work, with everything from Richard O'Brien's *Rocky Horror Show* to Athol Fugard's *The Island* [1973] to Trevor Griffiths *Comedians* [1975]. In the eighties, Max Stafford-Clark flew the flag for feminist writers like Timberlake Wertenbaker and Sarah Daniels, and in the 1990s Stephen Daldry rolled the dice on rock stars like Kane, Ravenhill, and Penhall.

Possibly no other building carries such a weight of responsibility for the future of contemporary drama, and its artistic teams must sometimes feel like Laurel and Hardy pushing the piano up a staircase of begrudging playwrights.

However, some artistic teams have done themselves no favours trying to define the building's 'identity' or 'message' by programming quick-fire responses to world events as if anyone outside of the building gives two shits what the theatre thinks. The danger of that approach is that aspiring writers start believing they must behave like journalists to get anything produced. Despite their noble intentions, if programmers divert writers away from their own creative instincts' – which may be *devoid* of left-leaning politics, which may instead be just something *stupidly joyous* or *fucking weird* – it risks limiting their playfulness and spontaneity at the first hurdle.

During the noughties, artistic directors Ian Rickson and Dominic Cooke generally placed their trust on the hunches of playwrights to create a diverse and eclectic theatre scene. When the fancy new auditorium re-opened on Sloane Square in early 2000, there followed a run of shows – including Kia Corthron's *Breath, Boom,* Marius von Mayenburg's *Fireface* and Martin Crimp's *The Country* – which, like *The Weir,* were so singular in form and style that first timers like me felt we could write whatever goddamn play we wanted.

Scribbling away with renewed energy, the millennium celebrations came and went. Simon and I were evicted from our flat in Gipsy Hill, so I moved back to Plumstead with my blues-guitarist buddy, Sharif. Friday nights were reserved for Tequila and jamming, but – for one reason or another – Sharif was rarely home, which meant I often had the place to myself.

Sat amongst the empty tequila bottles, I dug out a Sheffield-based play I'd written at drama school and decided to give it another go.

Giddy Little Kippers follows a group of 11-year-old kids who decide to play a football match against their teachers to show them 'who's boss'. Hodgy, the overly enthusiastic lead kid does everything he can to unite his mates, but they are far too caught up in their own problems to care. Bickering and tensions escalate until Hodgy discovers that their shy girl goalie, Rose, is keeping secrets that are more urgent than anyone imagined. Tears are shed, there's the beginning of a school romance, and, forgetting their silly grievance with the off-stage teachers, the kids play the match for each other instead.

Galvanized by the realism of Christopher Shinn's Manhattan comedy *Other People* [2000] and Roy Williams's West London scorcher *Lift Off* [1999] – I dug up memories of primary school to give it a personal touch. Specificity of setting and language were key, and I packed it with references to Pitsmoor, filling the dialogue with phonetically precise Sheffield dialect; '*your*' becomes '*yer*', '*give over*' becomes '*gi'oer*', '*no*' becomes '*naow*'. And just as every character in *The Weir* is experiencing a type of grief (however oblique), I decided that every character in *Giddy Little Kippers* should be experiencing comparable anxiety to Rose. Like a nucleus, it kept the story focused and avoided the need for eggy speeches that remind the audience what they're watching. As my writing progressed, in plays like *Boy* and *I'll Be the Devil*, I always made it a rule that every character – however minor – is a mirror image of the protagonist, even when their circumstances are less urgent.

Giddy Little Kippers was a sweet little play, with nice dialogue and funny scenes, but the problem was what to do with it.

During one ushering shift, I found a print out of the associate directors' home addresses that had been left on a desk backstage. Grabbing my notebook, I jotted them down, printed and posted numerous copies of *Kippers* and never heard anything back.

However, I also dropped a copy on the desk of associate director, Ola Animashawun, who managed the theatre's Young Writers' Programme, and when, in the spring of 2000, he called to arrange a meeting, I was elated.

The Young Writers' Programme had grown out of the Court's Young People's Theatre, which Ola had run with international associate, Elyse Dodgson, from their offices on the Portobello Road.

After the theatre's refurb, the YPT was renamed the YWP – to focus exclusively on playwriting – and was rehomed, across the alleyway from the main theatre, in London Undergound's old canteen building, enigmatically called The Site.

The Site had a large rehearsal/workshop space, as well as an open-plan office for Ola and the spunky YWP team of Nina Lyndon, Emily McLaughlin, Aoife Mannix and Lucy Dunkerly. There were also two or three smaller offices (or 'writer's rooms') dotted about the place, and a very pleasant garden (which, a few years later, homed the real-life chickens for Jez Butterworth's *Jerusalem*, providing the theatre with a constant supply of eggs).

An unsung hero of British theatre, Ola's passion for unlocking the creative potential of young people has springboarded the careers of hundreds of playwrights with initiatives like the YWP, Critical Mass and the National's Connections Festival. He also wears extraordinary jumpers and is very funny.

IMAGE 105 *Photo credit: Ola Animashawun, 2024. Photo reproduced with kind permission of @ Justine Themen.*

It was a brief meeting, full of chatter and laughter. Ola told me about himself, I explained a bit about myself. He'd enjoyed *Giddy Little Kippers* and suggested I submit it for the upcoming Young Writers' Festival. The deadline was sometime in June and the chosen plays would be produced in the autumn.

As the deadline approached, I knew I was going to send *Giddy Little Kippers* and, thinking it still had legs, another reworked version of *Starship Gaia*.

One morning I got out of bed and found *three* identical letters on the doormat. They were reminders that the deadline for Festival submissions was three weeks away, and, as such, I was convinced the gods were telling me to submit *three* plays for each of the *three* letters.

With only *three* weeks until the deadline, I thought I'd better get my skates on.

It was called '*Scallies*' to begin with.

I underlined the title and drew a picture of three . . . well, typical Sheffield scallies.

I scrubbed out *'Scallies'* and changed it to *'Made of Stone'* (from the Stone Roses' song)

I drew more pictures of the characters, creating an extensive family tree that included friends and workmates.

Gave them names and ages. Decided where they lived. Brainstormed a few facts about them and considered how they felt about each other.

I'll aim for fifteen or twenty multi-locational scenes. Sounds about right.

Ripping sheets of A4 from my notebook, I instinctively jot down a list of events that *might* happen to each of the characters based on what seems to be bothering them deep down.

This happens, *therefore* that happens, *but* this happens, *therefore* that happens, *but* this happens, *therefore* that happens, etc., etc.

Calling it the 'skeleton plot', I keep the sheet of A4 by my desk, ticking off each scene as I go.

But as I write, the play takes on a life of its own. The characters say and do things I don't expect. There are plot twists, revelations and new scenes I hadn't planned for.

I cross out, retitle or reorder the events of the 'skeleton plot' accordingly.

There are some terrific scenes, some are a bit too functional. I decide I'll rewrite them later. Get to the end first.

That bit's shit.

No, it isn't.

I like that speech though.

You'll probably have to cut it.

Alright, whatever. Just keep going.

Themes emerge. The characters become increasingly desperate.

It's more emotional than I imagined.

It reminds me of home. It reminds me of growing up.

I know these people.

I sometimes laugh at my own jokes. Shut up, dickhead, you're not there yet.

I slot in a scene that I'd written months ago. Easy peasy, saves me the arse ache of writing something new. Turns out it's the best scene in the play.

Some storylines are easy, some aren't.

Scenes that require a lot of stage directions, multiple exits and entrances, characters arriving at 'just the right time', are a massive grind, but I try not to rush them. It's a relief to get through to the other side.

Two handers, by contrast, are a breeze, and I'm fucking good at this.

Shut up, don't get cocky.

There's breath-taking excitement when the characters' start writing the scenes. I don't need the skeleton plot anymore; the challenge is trying to keep up.

Stay awake, remember to eat.

Pasta. Toast. Cereal. Endless coffee.

Chainsmoking, chainsmoking, chainsmoking. Working through the night.

Wake up. Ah shit, Sharif's back home.

Nope, that was the postman. Good.
I'm going a bit mad now.
I need to eat. Something decent, a bag of carrots. Have I got time to run to the shops?
Run to the shops.
Milk and cigarettes, chicken and chips. Fuck the carrots.
I need a shower.
There isn't time, just stink it out.
A pub, a car, a running track, a screaming baby and a giant pile of stones. Let the director work out the staging.
You're getting closer.
Albrecht Dürer's Saint Jerome is looming somewhere in my head, ready for the play's climax.
This is too easy.
Oops, don't speak too soon.
The bedroom walls dissolve, and I'm *inside the play* racing to the final lap.
Cheating. Putting words in the characters' mouths just to get to the end.
What is this play? Why am I writing it?
Who the hell am I anyway?
No time to stop. Deadline looming.
Throw in a reference to Kurosawa's *Throne of Blood*, and that bit about the mango.
And there's a nice line about the internet. Topical.
As the story reaches its crisis and conclusion, I like that no one's good or bad. Everyone's flawed like in real life.
It's sad in places. Some characters make questionable choices.
Did they make the right choice? Let the audience decide.
Finally, I reach the point where . . .

> *Elaine sits at the table. The meal begins.*
>
> *Long pause.*

Elaine Well, this is nice.

Lights fade.

Pressing print on the printer, I have no idea what I've just written except it's seventy-five pages with a title page.
I suppose it looks like a play, but does it work? Does it hang together?
It's a stinking pile of shit.
It's funny though.
It's a stinking pile of shit.
It isn't.
It is.
Shut up, man, the babysitting scene is funny.
No, it isn't.

It is.
You're wrong. It doesn't work on every level.
Whatever man, it's deadline day.
I jump on the train to Victoria Station, pop into the post office.
Buy an envelope. Shove the freshly printed *Made of Stone* into the envelope.
Race to Sloane Square, drop the envelope at the stage door.
Then came the waiting. Then came the waiting.
Weeks pass.
Sharif and I can't afford the rent.
I pack my bags and move into Rhyd's flat, making my bed on his living room floor.
More waiting. More tea and cigs.
Waiting.
Every day listening out for the phone.
Back to ushering shifts.

The autumn season was approaching, with fun-sounding shows like David Eldridge's *Under the Blue Sky,* Caryl Churchill's *Far Away* and Sarah Kane's *4.48 Psychosis* announced in the new brochure. There was also a gap for the Young Writers' Festival, with plays to be announced very soon.

It was sometime in July and Marina Carr's *On Raftery's Hill* was playing on the Court's main stage. I'm working the stalls, showing the audience to their seats, when I get a tap on the shoulder. 'You're Leo aren't you?'. 'Um, yeah ...'. 'I'm Ian, the Artistic Director. This is Katie Mitchell, one of our associates. I just wanted to say well done on your brilliant play.'

They left as quickly as they'd arrived, and my diminutive, dreadlocked co-usher called over from the fire doors: *'mate, you are getting pissed tonight!'*

I saddled my programme bag. Took my bench at the back of the stalls.

The house lights faded out and the discordant Irish fiddle echoed across Raftery's Hill.

Heart beating, grinning from ear to ear, it was the best shift I ever had.

Soon after, I received another letter from Willy ...

> Dear Leo,
>
> Many thanks for your last letter and, indeed, for all the good news therein. I'm so glad about the Royal Court doing your play. Many many congratulations. Of course I would love to come along to see it if I am able but please please don't think that you have to get me complimentary tickets. I'd be more than glad to buy my own.

IMAGE 106 *Excerpt of Willy Russell correspondence #2.* @ Leo Butler, 2024.

... and suddenly everything changes.

Within a few weeks I've bagged a literary agent, my show's on at the Royal fucking Court, and I'm having a beer in the bar when a young actress walks by.

ME: Man, she is fit as fuck!

RHYD: Then you should chat to her after the show, man, serious!

By Christmas, I'd finally left Rhyd's Peckham bedsit and moved into a shared house in East Finchley. My room was a playground of half-empty whisky bottles, blood-spattered guitars, half-finished scripts, hastily scribbled phone numbers from the night before, unwashed laundry and towers of art-house videocassettes.

In the New Year, Ian Rickson offers me an eight-week attachment at the theatre where I share an office with the super-talented and Tigger-like Simon Stephens who makes playwriting seem like *the most exciting thing on earth*. We smoke a lot of cigarettes, eat biscuits and inspire each other to write plays that could have belonged on the same album.

One Friday, I lock myself in the office and – on a diet of instant coffee and Safeway sandwiches – knock out the first draft of my next play *Redundant* over the weekend.

Stephens bursts into the office on Monday morning and laughs: *'fuckin' hell, Butler, it's smoky in here!'*

Two months later, *Redundant* wins the prestigious George Devine Award, which comes with a £10,000 prize, which I piss up the wall on holidays and drugs.

That summer, Dominic Cooke directs the shit out of the play on the theatre's main stage, and, once the curtain comes down, the West End's bars and night clubs become the backdrop for long drunken nights and a plethora of naughty dalliances that came and went.

Twenty-seven years old, a year since *Made of Stone* changed my life, I'm leaving a West End nightclub at four o'clock in the morning. Standing in the rain, waiting for the night bus to take me home, I ask myself –

What's the point of any of this success, if there's no one to share it with?

Christmas was approaching and 'N' was performing in a play at the Birmingham Rep.

I text her. She texts back.

Every Saturday night, she'd get the train from Birmingham, and I'd race from East Finchley to meet her on the doorstep of her flat on Lower Marsh, Waterloo.

We spent Christmas in Manhattan. We bought stupid hats and got tattoos. We ate sandwiches at Katz's Deli and toasted in New Year's with a George Harrison tribute band in Brooklyn.

By spring 2003, I was carrying my clunky PC up the stairs to her room, planning my third Royal Court play, and plotting when and how I was going to propose.

10

Births n' rebirths n' rewrites n' bellyaches

Of course, not all plays are written overnight. Aside from *Made of Stone* and *Redundant*, I think there's only one other play – *The Early Bird* – that I managed to write with such haste (in the final frantic weeks before the birth of our daughter).

In comparison, the first draft of *I'll Be the Devil* took me more than two years to complete. An epic historical play, several gruelling months were spent researching Catholicism and the occupation of Ireland in the eighteenth century. Tougher still was the play's fifty-page, multi-character Tavern scene (with swordfights, songs and game-changing plot twists), which felt more like choreographing a dance piece than writing a play.

Similarly, *All You Need is LSD* took three years as I struggled to find a throughline for the 300-odd pages of random scenes I'd been churning out. It was only once I volunteered to be injected with pure LSD while having my brain scanned by medical researchers that I realized *I was the throughline* and – once the lysergic wore off – could finally start shaping the material into something resembling drama.

Whatever the process, writing a play – like any birth – can be mired by complications, requiring plenty of gas and air. Even when you're commissioned by a posh theatre, deadlines, like due dates, come and go. Artistic directors – like midwives – might worry the play is premature, or – like social services – not even let you keep it.

I remember David Eldridge explaining how he doesn't submit a play until he's got it to the *'very best it can be'*, whereas I've frequently submitted drafts that still need tons of work. That's fine when you're collaborating with directors who understand the messiness of a writers' process, but some will (justifiably) read a new play in the belief that *this is the finished piece*, and you're left with a play that no one wants to touch.

Equally frustrating is when a draft is turned down because of something that hasn't happened yet. My comedy about the youth of Osama bin Laden, *Young Osama*, was rejected for fear of offending everyone, and, despite being faithful to the original text, my adaptation of John Bunyan's *The Pilgrim's Progress* was turned down because of ongoing concerns about *I'll Be the Devil*'s blasphemy two years earlier. And – like an interminable maze of foster care – I was once brought in to replace a writer on a musical, who himself had replaced two other writers, only to be replaced myself when the producers felt the script might be upstaging the songs.

Ultimately, whenever (and wherever) you submit a draft always involves a roll of the dice and its success depends on good timing or luck.

Whether it takes you two days or two months to write your first draft, I'd recommend Eldridge's advice of doing at least one rewrite before sending it out to theatres or competitions.

Feedback

First things first, give your rough draft to a couple of people to read.

If you hand your play over to family members or close friends, it's important to remember that they will want to encourage you no matter what.

You MUST welcome the flattery of your loved ones. First and foremost, they are the most likely to understand what your play's trying to achieve and, secondly, they're the ones who will keep you going when things get tough.

Don't hover over their shoulder while they read it.

Don't demand an explanation every time they react.

If you can, read the play out loud *together*.

Give the reader space and time to process their thoughts.

Don't be offended if the reader doesn't have any feedback except 'I liked it'. It's a lot of pressure to put on people (loved ones or friends) who aren't used to giving feedback.

Bear in mind that two readers will almost always have contradictory reactions. That's OK, you're not putting up a bookshelf or changing a fuse; art isn't functional, it's supposed to affect people differently. A range of opinions means you're doing something right.

And, of course, it's perfectly acceptable for a reader to completely misread your play or *not remember every damn detail of the plot*. You've lived and breathed your play for months, but the poor reader's only read it once so cut them some slack before you start grilling them.

Likewise, it's OK if a reader starts *playing the role* of a critic and starts criticizing everything because that's what they think they're supposed to do.

I remember running a session for a group of thirty aspiring writers at the Royal Court. As I didn't have time to personally critique each of their plays, I decided to split them into groups of two or three, so that they could give feedback to each other instead.

Ten minutes later, one of the students suddenly charges out of the class in floods of tears. Catching up with her round the back of the theatre, it transpires that her fellow student had told her *'I don't like your play, it's boring, I wouldn't pay to see it, you should seriously think about doing something else'*.

To smooth things over, I read the play myself and gave appropriate feedback. It wasn't boring, the reader was just being an arse.

Everyone has individual taste. I'm a fan of slow cinema, but I know Andrei Tarkovsky and Béla Tarr aren't for everyone. Likewise, I can't stand superhero films, but if a student wrote a play about Captain America I'd put my taste aside and give it the same respect as I would a seven-hour drama about Hungarian farmers.

What a reader likes or doesn't like is irrelevant. A good reader needs to shape shift their way into the writer's mind and work out what it is they're trying to achieve.

Like an actor getting under the skin of a character or a football pundit understanding the psychology and coaching technique of a particular team, it's only when the reader understands the *thinking behind the play* that they can help make practical suggestions to bring out the best of the piece. Whether it's *Uncle Buck* [Hughes, 1989] or *Uncle Vanya* [Chekhov, 1898], every story, like Laurel and Hardy's *The Music Box*, operates with the same set of valves.

Feeling awful for the tearful writer, I decided to lay some ground rules for giving and receiving feedback.

FOR THE READER . . .

- Words like 'rubbish' or 'boring' aren't allowed.
- Keep your taste in your trousers.
- Figure out what the writer's trying to do.
- Ask questions rather than give notes.
- Flattery is welcome.
- It's OK to be confused. Tell the writer when and where you were confused. The writer may reveal they were deliberately confusing you.
- Tell the writer what you want to know more about. The characters, their history, the situation or the world of the play, etc.
- Let the writer do the talking and ask questions.
- It's a conversation, not an interview.
- Treat the writer as you'd hope to be treated yourself.
- If you've got a 'burning note', don't keep it to yourself. But, equally, be sensitive with how you address it.

FOR THE WRITER...

- Don't get defensive. Be open to different interpretations. Nothing is an instruction, take what you feel is useful.
- It's OK to reject a note if you don't agree with it.
- Don't be offended if the reader was confused.
- The reader might have excellent suggestions or ideas. Steal them.
- The reader might offer an intelligent analysis of your play. Steal it.
- Ask the reader what they thought was happening in moments or scenes you're not sure about. Test if their interpretation correlates with your intentions.
- If the script's unfinished, ask the reader what they imagine might happen next. They might have some excellent suggestions.

Graham Whybrow, the Royal Court's literary manager of the 1990s and 2000s, helped me with my early plays and was one of the most skilful dramaturgs I've ever met. Rather than dryly doling out notes or pointing out where a script 'needs work', he would question why 'such and such a line' or 'such and such an event' happens at 'such and such point in a scene', not to expose its faults, but as a genuine line of enquiry. He would approach a script not as an expert, but as a first-time audience, asking *'is it your intention to make us think this thought or feel this emotion here? Why? If it's not your Intention what, as the dramatist, can you do to get the desired effect?'* In short, it was creative therapy, empowering the writer to do all the talking and take responsibility for their play.

When working with students on their plays, I generally try to employ Graham's method of asking questions rather than suggesting cuts. I might begin a feedback session with some positive comments like *'I fucking loved it'*, then I'll ask the writer what he or she thinks or feels about the current draft, adapting my thoughts to correspond with theirs.

But sometimes I'll go straight for the jugular. Having read hundreds of first drafts, I find I have an almost telepathic ability to tune into the writer's intention. As such, I can read any play – sometimes even *skim* a play – and instantly know what needs to be done. *'Get rid of the monologues ... cut those lines ... stop being so nice to your characters ... add another two scenes here ... you think your story's about vampires, but it's really about* that *character's grief.'*

But, then again, any suggestions are equally dependent on what I've had for breakfast, the state of the weather, the state of the world or how I'm feeling about life in general. With that in mind, I'll always remind the writer that even though I'm right, I may still be wrong.

The writer should remember that feedback isn't gospel. Don't think of your rewrite as correcting an essay for a teacher. Do whatever the hell feels right to you. It's your name on the script.

In my experience, most readers – from Aunty Ethel to the artistic director of a posh London theatre – will completely forget the notes they gave you by the time you've got round to a second draft.

Model box

Deep down, you already know what's right or wrong with your play. You're only using the reader to help clarify what you already suspect, and any fresh insights or suggestions are a bonus.

If you're reluctant to hand your play over to someone else, then you could always try staging a first performance of the play in your bedroom instead.

All you need is . . .

1. An empty shoebox.
2. Marker pens, biros, pencils, felt-tips.
3. Sellotape, glue, scissors. Blu Tack. Hairbands. Glitter. Bits of (coloured or white) card. Bits of string. Tissue paper. Paper. Cereal boxes. Wire. Bits of plastic. Any junk you can get your hands on.

Build a model of the play's set as you imagine it looking to an audience. Think about where you want the audience to sit.

Create a suitable design using your felt-tips, hairbobbles, glitter, etc.

You might even build little bits of furniture or doorways – like a mouse's house.

If you have multiple locations, think about how you will manage each of the scene changes.

Will it be a detailed, realistic set? Expressionistic or absurdist? Or an empty stage with just the bare minimum of objects or furniture?

Your model box doesn't have to be pretty or professional, just functional.

Think about how and where the actors will get on and off stage.

Build little models of all the characters that you can move around the set.

Or use Toy Soldiers or *Monopoly* figures – anything will do, even twigs stuck into blobs of Blu Tack.

Using a Dictaphone or voice-recording device, record the entire script – reading aloud all the parts yourself. It takes ages, but it's fun and worth it.

Playback the recording.

Moving the model characters around your shoebox – treat yourself to the first miniature performance.

Who knows what this exercise will reveal, but I guarantee it's an improvement on staring slack jawed at words on the page for the thousandth time.

A play is not a literary form like a novel or a poem. It's a guidebook for a LIVE EXPERIENCE with BODIES IN SPACE, so premiering the play in your shoebox will likely clarify which areas of the play are operating nicely and expose any bits that still need work.

Be prepared to hate everything you've written. That's natural.

Even if you think it's the greatest thing ever written, be honest about the moments where you're cheating or covering your tracks.

And if push comes to shove, put the rough draft in a drawer and get on with your life.

Come back to it when you've forgotten all about it.

Do I really have to do a rewrite?

Without Draft One, there's no play at all.

If you're lucky, Draft Two might generate some vague interest from a theatre or director. It might even be shortlisted for a competition or prize. If you're even luckier, someone might want to produce it. Or you might decide to produce it yourself.

Whatever the outcome, it's anyone's guess how many more versions you'll churn out before it finally reaches an audience.

Although *Made of Stone* only went through a couple of drafts, most of my subsequent plays went through several rewrites from first draft to press night. At least five or six before casting, another during the first two weeks of rehearsal once the actors put it on its feet, then some tweaks and edits during previews.

Boy went through about seventeen drafts over five years, and my most recent play, *Living* [Sheffield Playhouse, 2026], has undergone four major drafts over the space of a whole decade. Both plays were initially commissioned, then turned down by the Royal Court. *Boy* is set in the present day and *Living* spans a family's life from 1969 to the present day. As both plays were homeless for several years, what constituted the 'present day' kept changing and – with *Living* especially – I was endlessly rewriting to keep up with world events. As frustrating as it was, it was also nice to keep the characters alive – adapting to cataclysms like Brexit and the Covid-19 pandemic – a process that, in turn, deepened the overall gesture of the play.

First-time writers put themselves under a lot of pressure to make their script perfect straightaway, but, having spent many years mentoring new talent, it is very rare that a first draft is what you see on stage. Writers like Nick Payne, Polly Stenham and Anya Reiss all began with splurged-out drafts that were painstakingly reworked and refined all the way up to, and including, rehearsals.

Likewise, sitting in on the Royal Court's script meetings during the early noughties, I often read drafts submitted by some very famous playwrights that were a right old mess to begin with. Whether you're David Hare or David Who, it's good to remember that we're all just puzzling through, throwing paint at the walls to see what sticks. Don't give up just because you haven't got it right the first time.

I absolutely LOVE writing the first draft – it's magical, surprising and spontaneous. Rewriting, by contrast, is utterly nut driving. Even after twenty-odd years, 'N' despairs whenever I start a rewrite: *'Oh god, here you go again. You'll get stuck, have a breakdown, then eventually work it out like you always do.'*

I pride myself on being able to give sound dramaturgical advice to others, but – alone at my desk – I'm rubbish at taking my own. I often wish I had a 'Leo Butler' to send early drafts to because 'teacher Leo' is far more clear-headed than 'writer Leo'.

Sometimes it's obvious what needs doing to improve a draft, other times I'll convince myself the whole thing's horseshit. At my wit's end, I'll rip the script apart – deconstructing it, questioning everything – only to put it back together, months later, with only the smallest of tweaks, barely distinguishable from the first draft.

Which is why I love collaborating with others – directors, actors and other writers – when you can freely bounce around ideas without being distracted by that devilish voice in your head.

The trick is, partly, to remind yourself that a script is never finished.

I look back on plays I wrote more than a decade ago and find problems to fix that, at the time, seemed right as rain. Similarly, I can see where I made changes during or after a play's first production that, in hindsight, I needn't have changed at all.

But that's the nature of the beast. You evolve, your tastes and perceptions change with time. A script is a living thing. Sometimes you get it right, sometimes you get it wrong – and, given the enormity of the universe and the impermanence of life, none of it really matters anyway.

If you've ever embarked on rewrites, you'll know there is no one-size-fits-all approach – but, equally, you'll know you're guaranteed to hit some speedbumps and roadworks along the way.

The hotly anticipated second draft of *Redundant* was, for example, a bit of a disaster. For some stupid reason, I decided to change the play's structure from six short scenes to two long acts, which drained the play of any plausibility and momentum. Equally wrong footed was when I tried to be more politically explicit with excruciating out-of-character lines like *'New Labour? They don't care about people like us. We're like some forgotten fuckin' generation or somert.'* Or when I spent hours filling notebooks with character biographies that didn't result in anything except a half dozen overly long expositional speeches that wound up being cut anyway.

Thankfully, with the sound advice and dramaturgical dexterity of director Dominic Cooke, I restored the raw energy and structure of Draft One, while merging it with the best bits of Draft Two, to finally cobble together a much more credible Draft Three that we could take into rehearsal.

Lucky Dog didn't benefit from any extra character research or biographies either as the two lead characters revealed themselves to me as I wrote it. Of course, I'd constantly remind myself of what each character was trying to do to the other person in any given scene – the pianos and staircases that I talked about in **Chapter Seven** – but by far the most important thing was refining the pace and texture of the piece.

Likewise, the first draft of the vaudevillian *All You Need is LSD* was mammoth, so the key to rewrites was choosing what sketches and songs could be cut without losing the play's essence. Once I had a second draft, the play was then workshopped by Paul Hunter's madcap company, Told by an Idiot, who dispensed with the idea that 'writer-is-king', and would hack great bloody chunks out of the script at will. Their approach was a shock, but my bruised ego soon recovered once I admitted their decisions were (mostly) right. Sometimes it's about adapting to new approaches and, as with any feedback, being receptive to the ideas and creativity of others.

Before rehearsals of *Boy*, director Sacha Wares and I spent a huge amount of time discussing each new draft to get the script as tight as possible. Hidden away in the corner of a tiny Islington café, our conversations would last for hours as we interrogated *every line of dialogue*. When I couldn't immediately justify why 'such and such a line' or 'such and such a scene' moved the story forward, Sacha might suggest a cut or rewrite. I'd go away and think about it, and the next time we met – sometimes weeks later – I'd either convince her I was right or admit that I was wrong or come up with a compromise that pleased us both. Either way, we were rarely on separate tracks.

The play was originally written for a cast of eight, but once the Almeida snapped it up, it had evolved to a cast of twenty-six, along with a toddler, a baby and three dogs. Many of the scenes involve teenager Liam passing through populated areas of the city, including GP surgeries, train stations and nightclubs. I suggested that the surrounding dialogue could be improvised in performance, but Sacha encouraged me to write all the dialogue for all the hundreds of characters who pass – however fleetingly – through the scenes, even when fifteen characters are talking simultaneously.

By the time we started rehearsals, there were *three* versions of the play. The first was the published play and the second contained all the surrounding dialogues that the acting ensemble could choose from (some of which I included in the book's Appendix). The third version – scrawled in biro on scraps of paper – was a first-person monologue detailing all Liam's thoughts and feelings as he drifts from place to place. As Liam is so inarticulate, this version was presented to our lead actor, Frankie Fox, to help him access the character's inner life.

It was hard work, but nobody ever said writing was easy.

Copious notes are fine, but the one single thing that's helped the rewriting of all my plays is having someone – a director or friend of even the family cat – who's prepared to *listen* to me drone on about it.

And I've learned it's important not to fixate on trying to make it 'good' or to 'please' other people – as anyone's idea of what is 'good' can change from day to day.

Focus, instead, on whether the story is serving the idea or emotion you're trying to communicate. Focus on the truth and authenticity of the world and its characters. Know what kind of trip you're taking the audience on.

Check that each scene – or sequence – has a function to move the story forward. Keep your characters active, making choices – against the odds – to heave their pianos up the stairs.

Make a list of everything each character does in the play. Check for cause and effect: *this* happens; *therefore,* this happens, *but* this happens, *therefore,* this happens, etc.

Make sure your central characters are making choices that move the story forward. Don't let them be passive, unless they are *actively* passive.

Don't be afraid to cut sections that are holding the story up, even if they're beautifully written. Remember that this is just one play, so you don't have to throw everything you've got at it. Remember that there's no such thing as finished.

And at some point you'll duplicate a copy of the first draft and call it 'DRAFT TWO'.

You start on page one and work through the first scene. You read and examine each line of dialogue, refining them as you go.

If you're a perfectionist like me, you'll probably spend ages – weeks or months – working through the text until you're totally happy with it.

Or if you're super prolific, who knows! Maybe it'll be a total breeze!

You'll then start on scene two – or the next sequence of action. Repeat the process, double checking that each line of dialogue is motored by a psychological tactic.

Sometimes you'll have to write new scenes or sequences from scratch.

Once done, you'll want to reread and rewrite in much the same way as the others.

Keep going until you've got to the end of the play.

Read through the script again and make any further notes or changes.

Consider any question that someone may throw at you about the play – *Why does that happen? Why does that character say that? Why do we move to that location? Why have you written this play?*

If you feel you can answer any question about the play, then you're probably ready to stop.

Besides, there will always come a point where – sometimes out of sheer exhaustion or boredom – you can literally do no more.

As with the first draft, give it to a couple of people to read.

Or build another model box.

Or do something else entirely.

And, of course, it's still not finished.

Even when the director, actors, designers and stage crew have sunk their teeth into it, there's still the final piece of the puzzle – the audience.

Be prepared, they will tell you exactly what they think, and they never react in the same way twice.

11

The magic toybox

Wet behind the ears, I attended every day of *Made of Stone*'s four-week rehearsal, thinking my presence was requisite to its success, but, after twenty-five years, I've finally accepted that the writer's main job is supplying the biscuits.

Unless the director needs your opinion on 'such and such' a character or 'such and such' a scene, most of the day involves watching from the back – quietly giggling when an actor cocks up an entrance or forgets their lines.

And to be honest, it's not as if everyone *loves* having you around anyway.

No matter how many months of prep you may have done, the director's key collaborators are now their assistant and the stage manager. Stage managers – often the *coolest people in the room*, are also the unsung heroes of any show. From managing diaries, keeping note of every actor's entrance and exit, scribbling down each technical requirement, relaying messages to the lighting and costume designers, sourcing props, cleaning up spillages, organizing the day's schedule, organizing and emailing the next day's schedule, or being available for everyone's private concern or complaint – they practically run the show and neither they, nor the director, need to be badgered by an anxious writer wanting to know what time we're breaking for lunch. Once rehearsals move into the theatre, the play becomes a factory, an actual physical thing being built, so the stage crew – shifting ladders and setting up lighting rigs – don't want to be constantly tripping over your rucksack either.

Some projects, of course, do require the writer in the room. When director Eva Sampson and I collaborated with students at South London's famous BRIT school on *Decades* [Ovalhouse, 2016], some scenes were literally written in the room. Eva was as skilled at conjuring ideas from me as she was from our fifteen-strong cast of giddy youths. Even after I'd finally rattled out a script drawn from two terms of devising workshops, I remember Eva's palpable excitement when I mentioned a vague idea for a musical number. I dismissed the idea, but she persisted. I dismissed the idea again, but she convinced me to have a go. A few days later, the sprightly cast were up on their feet singing two vaudeville-style songs I'd composed – *Muck and Spit* and *Something Quite Nice About ISIS* – which, of course, turned out to be highlights of the final show.

IMAGE 107 *Clockwise from top: Saskia Collyns, Seamus McNamara, Ruby Holder, Joden Joseph-Wright, Ashleigh Brown, Esme Seber, Ffion Elen, Kate Ovenden, Humera Syed, Harvey Badger and Khai Shaw in 'Decades' (directed by Eva Sampson, Ovalhouse, London, 2016). Image from author's own archive.*

From Eva and Abigail Graham to Clare Lizzimore and Donnacadh O'Briain, I've had the pleasure of working with some wonderful directors over the years. Whatever their process and style, they need to know you trust them to teach your baby to walk, and you need them to know you trust them not to fuck it up.

IMAGE 108 *Director Ramin Gray and the author in rehearsals for 'I'll Be the Devil' (2008). Photo by Ellie Kurttz. Reproduced with the kind permission of @ RSC.*

The important thing is to have honest communication. As much as it's about respecting each other's creativity, it's also about admitting that you're both capable of being wrong. And, of course, to always maintain perspective and a sense of humour. A common trap is for the writer or director to think of the play as the *most important thing in the universe* when, in truth, it's a briefly glimmering speck of stardust in the vastness of the cosmos.

Whether a director chooses to spend the first few days putting the play on its feet or sitting round the table talking about the script, there comes a point (for the sake of the actors and your own sanity) when you must leave the script alone. Assuming you've spent months working on multiple drafts, you're probably pig sick of the thing anyway. You've done your bit. It's about letting the cast (and director) get on with their jobs and, like a magic toybox, letting it spring to life without your beady eye all over it.

I remember, for example, sometime in the second week of *Lucky Dog*'s rehearsals, the remarkable actress Linda Bassett asking if I might take a few days off to give her a chance to *'beat up the play without offending you'*. No problem, Linda, I've got a packet of fig rolls and a boxset of *The Sopranos* waiting for me at home.

Actors are what it's all about. They have the hardest job of all, and, whether you're Tom Stoppard or Tommy No-Mates, they're what the audience pay to see. When a play flops, the actors must soldier on while everyone else buries their head in the sand or, if it succeeds, soldier on while everyone basks in the glory. But let's be clear. Unless your play has no human beings in it at all, everyone else – writers, directors, designers – are just ghosts flapping around in the dark.

Students often ask me if the writer has a say in the casting, and – unless, say, you're in different countries – the short answer is 'yes', it should be in your contract. There have only been a couple of times when I've chosen to sit out of auditions either because I'm not available, or because I'm friends with the actor and it might make an already tense situation more awkward. But, for the most part, the writer and director take joint responsibility for who's playing who and on the rare occasion I've discovered the director's cast the play without my input, the slight warrants a complaint.

Made of Stone was no exception, and – with the expertise of casting director Julia Horan – it was fun to audition so many terrific Northern working-class actors, fresh out of drama school or at the early stages of their career whose readings often threw the characters in a completely new light.

By comparison, it was shocking how hard it was to find *any* young working-class actors for the cast of *Boy* just fifteen years later, giving further proof of how drama school training and access to the industry, has become the preserve of the middle class. It wasn't until casting director Amy Ball extended the search to local comprehensives and drama clubs that we were able to find excellent, authentic actors to fill the younger roles.

But no matter who turns up to an audition, there's no guarantee who's going to be the right fit. For a play like *Made of Stone,* our main objective was to build a believable family unit, so the actors' age and physicality were just as important as their performance and, inevitably, you'd feel terrible for turning an otherwise perfect actor down.

However you envisage the play in your head, it's the various temperaments of the actors who come to define its appeal. Each actor will bring their own creative process to the table and, as such, every rehearsal is a cauldron of possibilities and you'd better be prepared for some surprises along the way.

There may be frustrations, breakdowns, arguments, walkouts, lots of laughter, lots of tears and even the occasional romance. By the time the show's playing in front of an audience, the company will have either moulded into a functioning (albeit dysfunctional) ensemble – like *The Simpsons* – or they will be driven to madness by competing egos and personality clashes – like *The Texas Chainsaw Massacre* – biding their time for the whole damn thing to be over.

With that in mind, the writer-director team, when casting, will always be asking *'what will this actor be like to work with in a rehearsal room? Will they be a calm or levelling presence? Will they be a pain in the arse?'* With the sage advice of good casting directors like Julia Horan and Amy Ball, you learn to be alert to actors who waffle on too much or have been clearly sent by their agent under duress or might be drunk. And although it's exciting when someone offers a unique perspective on a role, it's a big no-no when – usually a telly actor – starts improvising or paraphrasing the text. Likewise, if an actor wants the job but has issues with the play and starts doling out notes, then my advice would be *'keep it in your trousers, mate. And don't fanny about with the lines'*.

Made of Stone had a terrific cast – including old mate Huss – who enjoyed partying as much as rehearsing, which was a plus, and our brilliant director, Deborah Bruce, approached the play with sensitivity and good humour.

IMAGE 109 *Clockwise from left: The cast of 'Made of Stone' (directed by Deborah Bruce, 2000) – Greg Chisholm, Nick Moss, Giles Ford, Sarah Cattle, Joanna Bacon, Huss Garbiya. Image reproduced from the author's personal archive.*

As it was only a three-week rehearsal, there wasn't time for much chin stroking, so most days involved putting the scenes on their feet, letting the actors do their thing.

After the first morning's obligatory (and nerve wracking) read-through, Deborah wasted no time in putting the first graveside scene through its paces. Nick Moss and Greg Chisholm played bereaved brothers Gary and

Pete with subtlety and humour, hitting the beats, adding nuance to the gaps between the lines. They asked questions about the backstory and if I didn't have an immediate answer, we'd come up with one together in the room. The scene was then repeated several times, with Nick and Greg adding fresh ideas and perspectives with each new turn. For a playwright who hadn't had anything performed since my stint at Rose Bruford several years earlier, it was a timely reminder of why a play is called a play.

By one o'clock, we'd go to the bar to join the rest of the Royal Court staff with our discounted lunch vouchers. If there was time, we might even disappear to the Duke of Wellington for a cheeky pint – which now, in an age of super-green salads and turmeric lattes, seems unthinkable.

Heading back to the rehearsal room, we'd move onto the next scene using the same process: *give it a go, fuck it up, ask questions, repeat.* Sometimes the cast nailed it straightaway, other times they'd hit speedbumps, but there was never a sense that we wouldn't get there in the end. I remember how the intimate bedroom scenes – requiring fearlessness from actors Sarah Cattle and Greg Chisholm – played out exactly as I'd imagined them, while other moments took on a whole new lease of life. When Joanna Bacon decided that her hungover mum, Elaine, should be glugging a pint of milk on her first entrance, it was such a precise, unexpected, detail, that I had to put it in the script. Similarly, the chemistry between Miles and Errol, played by actors Giles Ford and Huss, elevated what was on the page beyond measure and after a super-energized attempt at choreographing their own fight scene (with Huss being flung the length of the rehearsal room) everyone was a bit disappointed when a fight director was called in to make sure everyone was safe.

Although rehearsing a fight scene at the end of the first week may be perfectly fine for some directors, there are some who don't let the actors move a muscle until everyone's blue in the face from analysing the entire script – scene by scene, line by line. People call it 'tablework' and it's a forensic – albeit exhausting – means of character study, drawn from Stanislavski and popularised by Max Stafford-Clark in the 1980s.

Director Dominic Cooke, for instance, used it fastidiously during *Redundant*'s first two weeks, pushing the cast to deconstruct each of the play's seven scenes into hundreds of micro units of action. To top it off, every single line of dialogue would then be given a transitive verb to clarify the characters' motives: so, in this line, '*Lucy chivvies Darren*' or in this line '*Darren humours Lucy*', then '*Lucy seduces Gonzo*'. Such detailed analysis gave some of the actors a fog-free roadmap of psychological tactics to navigate their journeys through the show, while others just fell back on the same performance they gave on the first day's readthrough. As for me, the process helped me to iron out any of the script's weaker bits before I sent it off to the publishers.

Although they had different methods, both Deborah and Dominic were *writer's directors* who wanted to *serve* the text rather than spunk some regurgitated Schaubühne-esque meta concept all over it. As such, you were happy for them to lead the charge and use whatever the hell system worked for them.

I remember, for instance, when actors Lyndsey Marshal and Simon Trinder were over-thinking their 'psychological tactics' and Dominic suddenly transformed the scene by telling them to play their characters as if they were six years old. Or when he took the actors on a daytrip to Sheffield and got them to go shopping, in places like Argos and Top Shop, while still in character.

Similarly, when Sacha Wares led the twenty-six strong *Boy* company on a tour of West Norwood, it not only enabled the cast to root their characters to the various bus stops, doctor's surgeries and housing estates that I had in mind when writing, but it also helped the play's designers – Miriam Buether and Ultz – to drum up ideas for the overall look of the show.

In fact, when Miriam unveiled a high-concept travelator that wound its way through the audience – its thumping, industrial symbolism countered by the ultra-realism of Ultz's costume and wigs – we knew we were onto something good.

Similarly, Rae Smith and William Fricker's bear-pit design for *Faces in the Crowd,* which allowed the audience to look down like voyeurs into every nook and cranny of a Shoreditch flat, was equally impressive as it effortlessly solved the challenges of my almost-impenetrable text.

Whether their speciality is costume, set, sound or lighting, I've been lucky to work with some terrific artists whose creativity has transformed the plays way beyond anything that was on the page.

In the run up to rehearsals, the play's designer usually builds a scaled-down model of the set, to discuss with the director and the rest of the team – which is always tremendously exciting.

For instance, I'll never forget when designer Robert Innes Hopkins brought in the model-box for *Redundant* (pictured below).

IMAGE 110 *Robert Innes Hopkins' model-box for 'Redundant' (directed by Dominic Cooke, Royal Court, 2001). Image reproduced with kind permission from © Robert Innes-Hopkins.*

Robert had previously joined me and Dominic on a trip to Sheffield, where I gave them a whistle-stop tour of Lucy's neighbourhood. I remember Robert confidently marching up to the doors of a few choice flats and – sheepishly accompanied by me and Dom – persuading the bewildered residents to let him in to take polaroids of their walls and floors.

When he arrived at rehearsals, some weeks later, it was fascinating to see how he'd merged the play's set descriptions alongside specific details – such as the discoloured walls – that he'd photographed on our trip.

To top things off, Robert then revealed how the flat's ceiling would slowly rise to the top of the auditorium at the end of the play, accompanied by Gary Yershon's spine-tingling music. The effect would dwarf the bruised and battered Lucy as she watched the snow fall through the window, creating a gut-wrenching moment of poignancy to end the show.

Equally surprising was when Sophia Clist chose to design *All You Need is LSD*'s costumes based on my own (limited) wardrobe, or when *Lucky Dog*'s designer, Jean Kalman, quietly painted the set in the style of the pastel drawings I'd scrawled in my sketchbook weeks earlier.

Its director, James Macdonald, barely spoke a word either, but somehow – like some sort of magical cheshire cat – he managed to create a secure, creative space that allowed *Lucky Dog*'s actors – Linda Bassett and Alan Williams – to go freely to the dark side.

For such an emotionally gruelling play, *Lucky Dog* had a surprisingly upbeat rehearsal room, whereas – in stark contrast – the atmosphere surrounding my 2022 pantomime, *Cinderella* – despite the presence of sweet-natured performers like Gracie McGonigal and drag artist Gigi Zahir – was charged with inexplicable tension, for which I made myself scarce.

Thankfully, if you do find yourself hiding out at home for whatever reason, then there are always the daily rehearsal notes to keep you up to speed.

MADE OF STONE
REHEARSAL NOTES

Page No.   : 16

Date   : Monday 2nd October

To   : Deborah Bruce ; Leo Butler ; Liz Cook ; Nick Field ; Ola Aminashawun ; Aoife Mannix ; Sue Bird ; Bendy Ashfield ; Marion Mahon ; Rich Walsh ; Iona Kendrick ; Marion Marrs ; Emily Danby ; Max Foo ; Stage Department

General
- Costume fittings to be scheduled for Thursday
- We will be rehearsing in the Theatre Upstairs on Friday 10.15am – 5.30pm
- Is it possible to have another session with Jeanette Nelson ?

Props
- *Errol* may need a work bag as a convention for clear props off stage
- The newspaper in Sc.3. will be a *Sheffield Star*, which Leo's mum is posting down.
- We still need a packet of Embassy cigarettes for Pete (Sc.12)
- The trowels brought into rehearsal rm are plastering trowels, but need to be cement trowels with a pointed end.
- Elaine's contents of shopping bag, *examples* :
  Fray Bentos Steak and Kidney Pie
  12 x eggs (not free range)
  White sliced bread
  Cup a soups
  Sachet of Kwik Save coffee
  Tetley teabags (large box)
  12 x sausages (Kwik Save)
  2 x basic cheese & tomato pizzas (in clear plastic wrap, not boxed)
  Cheap cheese
  Tin of macaroni cheese
  Tin of Spag bog
  Bag of sugar
  4 pint milk
  4 x toffee yogurts

Sound
- The baby is no longer a 2 yr old, but a little baby.
- Could we have 5 x blank tapes to copy a dialect tape ?

Wardrobe
- Greg Chisholm / Pete would like to try the rock scene with padding. Even though we're using fake rock, it is starting to make his chest sore.

IMAGE 111 *'Made of Stone' rehearsal notes*, 2000 © Leo Butler, 2024.

Whatever their role in the machine, everyone works their socks off for the show, and, inevitably, emotions can be high and varied. I've never laughed so much during run throughs of *All You Need is LSD*'s silly Matrix-like sequence when the cast wrestle over a vial of acid on the roof of the Hammersmith Hospital . . .

IMAGE 112 *The author and 'All You Need is LSD's' co-directors Stephen Harper and Paul Hunter during rehearsal. Photo reproduced with kind permission of © Ben Wilkin at Benkin Photography.*

IMAGE 113 *From left, actors Sophie Mercell, Jack Hunter, Annie Fitzmaurice and George Potts in rehearsal for 'All You Need is LSD'. Photos reproduced with kind permission of © Ben Wilkin at Benkin Photography.*

. . . and, by comparison, I was moved to tears when I arrived at the Almeida to find Frankie Fox practising *Boy*'s 'long walk home' to the strains of Burial's *Night Bus*.

IMAGE 114 *Photo credit: Frankie Fox (Liam) in 'Boy' (directed by Sacha Wares, Almeida Theatre, 2016). Photo reproduced with kind permission from @ Tristram Kenton.*

In the script, the moment is a short, single stage direction, '*Liam walks home*', but thanks to the combined talents of the company it became a devastating five-minute sequence – bathed in muted light – worthy of Martin Scorsese at his finest.

Just as Frankie's performance was key to the play's success, so were the half dozen chaperoned teenagers who played, amongst other roles, the motor-mouthed schoolgirls that Liam attempts to befriend at a bus stop. As much as I tried to pepper the dialogue with authentic South London slang, some of it, inevitably, was a throwback to 1990s Sheffield with words like '*wicked*' and '*safe*'. Thankfully, the brilliant young actors were more than happy to collaborate, helping me rewrite the dialogue to bring it bang up to date with words like '*clapped*' and '*leng*'.

Scurrying back home to update the script, I would email any revisions – often late into the night – to the director, stage manager, and, of course, the proofreaders at Methuen Drama, who I would end up in long email exchanges like . . .

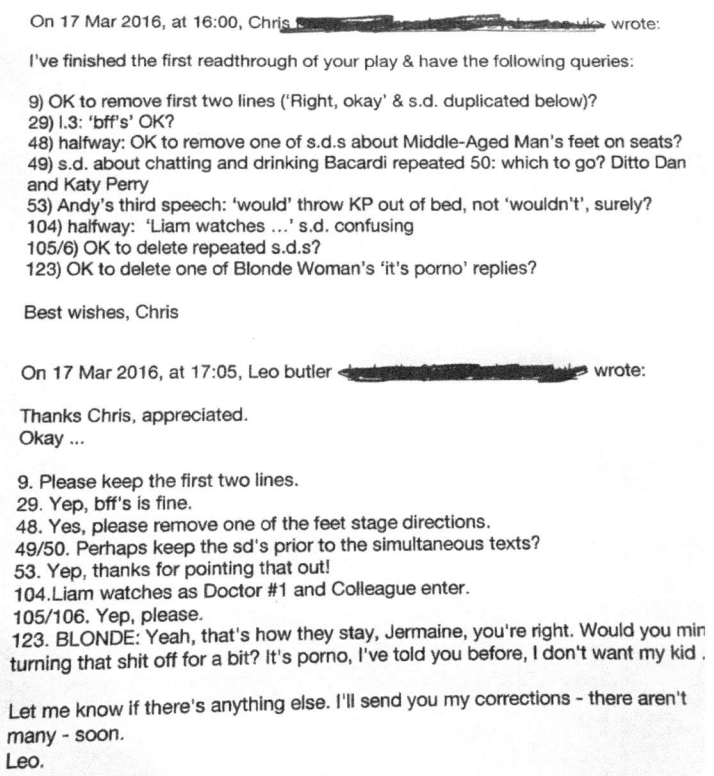

IMAGE 115 *Email correspondence with Methuen proofreader, 2016* © *Leo Butler, 2024.*

As a teenager, my shelves were lined with those familiar black-spined editions of Methuen anthologies by writers such as Joe Orton, Edward Bond and Caryl Churchill – their smart, reassuring covers disguising an abundance of unbridled filth. To finally join that club was as sweet as any drug and being busy with the proofs meant I could avoid those awkward rehearsals when – in plays like *Faces in the Crowd* and *Sixty-Nine* – the actors were getting naked for the first time, or when Roxana Silbert directed my mad adaptation of *Woyzeck* on the giant Birmingham Rep stage . . .

IMAGE 116 *'Woyzeck' (directed by Roxana Silbert, Birmingham Rep, 2018). Photo reproduced with kind permission from © Graeme Braidwood Photography.*

... and its 100-strong cast of local actors were suddenly losing their shit – like the play's titular hero – as they headed into week three.

Week three – as anyone who's ever worked on a show knows – is when everything falls apart. The actors panic, forget their lines, someone gets ill or falls off the stage, the sleep-deprived director has a breakdown, the designer rages at the perplexed stage crew who are doing their level best to hide their indifference, the set falls apart, props go missing and the producers feign buoyancy in the knowledge that tickets aren't selling. In short, everyone holds each other in contempt, bound together in unspoken mutual recognition that the whole thing's clearly a disaster.

The writer, meanwhile, when not busy putting his feet up at home, is suddenly called in by the theatre's press officer for a host of fancy newspaper interviews and photoshoots. As an unwashed nocturnal, the sudden attention takes some getting used to, but it's enjoyable swanning about like Lady Gaga for about five minutes.

IMAGE 117 *Leo Butler* Metro Life Newspaper Clipping, 11 September 2001. Reproduced with kind permission of @ London Metro Newspaper.

I'm generally happy to give interviews if it helps flog tickets, but it's very weird when a journalist asks you questions about the play and you realize you haven't thought about the damn thing for weeks. Sure, you've thought about the production, the performances and hundreds of transitive verbs, but in terms of its *meaning*? Christ, that's going back a bit. Cornered for a printable soundbite, you buckle up and waffle unsophisticated platitudes about *poverty of the imagination* or the government's broken benefit system. Why? Because to say you were just thinking about an ex-girlfriend sounds a bit shit.

With the press duties in the bag, you race back to the theatre for the technical rehearsals. A lot of people hate technical rehearsals as they often go late into the night and require infinite patience. Personally, I *love* seeing all the elements – set, costume, lights, music, special effects – come together to create a world that began as a dream or a hunch or a picture in your head. Amid the hammering and stubbed toes, there's a collective conjury at work, even if takes several days to achieve.

And as the first preview approaches, it's incredibly exciting to see your name on a poster or up in lights . . .

IMAGE 118 *'Redundant'* in lights at the Royal Court Theatre, 2001. Image reproduced from the author's archive.

Now all that's left is the audience.

Excitedly, you knock on the dressing-room doors to find the pale, shaken company still tending their wounds from that afternoon's disastrous dress rehearsal. Driven by blind panic and sheer necessity, everyone wishes everyone the best of luck while hoping to God it's not them who fucks it all up.

During the Young Writers' Festival, I remember not computing that *Made of Stone*'s 'press night' – which was still some days away – was meant to be its official opening night. Instead, I'd invited <u>everyone</u> I knew – friends, family – including Matt and our parents – to the very first preview, and the cast were horrified.

With The Stone Roses playing on rotation through the house speakers, the ushers check my ticket, and I nervously find my seat on the back row sandwiched between Deborah Bruce and Ian Rickson. Avoiding the various waves and thumbs ups from my mates, my nonchalance had gone AWOL and I was a bag of nerves. I can, in fact, guarantee, that if you ever catch sight of a playwright watching their own work, you'll be lucky to see the slightest *flicker* of enjoyment.

The houselights fade out, and the sound of a church bell tolling fades in as Nick Moss and Greg Chisholm take their places at their father's graveside.

Here we go.

Constant anxiety. Each new scene, every line of dialogue, creeps into view like Norman Bates looming behind the shower curtain in *Psycho*. You're sweating, your shoulders break bread with your ears. The plot holes are there for everyone to see. You suddenly realize how personal the play is. The audience laugh at things you didn't know were funny, but that witty line you slaved over for hours is met with total silence. That scene's great, the next one isn't. Wow, okay, that speech *is* moving. Wow, okay, the actors are *killing it*. You choke back the tears. *Wait, don't do that, don't cry at your own play! Be cool, dickhead.* Moments later, you're humiliated by that dreadful line in Scene Five, but it's followed by the splendour of Scene Six and – once more – you're in awe of your own genius. The plot twist you'd become so used to through rewrites and rehearsals suddenly get its giant gasp. Now, here comes the big Saint Jerome moment . . . *Come on!!* Man, there's no feeling like it. The electric charge of the here and now.

The lights fade, and the audience erupt into cheers and applause.

Swaggering out of the auditorium like Billy Big Bollocks, you're met with bear hugs, fist bumps and several shots of Tequila at the bar.

Nursing a colossal hangover, the director calls you up the following morning and suggests *'we should have a think about a couple of cuts in Scene Four'*.

Critics

Just as I'd mistakenly assumed 'opening night' was the first preview, I hadn't registered there would be actual newspaper reviews of *Made of Stone*. Over the following weeks, my parents would call to say they'd read 'this or that' in *The Guardian* or *The Times* or some other posh rag. Although the reviews were good, the experience of being reduced to a star rating was a shock, and it heralded a destabilizing element of a professional writer's life that no 'rules of good feedback' ever prepares you for.

It's odd that, after all the effort that goes into making a play, so much attention is paid to a single performance and the opinions of a few pundits who might not always be the play's target crowd.

Even before the reviews roll in, the anxiety of putting your baby in front of an audience of peers, critics and future employers – and then having to *talk to people in the bar* afterwards – is enough to make even the hardiest playwright crumble. On *Boy*'s press night, for example, I avoided the throng by hanging out under a streetlamp, smoking roll ups with my agent, while Sacha Wares and Miriam Buether hid in a dressing room backstage until it was all over.

And when the reviews do finally trickle in?

Well, I mean . . . I never thought any of my plays would win a Nobel Prize or anything, but five years is still a long time to slave over a show that's then mauled by a broadsheet for *'sentimentally maundering about how nice it would be to see the world through the eyes of children'*, as if that were a bad thing.

But for every mean-spirited critic, there's usually someone – in this case, a student from the University of Bath – who runs over to tell you that the same 'sentimentally maundering' *All You Need is LSD* is, in fact, *'the best play of all time!'* Although their assessment may have been a bit of a stretch, the compliment was a nice reminder that you're not in the business of making soap.

However, whether they admit it or not, critics can affect livelihoods. For every writer that's showered with five-star reviews, there's a Sarah Kane or Joanna Laurens – both young women, funnily enough – who are chucked under the bus for *getting it wrong* by people – usually middle-aged men, funnily enough – who couldn't write a play to save their lives.

And if a playwright tells themselves *'well, they can't all be wrong if they all think it's shit'*, it's worth remembering that a well-known reviewer once confided: *'people think we don't talk to each other, but we do.'*

When a new play's hit with negative press, it's common for the writer to wear it like a badge of honour. *Of course they didn't like it. They didn't like 'Five Gold Rings' or 'Blasted' either.* Sometimes there's truth to that, sometimes there isn't. Either way, we're only human, criticism can hurt, and we protect ourselves with reciprocal spite or humour.

After *One Man, Two Guvnors* [2011] opened at the National Theatre, I remember bumping into its author, Richard Bean, and congratulating him on its glut of raves. 'Yep' he replied, *'turns out they were right all along.'*

Don't get me wrong, I like critics, and I've stayed friendly with a few of them over the years. While teaching at the Royal Court, I often invited Michael Billington and Aleks Sierz to share their insights with the groups, which was always a treat. And even if I don't always agree with their views and reviews, their passion for the artform – as with most film or book critics – is undeniable. The default vitriol of some of their peers, on the other hand, makes you wonder if they enjoy going to the theatre at all.

'You realise they're all going to hate it, don't you?' warned Ramin Gray the night before press night.

I should have heeded his words. After *I'll Be the Devil* was savaged by the press in 2008, I'll admit I had a bit of a breakdown. Forcing myself to keep my shit together for the actors' sake, I returned to the theatre to find the actors were keeping their shit together for my sake. Ramin, bless him, didn't seem phased at all, but the hostility still cut deep. During the rest of its short run, I'd periodically sneak into the theatre to watch a matinee and think, *'I don't get it; I love this crazy show.'*

IMAGE 119 *Photo credit: Billy Carter (Capt O'Connor), Tom Burke (Dermot), Colm Gormley (Corporal Finnigan), Gerard Murphy (Capt Browne), J D Kelleher (Capt Skelton) and Edward MacLiam (Capt Farrell) in 'I'll Be the Devil' (directed by Ramin Gray, RSC/Kiln, 2008). Photo reproduced with the kind permission of @ Tristram Kenton.*

A huge fan of David Eldridge's work, I was deeply moved when he wrote a flattering defence of *I'll Be the Devil* on his blogpost, in which he criticised . . .

> . . . the limitations of the reviewer who appears to have never seen a play by Edward Bond or looked at the work of Goya. *I'll be the Devil* is a triumph of compression, and the utter conviction and plausibility with which an English thirtysomething writes eighteenth century Ireland is awesome.

Convinced I was the worst dramatist of all time, his kind solidarity was a big help. Playwrights, in general, are a close and supportive group and, given that we've all shouldered a bit of grief from journalists (or, indeed, badly behaved theatres) from time to time, we generally rally round to support each other when it counts. To quote that well-known reviewer: '*people think we don't talk to each other, but we do.*'

However, when – just a few months later – my next play, *Faces in the Crowd*, got a similarly vitriolic response, I decided to hang back and throw my energy into my teaching, as well as picking up my guitar for *Alison! A Rock Opera,* and it took years to get back into the playwriting saddle for *Boy*. Thanks to the critical drubbing of *Devil* and *Faces*, my 'risky reputation' had been cemented (even at the Royal Court), and it took Sacha Wares's dogged determination to give the play a home.

But, before you unpack your violin, it's worth mentioning that even when *Boy* was showered with praise, it transpired I could still be a miserable git. Unlike the halcyon social-media free days of 2008, there was now a constant ping and twitter of online discourse which, although working wonders for my ego . . .

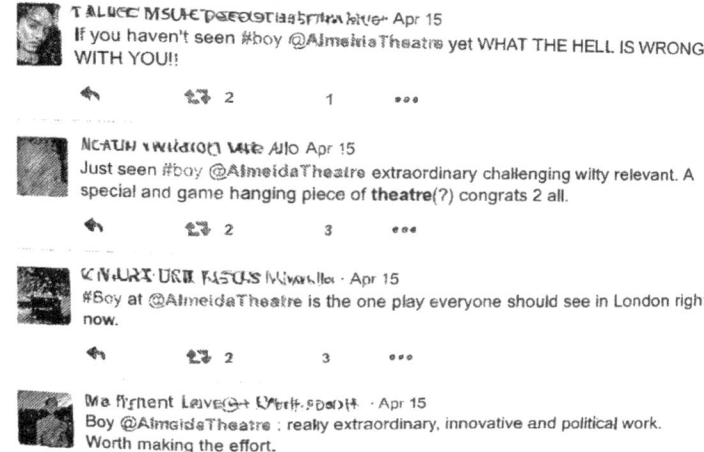

IMAGE 120 *Twitter feed on 'Boy' at the Almeida, 2016 @ Public Domain.*

. . . could equally make me want to vanish, out of sight, on top of a double-decker bus. Like Liam in *Boy*.

Whatever the show, the reviews roll in over a few short days and sometimes they're good, sometimes they're bad. Sometimes the good ones totally miss the point, while the bad ones – though bad – still manage to make good points.

The trick is not to read them. Or, if you can't resist, to take them with a giant pinch of salt. Ultimately, the play is over as soon as it began.

Here today, gone tomorrow. Up in smoke – poof! Bye bye!

It is, of course, common to grieve for the show once it's gone, but it's equally likely that you and everyone else – director, actors, stage manager and designer – will just move onto something else. Perhaps you were already up to your neck in another script before rehearsals began, so the whole thing felt like a day off from your real job anyway.

As I've repeatedly said in this book, it's not the result but the process. If you're going to write or rehearse a show with any expectations, do yourself a favour and have no expectations at all.

For instance, I never expected *Redundant* to win the George Devine Award or that I would be the youngest playwright since John Osborne to have a play on the Court's main stage. Neither did I expect its big opening night (13 September 2001) to be completely derailed by the 9/11 terror attack – especially when the script contained a line that said, '*somebody should bomb this bloody country. Bin Laden, yeah, he could do it.*'

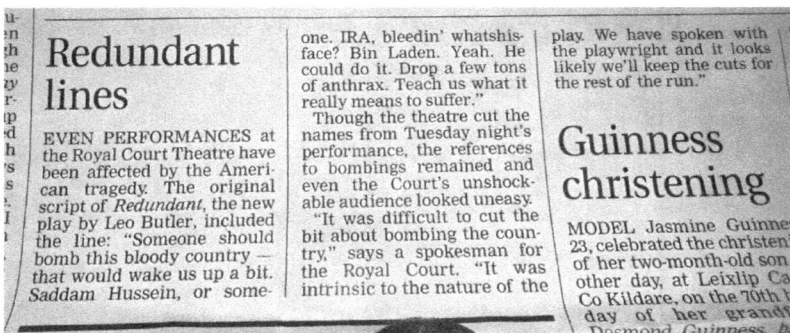

IMAGE 121 *Clipping from* Evening Standard, *13 September 2001. Reproduced with kind permission of @ Evening Standard Newspaper.*

After a crazy couple of weeks – packed with conflicting emotions and dwindling ticket sales – I never expected to have my spirits lifted when hundreds of rowdy London teenagers piled in for the school's matinee performance. Once they got over the weird Northern accents, the kids – unphased by the violence, drugs and profanity – were on their feet, cheering at every twist and turn, roaring at the rude jokes and heckling the characters when they said something stupid or turned violent. In the post-show discussion, some of the kids said it was great to see *people like them* represented on stage and it made them want to act or write themselves.

Given the response, it was no surprise that I chose to write my next play for Theatre Centre, a theatre-in-education company who tour new plays around UK comprehensives.

IMAGE 122 *Leigh Kelly (Batman) and Mark Oliver (Mary) in 'Devotion' (directed by Liam Steel, Half Moon Theatre and Theatre Centre UK Schools Tour, 2002). Photo reproduced with the kind permission of @ Hugo Glendinning.*

Devotion [2002] – an absurd, comic piece about three children escaping a warzone in a burnt-out car – was masterfully directed by Liam Steel and featured a funny young cast. With no fanfare or publicity, it was exciting to put it in front of large audiences of kids who, like those at *Redundant*'s school's matinee, seemed directly impacted by the show.

But, then again, how do we define impact? I've been hugely impacted by the raw emotional force of *A Raisin in the Sun* as much as I've been impacted by the jaw-dropping magic of *Harry Potter and the Cursed Child* [Palace Theatre, 2016]. I've watched important political shows that have stayed with me for about five minutes while dismissing seemingly lifeless plays that have stayed with me for years. And even if those kids were impacted by *Devotion* or *Redundant,* did the experience change them in any meaningful way or did they just move onto the next lesson? A person might claim that theatre should be 'a force for change', but what kind of change are they aiming for?

I remember asking a group of students to name any plays that had either successfully challenged or changed their political views, and being met with a wall of complete silence. When, a few weeks later, I invited *Guardian* critic Michael Billington to meet the class, I decided to ask him the same question. After a moment's pause, Billington responded with, *'No, I can't remember anything that's changed me politically, but I've seen hundreds of plays that have altered my consciousness.'*

Whatever claims you have about your play's meaning, you can never really know how it's going to affect or alter someone's mind. Once the show's been and gone, chances are you'll dig out the script years later and discover it's got a whole new meaning anyway.

Just as joining the Sheffield Youth Theatre impacted so much of my life, I believe the most important thing is giving people the opportunity – whatever their background – to not just have access to good theatre, but to take part in it themselves. That's where you see genuine impact happening, and it's partly why I decided to support – or, rather, *compliment* – my own playwriting by encouraging others to have a crack at it themselves.

12

What the f*ck is a dramaturg?

With zero teaching experience, I was employed as the Royal Court's writing tutor in the autumn of 2005.

Following in the footsteps of Nicola Baldwin, Hanif Kureishi and Simon Stephens was daunting at first, but I soon found my feet and the theatre kept me on until autumn 2014. Not long after I left, I met a leading artistic director to pitch an idea for a new play, who shook my hand and said '*sorry, but it's not something we'd be likely to commission, but thank you for discovering all those writers and changing the face of British theatre*'.

The truth is I was lucky. In 2006, Dominic Cooke became the new artistic director and looked to the Young Writers' Programme (YWP) to fill the stages with debut plays. I was luckier still that every single one of my groups – roughly four per year, with more than twenty playwrights in each – was jam-packed with extraordinary talent. When you've got people like Polly Stenham, Bola Agbaje, Brad Birch, Jonathan Schey, Isley Lynn, Ali McDowall, Rachel De-Lahay, Sarah Solemani, D C Moore, Alia Bano, Cordelia Lynn, Arinze Kene, Lou Brealey, Luke Barnes, Deborah Pearson, Eve Leigh, Yve Blake, Ellie Kendrick, Michael McLean, Gareth Farr, Yasmin Joseph, James Fritz, Anya Reiss, Daniel York Loh, Zawe Ashton, Ambreen Razia, Monsay Whitney, Simone Saunders, Alexandra Wood, Matilda Ibini, Ella Hickson, Jake Brunger, Nick Payne, Rose Lewenstein, Luke Norris, Penny Skinner, Karis Halsall, E V Crowe, Hammaad Chaudry, Stacey Gregg, Molly Davies, Rory Mullarkey, Mufaro Makubika, Marcelo Dos Santos, Nessah Muthy, Rob Hayes, Pamela Carter, Ming Ho, Poppy Corbett, Daniel Karasik, David O'Brien, Dean Stalham, May Sumbwanyambe, Joe White, Elise Hearst, Sarah Kosar, Subika Anwar-Khan, Nick Cassenbaum, Simon Longman, Natalie Mitchell, Paula B. Stanic, Jon Brittain, Lucian Huxley-Smith, Margaret Parry, Kenny Emson, Sarah Simmonds, Bam Abedi-Amin, Chris Thompson, Sonia Jalaly, Kyoung H Park, Duncan Macmillan, Janice Okoh, Suhayla El-Bushra, Tom Holloway, Phoebe Éclair-Powell, Beth Steel, Miriam Battye, Sarah Hanly, Elinor Cook and Alice Birch, amongst others, then the only thing a teacher has to say is '*write*'.

Some commentators, or subsequent artistic teams, tried to argue that the YWP only catered for middle-class university grads. I can vouch that Ola Animashawun, Clare McQuillan and Nina Lyndon – and the whole YWP team – worked tirelessly to ensure there was diversity of gender, ethnicity and class. Likewise, the YWP made sure to be inclusive of writers with mental and physical disabilities, as well as finding ways – sometimes via financial support – to invite young (and old) writers from anywhere across the country. Alongside the Court's international work, it did feel, for a few years, that the building was continuing George Devine's legacy of shaping a vibrant theatre culture – or 'sharpening the spear of the spearhead' – for future generations.

As well as the Royal Court, I've also taught at numerous drama schools, colleges and universities. It's been a joy to run sessions for companies like Cardboard Citizens, as well as theatres like the Young Vic, the Crucible, and, as I write this book, The Marlowe in Canterbury, for whom, as their dramaturg, I've helped discover a hidden community of awesome Kent-based talent.

Whether it's a one-day workshop or a twelve-week course, the meshing of individuals creates a unique group dynamic, and, as course leader, it's important to stay receptive to its peculiarities and needs. The trick is how to structure each session and foster an environment that serves both the individual and the whole. If I have any singular talent, it's the instinctive way I can tap into a group's vibe and spontaneously change the direction of a session to give them what they don't realize they need.

Whatever a group's personality, the first couple of sessions – like the opening of a play – are usually tinged with anxiety. However, once everyone gets over their nervousness and bonds – which, after a few weeks, they always do – you can almost taste the inspiration flowing around the room. The hope is that everyone learns something new – about drama or themselves – and makes friends along the way. And even if someone decides never to put pen to paper again, perhaps there's something about the holistic approach that makes a difference to other aspects of their lives.

However, I'd be lying if I said I wasn't made up when writers like Rachel De-Lahay or Rory Mullarkey were suddenly catapulted to fame, or when, in 2010, BBC's *Newsnight* ran a celebratory feature on our work. It was equally gratifying when the Young Writers' Programme was awarded a Praemium Imperiale Award by the Japanese Arts Association. Dominic Cooke and I were hosted by Queen Elizabeth and Prince Philip at Buckingham Palace to receive the award, which went against my anti-royalist stance, but, of course, they were charming as fuck. When we met Her Royal Highness, I suggested she join one of the writers' groups. '*Who, me?*' she gasped. '*Oh aye, you'd love it*' I said, before being quickly whisked away by Chris Patten. I would have *loved* to have got a brilliant new play from the Queen, no doubt full of profanity and mindless violence, and I'm sure she would have enjoyed the ball games too.

Some might imagine a writing course to be a dusty old thing, with rows of socially awkward, ink-stained misfits hunched over desks. But what's the point of that when you can be socially awkward at home? While we've got three or four hours in a rehearsal room, I prefer to keep the writers on their feet, acting out scenes, debating ideas or playing games like 'zombie-tag' or keepy-uppy.

Keepy-uppy is basically thwacking a ball around the room, keeping it up in the air for as long as possible. You're not allowed to catch it or use two hands, but you can use other limbs – head, foot, arse – if hands aren't accessible. With each fresh thwack of the ball, we count upwards in unison and the aim is to reach as high a number of hits as possible. If someone drops the ball or if it's accidentally flung out the window, then you pick it up and start again.

I nicked the game from the Court's International Associate, Elyse Dodgson, who was, amongst many other things, the Queen of keepy-uppy. When Winsome Pinnock and I joined Elyse on a trip to South Africa, the group of local writers managed to reach more than 100 keepy-uppies without breaking a sweat. British writers, on the other hand, are lucky to reach ten or fifteen without sustaining an injury or giving up with ironic self-congratulation.

There's a dramaturgical lesson in keepy-uppy, as – like any sport – it follows the same pattern as any good scene. Rather than a ball, the playwright keeps the tension and suspense thwacked up in the air, using a range of tactics – head, foot, arse – to move the scene forward with increasing stakes. Once the ball drops, the scene – or unit of action – is over. In the first scene of *King Lear*, for example, Cordelia drops the ball when she says '*nothing, my Lord*'. Lear, seized by indignant rage, picks up the ball and starts the scene again.

However, the main objective was to get the students energized, embarrassed and egoless. If you're able to fling yourself around the room like a demented crane fly, then reading out a few pages or some half-baked scene you've just written is going to be a breeze. Ultimately, I don't care how many brilliant plays you may or may not have written, you're in the same boat as the first-time playwright who's written sod all.

While at the Royal Court, I ran three or four 'Introduction to Playwriting' courses per year, and each of their twelve, three-hour long sessions tackled a different aspect of dramatic *writing – character, structure, narrative, etc*. If you flick to The Twelve-Week Course in the **Appendix**, you'll find a more detailed description of the course. If you're ever running a writing group, feel free to use it.

In my experience, most playwright teachers do versions of the same exercises, it's just the style and vocabulary that's different. For instance, playwright John Donnelly teaches how to sustain a plot by mapping a character's psychological transgressions, which is basically the same as my Laurel and Hardy class – only smarter – and both can be traced back to Aristotle. Likewise, I remember Tanika Gupta teaching the 'invent a play based on the life of Michael Jackson' exercise and being taken aback as I thought that I'd invented it! In truth, I'd probably pinched it from someone else, who pinched it from someone else, who probably nicked it from Stephen Jeffreys or Noël Greig without realizing.

Similarly, I could always count on my 'assistant' or 'number two' – who was generally a fellow practitioner, such as Kenny Emson, Chris Sonnex, Lucy Prebble or Duncan Macmillan – to be whip smart and super articulate when I forgot what we were meant to be doing or got lost on one of my customary rambles.

Other perks included guest speakers, such as Debbie Tucker Green, David Hare, Tim Crouch and Caryl Churchill, who were always good value and provided alternative perspectives. I remember, for instance, explaining how the YWP functioned to a genuinely baffled Wallace Shawn who turned to the group and asked, *'Why does there always have to be a new Sheriff in town?'* And when his epic *Rock n Roll* was produced in 2006, Tom Stoppard admitted to the class that although writing plays is a *'fucking nightmare, what's great is you're essentially writing a very thin book'*.

The twelve-week course always ended by giving the students a two-month deadline to finish and deliver their new play. Each play was then read by at least two members of YWP staff, and the writers were sent written feedback.

Based on that feedback, a smaller bunch of writers were then invited back for an 'advanced group', in which the writers could either develop a play they'd already written or start something new,

The structure of the 'advanced group' was never set in stone, and its looseness allowed me to try out new exercises, such as **Chapter Five**'s 'ideas bank' or 'conjured images'. I have fond memories of improvising as-yet-unwritten scenes with terrific writer/actors like Daniel York Loh, Ambreen Razia and Luke Norris. Or not-so-fond memories of trying to squeeze twenty-five individual tutorials into the space of a three-hour session while steadily losing all sense of time or what my name was.

As before, the writers were given a two-month deadline to finish their plays and some excellent submissions, like Alexandra Wood's *The Eleventh Capital* [2007] and Bola Agbaje's *Gone Too Far!* [2007] wound up having Theatre Upstairs productions.

However, I was also frustrated by the protracted deadlines, with no time to work on rewrites, and so, in 2009 I created a 'supergroup', inviting a dozen of the best writers from the previous groups to join a super twenty-five week course.

Some of the Royal Court staff didn't like the name 'supergroup', which I saw as a playful nod to bands like Cream or the Travelling Wilburys, and after I left, in 2014, the theatre kept the course, but boringly renamed it 'the long-form group'.

Rather than a paltry three-hour meeting, each supergroup session would include an afternoon *and* evening class, making it a minimum of seven hours per week. The lengthy timescale meant that we could offer the entire process of conceiving, writing and rewriting a new play without breaks. The writers would also, by default, start to feel like they were *part of the fabric of the building* (just as I did as an usher), which would only build their confidence.

The inaugural supers included writers like Nick Payne, Anya Reiss, Penny Skinner, E V Crowe, Hammaad Chaudry, Molly Davies and Alia Bano, who agreed to be guinea pigs as I figured out how to structure the new course.

When I first started, I'll admit I robbed a fair few writing tasks from the likes of Simon Stephens and Nicola Baldwin, but I soon realized the most effective method was to replicate my own writing process. Even if that process didn't work for everyone, it at least provided a template for students to fight against and formulate their own.

For instance, thinking back to how I'd tackled the first draft of *Redundant* by locking myself in the theatre overnight, I decided I'd lock the students in the theatre too.

One warm Friday evening, the supergroup writers cautiously arrived at the theatre at 5.00 pm and they had until 9.00 am to finish their plays. Some chose to lock themselves away in the small 'writers' rooms' or tuck themselves away in corners by the bogs. But, as nothing gives you a kick up the bum than being surrounded by others who seem to be writing more than you, most shared the large fold-away tables I'd set up that afternoon.

Pizza was ordered. Pizza was eaten.

I remind them of the popular playwrights' mantra *'don't get it right, get it written'*, then head into my office, unroll a sleeping bag and get my head down.

Tapping of keyboards from the other rooms, the constant rumble of tube trains. In the wee small hours, the thud and clang of train workers' boots pacing the deserted tracks are followed by disarming moments of silence.

9.00 am. The writers pack their bags and lumber out the building like extras from *Dawn of the Dead*.

See you next week guys! Make sure to clear your cups away!

Unless memory fails me, I believe E V Crowe wrote a rough draft of *Kin* [2010] and Penny Skinner wrote a nuts-and-bolts version of *The Village Bike* [2011], two fabulous plays that the Court went on to produce. The prolific Anya Reiss probably wrote about ten plays before midnight, and Nick Payne puzzled through a rewrite of *One Day When We Were Young* [2011], which would eventually be produced by Paines Plough.

Following the lock in, I then made sure the supergroup writers had ten or fifteen sessions for discussion and rewrites. Each week, one of the writers would bring in their rough draft and they'd either read it out themselves, or we'd read it aloud as a group. The reading would be followed by two or three hours of detailed group feedback and advice. Some of these discussions could become heated or veer off into political debates or sometimes we'd just talk about fonts.

The closeness of the group meant there was sustained mutual respect, and nothing was out of bounds. On rare occasions that a writer offered only a few pages to read out, great care was taken to help them work out why the idea wasn't quite gelling yet. It didn't matter if the person next to you was already deep into their second draft, we'd all been there at some point.

Twenty-five intense, but enjoyable, weeks later, all that was left was to alert the rest of the theatre that there were a bunch of exciting new plays coming their way.

The Royal Court script meetings were traditionally held on Friday mornings and included the artistic director, the literary manager and a clutch of associate directors and scribes. Whether it was a new Sam Shepard or 'Untitled by Unknown', each submission was discussed with unflinching honesty and a genuine eye on programming. Using an infamous, bingo-like grid – or, as Richard Bean called it 'The Matrix' – everyone would vote on the plays, using options such as 'production', 'reading', and 'over my dead body', and the artistic director would often base their decisions on that. It was a remarkably democratic process.

When plays like *Kin* and *The Village Bike* scored a full house on the matrix, it was, of course, enormously rewarding. But, as the Royal Court couldn't produce *every play* that the groups produced, it was equally exciting when plays such as Ella Hickson's *Boys* [HighTide, 2012], James Fritz's *Parliament Square* [Bush Theatre, 2017] and Michael McLean's *Years of Sunlight* [Theatre 503, 2017] found a home elsewhere.

Although they were never produced, there were also a plethora of brilliant plays by the likes of Lucien Huxley-Smith, Hammaad Chaudry and Maxine Quintyne-Kolaru, which, for me, remain as memorable as any big hit.

And whereas Alia Bano and Anya Reiss leapt straight from a group to a production, other writers – such as Alice Birch and E V Crowe – held their nerve and persevered for a few more years until the rest of the world caught up.

In truth, there's not much difference between the aspiring and so-called professional playwright, so, in 2011, I set up an admittedly daft titled 'mega group'. The mega group invited the current roster of commissioned Royal Court writers to meet one evening a week with the aim of giving them the same care and attention we'd give to any newcomer and, crucially, keep them connected to the building.

They were randomly structured sessions, led by writers such as April De Angelis, David Eldridge and Mike Bartlett themselves. For instance, one week we'd sit round a table and read Chekhov's *The Seagull*, with Alexi Kaye Campbell performing a rather brilliant Trigorin, while the next week Gregory Motton provoked everyone into a rather un-brilliant, but certainly memorable, slanging match.

Gradually establishing a reputation as a decent dramaturg – given that no one really knows what a dramaturg is – it was only a matter of time before I started being invited to run workshops and sessions outside of the Royal Court.

I remember, for instance, the Young Vic theatre packing me off to Cairo to run a workshop with local playwrights during 2010s tumultuous Arab spring. An interesting idea on paper, the reality was I spent a lot of time avoiding armed police by hiding in an underground, jungle-themed café, smoking shishas.

When we returned to the workshop space, the Egyptian writers produced some powerful verbatim work in response to the uprising. I remember attempting to present some of the work amid the protests on Tahrir Square, but the writers felt – quite rightly – that their safety was more important.

Who said making theatre had to be safe?

Zigzagging through the slums of Lagos in the back of a bulletproof van isn't something you'd usually associate with a playwriting class either.

Neither is being staked out by Robert Mugabe's secret police while rehearsing at the Harare Garden Theatre.

The 6.7-magnitude earthquake in Chile was equally unusual, as was the time our South African workshop space was surrounded by hungry baboons.

Then again, nothing was usual about the woman who organized and led these trips, and who – above anyone else – not only taught me how best to work with writers, but who continues to remind me that playmaking does – against all the odds – have the potential to transform lives.

As much as Elyse Dodgson was the Queen of keepy-uppy, she was also the most dedicated theatre artist I've ever met.

Elyse

When I first met Elyse she was stationed in a corner of the Royal Court's open-plan office, her unmistakeable Anglo-American voice booming across the partitions as she planned and financed several international playwriting workshops at once.

Raised in Brooklyn's Brighton Beach, Elyse moved to London at the tail end of the sixties. An unashamed flowerchild, she was passionate about theatre, and, as she later claimed, fell instantly in love with the revolutionary spirit of the Court.

It would take a whole other book to describe all the events that led to her – by then a doting mum of two kids – being first employed by Max Stafford-Clark in the 1980s and then promoted by Stephen Daldry to international associate in the mid-nineties. But, for the eighteen years that I knew her, such was her dedication to the role, that it's hard to think of her doing anything else.

From Brecht and Soyinka to Mustapha Matura and David Mamet, the Royal Court has, since its inception, led the way in bringing the work of international playwrights to the UK. Elyse amplified that reputation by creating (and raising the money for) a series of British Council partnered projects that built bridges between theatre makers across the world.

Aptly titled 'Dodgy Tours', Elyse enlisted a who's who of British playwrights and directors – usually two for each tour – to join her on a year-long project working with an array of local writers from a chosen country.

Although she'd tell anyone who listened that her favourite country was Palestine, she was equally at home in India, Mexico, China, Cuba, Argentina or Syria. In fact, over the course of twenty-five years, she worked in more than seventy different countries giving hundreds, if not thousands, of talented young artists a transformative experience that would send, in her words, *'ripples across the culture'*.

There were usually three, two-and-a-half week workshops per year – always with the same team. For instance, Nick Payne, director Richard Twyman and I joined Elyse in Chile, while Winsome Pinnock and I joined her in South Africa and Zimbabwe.

With roughly twenty writers in each group – as well as translators and members of the British Council – the workshops would ideally take place in a theatre space or some sort of conference room big enough for us to play lots of keepy-uppy.

In partnership with the country's local theatres, Elyse would personally select the playwrights, taking great care that there was an equal gender balance, and that there were as many first-time writers as there were those with experience.

As we all stayed in the same accommodation – be it the Sherlock Holmes themed hotel in Nigeria, or the thatched wooden cabins in the mountains of Magaliesberg – the workshops would start early in the morning (with keepy-uppy) and might last way into the night (with games of 'Mafia' or Karaoke).

Here's Elyse, Nick Payne and I with the brilliantly talented Chilean writers . . . .

IMAGE 123 *Clockwise, from left: The author, Emilia Berger, Pierre Costa, Florencia Martinez, Begoña Ugalde, Camila Le-Bert, Nick Payne, Cláudia Jimenez, Andrés Kalawski, Elyse Dodgson, David Arancibia, Daniela Contreras, Bosco Alvarez, Gerado Oettinger and Juan Andrés Rivera. Santiago, Chile, 2012. Photo courtesy of © Elyse Dodgson archive.*

Or Winsome Pinnock and I with the South African group . . .

IMAGE 124 *Clockwise, from left: Dominique Gumede, Nobantu Shabangu, Genna Gardini, Napo Masheane, Winsome Pinnock, Neil Coppen, Amy Jephta, Mongiwekaya, Mandi Vundla, Omphile Molusi, the author, Eliot Moleba, Tau Maserumule and Mpapa Simo Majola. Magliesberg, South Africa, 2014. Photo courtesy of © Elyse Dodgson Archive.*

The workshops would include a plethora of games, exercises, discussions, group tasks and individual mentorship. Each of the writers would then develop a brand-new play from scratch that would be workshopped, showcased and might, ultimately, be produced back at the Royal Court or at a partner theatre in their own country.

The aim was never to wade in like dramaturgical imperialists, but to merge our disciplines to create original, groundbreaking work. Although her preference was for overtly political voices, Elyse never dismissed a writer's individual taste or style.

In Chile, I remember how she pushed writer David Arancibia to plunder his Mapuchian heritage to create an impassioned, personal polemic, while also encouraging Bosco Alvarez to pursue his expressionistic, Lynchian tale of General Pinochet's nurse. Camila la Bert, meanwhile, peppered her contemporary Santiago-set romantic comedy with Phil Collins hits.

In South Africa, the group were so energized that Elyse urged them to form their own playwriting collective to take on the establishment. As a result, writer/directors like Neil Coppen and Napo Masheane went on to run companies of their own, while Mongiwekaya's razor-sharp police thriller *I See You* [2016] was produced at the Court in partnership with the Market Theatre in Johannesberg.

Sometimes the plays weren't performed at all, but the partnerships with writers and theatres – such as in Palestine or Cuba – might last for decades. When a country was thrown into political upheaval or war (such as in Syria), Elyse would take great care to stay in contact with the writers and try to help them – personally and artistically – as much as she could.

And, of course, the experience could be just as invigorating for those of us travelling on a temporary visa. In fact, there are so many directors (like Dominic, Ramin and Sam Pritchard) and playwrights (such as April De Angelis, Tanika Gupta and David Greig) who were blessed to take part on a Dodgy Tour – and have countless anecdotes of their own – that I feel a bit awkward writing about her as if I was some kind of authority.

As I write this, I can almost hear Elyse wanting to correct me or tell me to mention all the other projects – the International Summer Residencies, or producing work by writers such as Vassily Sigarev, Guillermo Calderón, Natalya Vorozhbit and Amir Reza Koohestani, as well as her collaboration with Alan Rickman and Katherine Viner on *My Name is Rachel Corrie* [2005] – that she worked tirelessly on too.

She would also say that it was about 'the writers, not her', or that none of it would have been possible without Stephen Daldry, but – conversely – that she raised the fucking money by herself and the whole international department would have collapsed without her.

And, of course, in all but name, it did.

In October 2018, Elyse, Nick (Payne) and I ran a two-week workshop with Peruvian writers in Lima. One evening, we went for Chinese food and talked about, amongst other things, our favourite Woody Allen films, our favourite desserts and how Elyse wasn't going to let the new Royal Court team – however much they tried – force her out of her job.

Later, there were pisco sours on the roof of the theatre with the rest of the group, and the next day I had to catch a plane back to London for an emergency back home (which turned out fine). As there was only one more day of the workshop left, the three of us arranged to meet up at the Royal Court in a few days' time to plan the second trip.

Before heading to the airport, Elyse arranged a lunch for everyone, at which I was given a surprise farewell with red balloons and silly paper hats.

Here she is (pictured below), at the lunch, enjoying my embarrassment . . .

Four or five days later, the Court's artistic director, Vicky Featherstone, made the difficult phone call to tell me that Elyse had suddenly passed away at home.

I was dumbfounded.

Her memorial at the Royal Court, a few months later, was a wonderfully cathartic thing. The auditorium was jam-packed with friends, family and colleagues from more than three decades of theatre history whose lives she'd touched in so many ways. And we played a big game of keepy-uppy across the stalls.

IMAGE 125 *The author and Elyse Dodgson (centre right) in Lima, Peru, October 2018. Image reproduced from the author's archive.*

But however moving the memorial was, Elyse's legacy is bound in the ripples she made across the world. She was a force of nature, and she could be *terrifying* if you ever got on the wrong side of her. But she also had a terrific sense of humour, was a doting grandmother and had a gentleness borne out of deep maternal care for the writers she worked with, genuinely believing their work could change the world. And maybe it did, maybe it still does. In an industry that can be dogged by cynicism, censorship, injustice, entitlement, competitiveness, back-stabbing, economic failure and in-fighting, I think about her a lot.

'Well, *why does anyone carry on?*' I can hear her say, '*You just have to.*'

13

Now and then

As I write this, in the winter of 2024, the newly appointed Royal Court artistic director, David Byrne, has just issued a statement saying *'few new playwrights truly believe that sending a play cold to a theatre is a viable route to a career anymore – and nothing has replaced it. The drawbridge is up. The open routes that once filled stages with new talent feel blocked.... Playwrights, who should be bold and brave, are increasingly nervous of making art that isn't instantly appealing to the loudest voices.... These are big challenges.'*

There have always been big challenges, but, as David says, it does feel like new writing (arguably, the entire industry) has stalled at the drawbridge.

When I first started – in the early noughties – it was never easy to get noticed, but there were far more opportunities for emerging writers and directors than there are today. The reasons, I feel, are as much to do with poor management as they are to do with economics.

I remember Ian Rickson talking about the need to bankroll riskier work by programming one guaranteed hit per season. A shrewd plan that also reflected a commitment to theatre artists whose work might be deliberately off kilter or divisive. In short, theatres like Rickson's Royal Court embraced George Devine's mantra of *'a right to fail'*.

Even after the financial crash of 2008 (and the barbaric cuts to state-subsidised arts), many UK theatres ploughed on producing new plays by the barrel full.

Indeed, it's arguable that theatres began *over-commissioning* new plays as they frantically searched for the 'next Polly Stenham or Mike Bartlett'. But, as it's impossible to search for the next anyone, they were simultaneously nervous about bankrolling anything that couldn't guarantee a return.

As part of their search, budgets were spent on creating 'new Work departments' who were employed to discover and nurture new voices and, through a process of 'research and development', iron out any critical or financial risks. Rather than simply producing debut plays within, say, the protective framework of a Young Writers' Festival, 'R & D' – as it became known – entailed workshops, readings and dramaturgical meetings with zero commitment to producing. As a result, the playwright might spend months or years improving (or, in some cases, sapping the life out of) their play – for no money – satisfying no one – only for it to be left gathering dust once everyone's moved on to something else.

Even worse was when a theatre made a commitment to producing a play, then failed to produce it, while denying they ever made a commitment in the first place. For this to happen once is bad enough, but when it happened to multiple playwrights (and from one of the country's most beloved theatres), then the damage was felt throughout the culture. One senior playwright once remarked that *'theatres build their reputation off your work, then never return your calls'*, while other playwrights have given up writing altogether.

Then came Brexit, the Covid pandemic and the cost-of-living crisis.

Ask around and you'll find many theatres have no money, or have shut down or on the brink of shutting down.

As everyone knows, ticket prices have shot through the roof.

Theatre producers are increasingly offering themselves up as partners to million-dollar franchises.

You've read the book, watched the film, bought the lunchbox, now see the play!

Playwrights who once pondered the value of art, now sit around brainstorming Disney or HBO adaptations that they can try pitching to West End producers. *Avengers Assemble: The Musical* may sound like a dismal idea, but I guarantee it's being discussed.

In recent years, it's been reassuring to see challenging work like Ivan van Hove's adaptation of *A Little Life* [2023] and Chris Bush and Richard Hawley's *Standing at the Sky's Edge* [2024] packing out West End venues, but should a single ticket cost more than £200? Who are we making it for anyway?

Meanwhile, writers – and their employers – wrack their brains for that super-successful one-person show that they can offer to a celebrity actor or popstar.

Such commercial ventures have always existed, and they may have saved the industry from collapse, but serious actors and directors need work too.

Despite the overdue wake-up calls of the #MeToo and BLM movements, there's a risk of intelligent debate being reduced to point scoring on social media, with opposing sides trivializing or weaponizing issues for personal gain.

Young writers feel the pressure of being cancelled by their peers even before they've written anything. Who is allowed to write what? What is acceptable/permissible? What does my play say about *me*?

Theatre is not a profile banner. It's a mirror to the world. Would you put your dreams or nightmares through a board of censors?

Ah, fuck it.

In my experience, most theatre folk are decent, well-intentioned people, and the industry's capacity to survive in the face of economic and cultural change is, frankly, astounding.

I remember the joy of taking my seat to watch Kae Tempest's *Paradise* at the National Theatre in the summer of 2021. Covid remained a threat, the theatres were in disarray, but here we all were. A sea of face masks clamouring for that collective, live experience.

As technology and AI conspire to separate ourselves from ourselves, we're going to need that physical shared experience – whether it's *4.48 Psychosis* or *Peppa Pig's Fun Day Out* – more than ever I think.

Look on any theatre's website or pick up their brochure and you'll find good people still trying to create good work. Unlike other industries, theatres (no matter where they're based or who their core audiences are) generally want the best for each other. They depend on it.

And, of course, without investment there isn't any industry at all.

Governments need to stop seeing the creative industries as a luxury or an afterthought. They need to properly budget for arts education in schools (particularly those in working-class communities) as kids need room to dream as much as they need algebra or physics.

As for navigating the industry as a so-called professional, I still get disappointed or fucked off. There are times I can't get arrested. I've defiantly announced I'm giving up writing plays for good, only to find myself – out of nowhere, to my astonishment – back in the playwriting saddle working with fellow artists to create those brief moments of magic in a rehearsal room together.

Two dozen – produced or unproduced – plays since I first performed *Happy Hospital* in that school hall back in 1983, I've survived by the skin of my teeth and, largely, thanks to the talent of many of the people I've mentioned in this book.

Insistence, perseverance, honouring the allies you make along the way.

Teaching has kept me rooted. I love my students and learn as much from them as they learn from me.

Sitting down to write a new play, I encounter the same challenges as I did when I wrote *Giddy Little Kippers* all those years ago. *What the fuck's going on? Who are these characters?* I find that reassuring somehow.

You're still chasing those breathtaking moments when the characters take over the story and you're struggling to catch up.

You grow up, get married or settle down; things change. You might stop writing about 'me and my mates' and dip into deeper pools of imagination and experience.

You become a parent; things change. You might question your moral responsibility at the heart of your work. What you're putting out into the world has deeper implications. Until the kids grow up and leave home, that is. Then you're back to square one.

You get older; things change. You may not have the luxury of time anymore. Is it any wonder that the work of writers like Beckett, Pinter and Churchill became more precise, more distilled? You begin with a community; you end with a mouth suspended in space.

You might retreat into history or nostalgia to make sense of the present.

You might consider whole lifetimes rather than individual chapters of a character's life.

You might consider what the purpose of a good story is. How imagination and art have impacted your own life, and how they might impact the lives of those you leave behind.

You might even write a book about your experiences.

You look around and people you love fade away. Disease robs them of their memory, their speech and emotional reflex. The books on their shelves go unread.

Like the final line and the final blackout on the play's final night – poof! Up in smoke! Gone forever.

Well, almost.

The cat wakes me up with a '*meow meow*' and I'm still that kid who wants to have a go at *everything*. I'm sitting in my garden shed, pretending to write for the sake of a badly taken selfie . . .

IMAGE 126 *The author pretending to write, 2025. Image reproduced from the author's archive.*

Perhaps I'll write scripts indefinitely. Perhaps I'll sit on my arse and pick up my guitar to strum a tune every now and then. Make up for lost time with family and friends.

Ultimately, everything turns to dust.

Reading new work from my students, or, indeed, another film script that our daughter has miraculously written overnight or racing across town to sit in a rehearsal room with a company of likeminded misfits . . . well, I'm reminded how we all share this insane, rather beautiful, desire to express something from somewhere deep within ourselves.

Even when we can't put it into words or have nothing profound to say, it's the reaching out that matters. Whether you're a social butterfly or a master of solitude, it's the array of connections with audiences, collaborators, mentors, friends, sometimes lovers – that gives the game its juice.

As I reach the end of this book, I realize that – as a writer – my proudest achievements and happiest memories aren't a packed house or a glowing review.

Some are hidden away in the memories of schoolkids who came to see *Devotion* and *Innocent Creatures*. The little girl who felt inspired by *Cinderella* to 'change the world'. The young people who said *I'll Be the Devil* or *Boy* altered their perception of what theatre can do.

Some are 'N' squeezing my hand at the climax of *Lucky Dog*, or Bea singing along with Cinders from the stalls. Playing *Alison!* with the band in a pub in East Croydon. The schoolkid who joined a half-term playwriting course and now has a glittering career and a family of their own. The student who didn't become a success, but whose play still sits with me.

Some are getting revenge on CHARACTER C. A letter from a famous writer telling me it's all going to be okay. Some are working with friends or making great friends. Childhood, and my brother. Martin Murray-mints. A student house in Plumstead. A family home in Pitsmoor. Charlie Chaplin and The Beatles. David Lynch and Akira Kurosawa. Beckett. Dennis Potter. Memories of *Threads*. *A Midsummer's Night Dream* in the Botanical Gardens at dusk. My parents, of course. It's the connection with family I never met. John Gordon Barber training his greyhounds in 1948.

Above all, it's giving a voice to people who didn't have one before. Liam in *Boy*, Lucy in *Redundant* or Sue in *Lucky Dog*.

It's everyone who shuffled onto the page, however fleetingly, in one scene or another; the journeys they took me on, the things they taught me, the people who brought them to life.

It's the strong, beautiful women who've shaken me out of daydreams. My amazing mum. Forces of nature like Meg Jepson and Elyse Dodgson.

And the strongest and most beautiful of all, my wife and daughter.

And if, like twenty-year-old me, you're printing out that first play somewhere and struggling to know what to do.

It's true about the drawbridges; there may be fewer places to send your work than when I first started. But don't worry, it won't be for long.

There are still legion more opportunities than when the first working-class playwrights crawled out of their primordial bedsits back in 1956.

There are, and always will be, hurdles.

But the intention is where it begins.

If you're reading this book many years in the future, then – *hello from the past!* – you know more than we do. Did things work out? What are you going to see tonight? What worlds or people are you creating? For whom?

Great work will always find its way through the paving stones.

After all, theatre has survived for more than 2,000 years and, if ancient ritual's your bag, you can probably add a further 10,000 onto that; talk about pushing a piano up a staircase!

Persevere. Start today.

Appendix

Q & A exercise

From **Chapter 2: Getting Started,** 111 questions for you to answer in your own time and space. Answer them alone, in private, not to be shared. Dispose of answers in an appropriate way.

The questions can also be answered as a character, for research and backstory.

1. How are you today?
2. What's going on in your life right now?
3. If a genie offered you three wishes, what would those wishes be?
4. Describe your home and what it means to you.
5. Who is the most important person in your life and why are they so important?
6. How do you hope things will work out for your most important person in the next few years?
7. What do you hope for yourself for the next few years?
8. Is there one person that your life would be much better without and why?
9. Who or what makes you laugh?
10. What, if anything, keeps you awake at night?
11. How do you describe yourself politically?
12. What, in your opinion, is the biggest problem facing the world today?
13. Do you have an opinion that you would not readily share with other people? What is it?
14. What, in your opinion, is the biggest problem in your life at the moment?
15. What is one of the worst things you have ever said to someone else?
16. What is one of the worst things anyone has ever said to you?

17. What did you say in response? What do you wish you'd said in response?
18. What's the best (or loveliest) thing that anyone's ever said to you?
19. What's the thing you're most proud of? (The best thing you've ever done)
20. What's the thing you're most ashamed of? (The worst thing you've ever done)
21. What's the worst thing that someone's done to you?
22. What's the worst thing you've done to someone else?
23. Who do you most want to hold/touch and why?
24. What is the smallest thing you are proud of?
25. What is the biggest thing you are proud of?
26. Is there one mistake you keep making? How do you fix it?
27. What do people say about you behind your back?
28. What do you say to those people behind their backs?
29. What do you like about your physical appearance?
30. What do you dislike about your physical appearance?
31. What do other people like about your physical appearance?
32. What words or phrases do you overuse?
33. What or who is the sweetest thing? Why?
34. What or who is the cutest thing? Why?
35. What or who is the scariest thing? Why?
36. What or who is the best thing? Why?
37. What or who do you most despise? Why?
38. What would be the best way to hurt that person?
39. What's the biggest problem in the world right now?
40. What would be the best way to solve that problem?
41. How can you make a difference to the world?
42. When and how have you made a difference to someone else?
43. Who made a difference to you? How?
44. When did you last help someone in need?
45. Who can you help tomorrow?
46. If Father Christmas was to give you a brilliant present (something that can be unwrapped), what would it be?
47. If you could live in a movie or TV show or play, what would it be and why?
48. What's the most moving play/film/artwork you've ever seen?

49. What were you like as a child?
50. Where was home? How does home make you feel?
51. What was your bedroom like?
52. What was on your bedroom walls?
53. What can you see out of the bedroom window?
54. What's outside the door?
55. What can you hear? What are you doing?
56. As a child, what was your worst day?
57. As a child, what was your best day?
58. Who was your best friend as a child and what was the best thing you did together?
59. What did the people who raised you teach you, and what did they fail to teach you?
60. What would you say to them now?
61. What is your abiding memory of school?
62. What would you change about school?
63. What would you still like to learn at school?
64. Who was your first crush? What did you like about them?
65. What would you say to them now?
66. Where and with whom (if applicable) did you lose your virginity?
67. Where and with whom was the best sex of your life?
68. Where and with whom was the worst sex of your life?
69. Who do you most want to have sex with today?
70. What's your favourite drink? Or drug? Why?
71. When were you most drunk? Or high?
72. Where is the best view in the world?
73. Where is the best place in the world?
74. Where's the best place to walk?
75. What's the most exhilarating feeling?
76. What and with whom was the best night out you have ever had?
77. What's one of the biggest arguments you ever had with somebody? Who started it? Why did it happen? Who won the argument? How was it resolved?
78. What was the most meaningful/important conversation you ever had with someone else?
79. If you could erase one memory from your life, what would it be?

80. If you could re-live one memory from your life, what would it be?
81. What's the thing you should've said, but didn't?
82. What have you sacrificed?
83. What keeps you going?
84. Who is the love of your life? What would you like to say to them?
85. What are you going to do next?
86. Describe a dream you've had.
87. Describe a fantasy you've had.
88. Describe a fear you've had.
89. What does the devil look like?
90. What does heaven look like?
91. What happens to you after you die?
92. What song would you like played at your funeral?
93. What would you like people to say about you after you die?
94. What do you hope people don't say about you after you die?
95. How are you going to improve your life? How can you be a better person?
96. What do people have to learn to accept about you?
97. What do you need to accept about yourself?
98. What do you need to accept about other people?
99. What do you most want to say to your loved ones?
100. Why do you work?
101. If you could change your job, what would you do? Why?
102. What's so good about money? What do you like to spend money on?
103. If you had a million pounds, what would you buy?
104. If you lost all your money, what would you do?
105. Have you ever prayed? When did you last pray?
106. How has religion improved your life?
107. What's the most important thing life has taught you?
108. What is one of the biggest sacrifices you have ever had to make?
109. What or who makes life worth living?
110. If you could meet your 10-year-old self now, what advice would you give to them?
111. What advice would your 10-year-old self give to you now?

The twelve-week course

A more detailed outline of the introductory twelve-week course, as described in **Chapter Twelve**. Feel free to use or adapt.

Week 1

Introduction. Ball games, name games.
Writers split into pairs to introduce themselves, then report what they've learned to the whole group.
Put together a reading list. Discuss hopes and needs for the course.
A short bit of writing, such as the *'If you're really really stuck'* exercise from **Chapter Five**.

Week 2

The **Chapter 2** Q & A exercise, with half an hour or more of freestyling writing.
The questions are followed by one of the four or five exercises, also outlined in **Chapter 2**.

Homework: Prepare a scene from the freestyling exercise to share with the group next week.

Week 3

Read the scenes aloud in small groups. This isn't to show off, but to get into the habit of sharing work.
Group leader instructs the writers on the rules of giving feedback; flattery is welcome. Enquire, but don't dictate, etc. Subjective taste is irrelevant.
If anyone's pleased with their work, share the scene with whole group. Group leader gives feedback and thoughts.
Have a break.
Explore political themes, by brainstorming what everyone thinks the most important political or social issues of the day are.
Split everyone into smaller groups. Challenge each group to conceive, write and present a short scene from a play that explores their chosen political theme.
Watch the scenes back, which is fun.

Discussion on different types of theatre, and whether political theatre can be successful or not. Let the students lead the conversation, making sure the shy writers aren't left out.

Homework: Read a play, any play. Or perhaps everyone read the same play. A relatively short one, like Caryl Churchill's *Far Away* or Buchner's *Woyzeck*.

Week 4

Watch Laurel and Hardy's *The Music Box*.
As in **Chapter Seven**, present and explore the so-called rules of narrative, in comparison with the plays you've read, ones you already know.
    In small groups, pick your chosen play, or a film or TV show, and trace it against *The Music Box*.
Discuss each group's discoveries and insights with everyone.
If there's time, give the students a few minutes to consider the narrative rules in relation to their own play idea.
Share/feedback in smaller groups, or with everyone.

Homework: Get a new notebook. Make sure to write in that notebook every day for a week. Thoughts, ideas, random nonsense.

Week 5

Character study. Take a character you're already exploring or conjure one from thin air.
The group leader asks the questions from either **Chapter Two** or **Chapter Seven**, and each student hopefully discovers backstory and details they didn't have before.
Write a two-hander scene with that character and someone else that's close to them. Consider the setting and time of year. Why they're meeting, and who set up the meeting. Consider the characters' wants and objectives (their pianos and staircases) and how they *avoid* conflict to get what they need. Decide who wins and who loses at the end of the scene, or just discover that as you're writing.
Share what you've written in pairs or threes, and, if there's time, with the whole group.

Homework: Go out somewhere. On a bus or train. Or sit in a café. When someone interesting starts talking – record or transcribe – or record *then* transcribe – them talking. Be careful and respectful. Pay close attention to their rhythms of speech, dialect, repetitions, etc. Think about your own characters' dialogue and how their patterns, rhythms, vocabulary and turn of phrase reveal interesting insights about them.

Week 6

Structure. Use the exercises from **Chapter Nine** to explore different ways of structuring a play.

In groups, use existing, well-known plays and try drawing up a plan of how you might structure them differently. What does it do to the play? Does it change the themes and ideas?
In the second half of the session, think about your own play idea and try each of the three or four structures to see which one works best.
Draw pictures, diagrams, write bits of scene.

Feedback what you discovered in pairs or threes, or to the whole group.

Week 7

Group leader reads aloud one of his or her plays to the group. In my case, something like *Lucky Dog* or *Redundant*.
Group leader explains the process of writing the play and takes questions.

If group leader doesn't have – or doesn't want to read – a play of their own, then read a good play together and discuss how the playwright is developing the story and characterization in each scene.

Annie Baker's *The Flick* and Chekhov's *The Seagull* are recommended, but any play will do.

Homework: Work on your play.

Weeks 8 and 9

Group leader meets with each student individually to discuss their play idea. An informal conversation, dependent on each students' needs.
These tutorials are exhausting for the group leader, but they can be indispensable to the students – especially those who are shy, or unsure about what they're writing.
Group leader stays receptive and tries to offer at least one piece of practical advice.
While the individual tutorials are taking place, the rest of the group stay (in another room, if possible) and work on their plays. Writing and planning time.

Week 10

Based on the previous week's tutorials, the group leader creates an individual writing challenge for each student.
It might be working on a character's backstory or writing a scene they haven't written yet (or that doesn't appear in the play).
It might be you ask the student to try an alternative structure, or you might provoke the writer to find *the hidden* play and to work their personal connection to the material.

It might be you ask the writer to pretend to be a theatre critic and review the first night performance of their (yet unwritten) play, or you might pair two writers' together to share their material.
It is up to the group leader to think carefully about each of the students' ideas and suggest exercises that you think will be helpful, but not disruptive to their process.

Homework: Write and prepare a scene from the play to share with the entire group. Think about how you want to be read. By other members of the group or read aloud by yourself.

Week 11

The group shares the scenes from their plays. Feedback, questions and support.

Week 12

On scraps of paper, the students write one thing they're feeling confident about, and one thing they feel anxious about.
We discuss all the answers as a group.
The 'anxious' scraps of paper are burned or eaten in some kind of silly ceremony.
A game of keepy-uppy. Perhaps a visit from the artistic director, literary manager or another writer.
There's cake.
Group leader gives an inspiring speech. Takes final, practical questions about delivering the play and what happens next.
Goodbye, and good luck.

Some plays and films

Here are a few of the plays and films that have had an impact on my writing life, and that I think you might enjoy.

Plays

Krapps Last Tape by Samuel Beckett (1958). How Beckett manages to use a simple theatrical device (a tape player) to summarize an entire lifetime – with maximum efficiency and heart-wrenching dramatic irony – is a lesson for anyone who ever wanted to write a play.

Road by Jim Cartwright (Royal Court, 1986). *The Cherry Orchard* of the North. I remember watching Alan Clarke's screen version on Channel Four when I was a kid. There's no black-and-white morality in Cartwright's collage-like depiction of working-class life in the throes of Thatcherism. The characters can be as ugly as they are sympathetic. Funny, brutal, and still, sadly, relevant all these years later.

4.48 Psychosis by Sarah Kane (Royal Court, 2000). I was an usher on the very first performance of this show (shortly after the author's tragic death). I needed a stiff whiskey afterwards. The opening of the window at the end of the play (an *actual window* overlooking Sloane Square from the Royal Court's Theatre Upstairs), remains one of the most moving theatrical experiences I've ever had.

King Lear by William Shakespeare (1606). Better than the Bible.

The Caretaker by Harold Pinter (Arts Theatre Club, 1960). *Pinter-esque* suggests a po-faced pretentiousness that isn't really true of Pinter's writing. It's easy to forget just how *weird* and *funny* and (not always, but often) *unashamedly working class* plays like *The Caretaker* really are.

A Raisin in the Sun by Lorraine Hansberry (Ethel Barrymore Theatre, 1959). Nothing beats a classic American drama. Every line of dialogue is perfect, every character a killer part. The *crafting* of action, the handling of exposition . . . man, just everything about it is perfect.

Machinal by Sophie Treadwell (1928)/Woyzeck by Georg Buchner (1836). I could eat both these plays for breakfast.

Where the Shot Rabbits Lay by Brad Birch (Royal Court, 2012). A delicate, moving story of a recently divorced father teaching his son to shoot rabbits. Not much happens, but everything happens. Rather like Kelly Reichardt's wonderful 2006 film *Old Joy*, just the kind of drama I aspire to write.

Tourism by Rory Mullarkey (2010). This visceral, episodic story of a young man travelling across Central Asia (seemingly without purpose) is sharper and more nuanced than its sparce form suggests. And it's mad as a box of frogs.

Little Russians by John Donnelly/The Letter of Last Resort by David Greig (Tricycle Theatre, 2012). Part of Nicholas Kent's excellent anthology *The Bomb: A Partial History*, which explored the history and impact of nuclear weapons. Grieg's *Letter of Last Resort* chills you to the bone, Donnelly's gag-tastic *Little Russians* tickles your bones.

The Writer by Ella Hickson (Almeida, 2018). No f*cks given.

The Book of Mormon by Matt Stone, Trey Parker and Robert Lopez (Eugene O'Neill Theatre, 2011). No f*cks given.

The Oresteia by Robert Icke (Almeida, 2015). Writer/director Icke is an alchemist, turning these centuries-old stories into something completely present and utterly plausible. Massive beast of a play, three plus hours long. Possibly the best night I've had at a theatre. The rightful heir to Peter Brook.

Posh by Laura Wade (Royal Court, 2010). I've never felt an audience more alive and divided as watching Wade's fast and funny story of awful public schoolboys at their most casually reprehensible. Look around at your fellow audience members. Who is laughing *with* the characters, who is laughing *at* the characters? What does that tell you about who we are? A canny and clever (and brilliantly written) piece of political theatre.

People Places and Things by Duncan Macmillan (National Theatre, 2015). The most accurate depiction of drug addiction I've ever read. Masterful writing.

Far Away by Caryl Churchill (Royal Court, 2000). Even in her seventies and eighties, Caryl Churchill remains the youngest playwright on the block. *Far Away* is the Brothers Grimm meets the Chapman Brothers via Hieronymus Bosch. Any play with the line *'who's going to mobilise darkness and silence?'* deserves untold praise.

Kin by E V Crowe (Royal Court, 2010). I'll never forget this beautiful, episodic play about eleven-year-old girls at boarding school. I had to rush to the gents and have a little cry afterwards. It was the poster of the hamster that broke me.

Films

Satantango (Bela Tarr, Hungary, 1994). Heavyweight Hungarian director Bela Tarr presents an extraordinary seven-hour meditation on impoverishment, cruelty and cows. Unashamedly slow. Unforgettable.

Land of Silence and Darkness (Werner Herzog, Germany, 1974). Herzog's astonishing documentary concerns a community of elderly blind/deaf people helping each other to experience life to its fullest. Genuinely uplifting.

A Separation (Asghar Farhadi, Iran, 2011)/Leviathan (Andrey Zvyagintsev, Russia, 2014). Farhadi and Zvyagintsev deliver stories (and characters) with the complexity of Ibsen and the edge-of-your-seat suspense of Hitchcock. If a film is a meal, both deliver multiple courses.

Raining Stones (Loach, UK, 1994). Easily my favourite Ken Loach film. It's funny, politically razor-sharp, and relies on neither cheap shocks, broad strokes or cheap sentimentalism. And it has Ricky Tomlinson.

Come and See (Elem Klimov, Belarus, 1985). I made director Ramin Gray watch this before we started rehearsals for *I'll Be the Devil*. I'm not sure he ever forgave me. The purest war film ever made. Hold tight, it takes no prisoners.

Young Frankenstein (Mel Brooks, USA, 1974). The funniest, most perfect script, thanks to Gene Wilder and Brooks. A perfect movie in every way.

The Day the Earth Caught Fire (Val Guest, UK, 1961). A little-known British sci-fi movie that is surprisingly prescient and has one of the best line-by-line screenplays (by Wolf Mankowitz and Val Guest) I've ever read.

Through a Glass Darkly (Ingmar Bergman, Sweden, 1961). I could choose any Ingmar Bergman film *(Persona, The Magician* and *Fanny and Alexander* being personal favourites)*, but *Through a Glass Darkly* is a particularly good one for writers being, partly, about the personal cost of writing. And it has Max von Sydow on top form.

Singin' in the Rain (Stanley Donen/Gene Kelly, USA, 1952). Pure joy.

Alice in the Cities (Wim Wenders, Germany, 1974). I watch Wim Wenders' Road trilogy – including *Wrong Move* and *Kings of the Road* – at least once a year. Something about characters adrift, searching for purpose, in a homeland that feels nothing like home is peculiarly comforting. *Alice in the Cities* is the one that really gets under my skin.

Mulholland Drive (David Lynch, USA, 2001). It's the gift that keeps on giving.

L'Avventura (Michaelangelo Antonioni, Italy, 1960). Antonioni's film is both a ravishing portrait of desire as well as a savage critique of the nihilism of the modern world. Like a classic episode of *The Simpson* (set against a backdrop of the Aeolian Islands), the narrative twists and turns, constantly pulling the rug from under your feet, until you're left wondering what in God's name you've just watched. And it has Monica Vitti.

Meantime (Mike Leigh, UK, 1983). Those early Mike Leigh films feel like coming home.

News From Home (Chantal Akerman, USA/Belgium, 1971). Real-life letters from home (aka Belgium) written by Akerman's mother, read by Akerman herself, and set against long (often static) sequences of New York's streets and subways. Another comfort film for this fan of slow, seemingly undramatic, cinema. The final shot of Manhattan shrinking into the distance is profoundly effective.

The Hidden Fortress (Akira Kurosawa, Japan, 1958). The Shakespeare of cinema, Kurosawa, gives us laughs, thrills, action and excitement, perfectly combined in a story that George Lucas famously ripped off decades later.

The White Ribbon (Michael Haneke, Germany/Austria, 2009). Fascism doesn't goosestep into town. It breeds imperceptivity in the schools, churches and kitchens of the town folk. Haneke's subtle, yet terrifying, drama is as much a warning for humanity as it is an example of nuanced, subtextual storytelling at its best.

Taxi Driver (Martin Scorsese, USA, 1976). We've all been there.

BIBLIOGRAPHY

Agbaje, Bola, *Gone too Far!* (London: Methuen Drama, 2007)
Albee, Edward, *Who's Afraid of Virginia Woolf?* (Vintage Classics, 2001)
Allen, Woody, *Manhattan* (London: Faber, 2003)
Arden, John, *Live Like Pigs* (London: Methuen Drama, 1994)
Baker, Annie, *The Flick* (London: Nick Hern Books, 2016)
Bean, Richard, *One Man, Two Guvnors* (London: Methuen Drama, 2016)
Bean, Richard, *Toast* (London: Oberon, 1999)
Bean, Richard/Coleman, Clive, *Young Marx* (London: Oberon, 2017)
Beckett, Samuel, *Happy Days* (London: Faber, 2010)
Beckett, Samuel, *Krapp's Last Tape* (London: Faber, 1960)
Beckett, Samuel, *Not I* (London: Faber, 2004)
Beckett, Samuel, *Waiting for Godot* (London: Faber, 1965)
Bennett, Alan, *A Cream Cracker under the Settee* (London: Picador, 2003)
Berkoff, Steven/Kafka, Franz, *Metamorphosis* (London: Amber Lane Press, 1988)
Birch, Brad, *Plays One: Where the Shot Rabbits Lay; Even Stillness Breathes Softly Against a Brick Wall; The Brink; Black Mountain* (London: Methuen Drama, 2018)
Bond, Edward, *Early Morning* (London: Methuen Drama, 1968)
Bond, Edward, *Saved* (London: Methuen Drama, 1977)
Brecht, Bertolt, *Mother Courage and Her Children* (London: Methuen Drama, 1986)
Brook, Peter, *The Empty Space* (London: Penguin Modern Classics, 2008)
Büchner, Georg, *Woyzeck* (Oxford World's Classics, 2008)
Bush, Chris, *Standing at the Sky's Edge* (London: Nick Hern Books, 2021)
Butler, Leo, *All You Need is LSD* (London: Methuen Drama, 2018)
Butler, Leo, *Boy* (London: Methuen Drama, 2016)
Butler, Leo, *Decades* (London: Methuen Drama, 2016)
Butler, Leo, *Devotion* (London: Aurora Metro Press, 2002)
Butler, Leo, *Plays One: Made of Stone; Redundant; Lucky Dog; The Early Bird* (London: Methuen Drama, 2008)
Butler, Leo, *Plays Two: Airbag; I'll Be the Devil; Faces in the Crowd; Juicy Fruits; Sixty-Nine; Do it!* (London: Methuen Drama, 2016)
Butler, Leo, *Innocent Creatures* (London: Methuen Drama, 2023)
Butterworth, Jez, *Jerusalem* (London: Nick Hern Books, 2009)
Carr, Marina, *On Raftery's Hill* (London: Faber, 2001)
Cartwright, Jim, *Road* (London: Methuen Drama, 1986)
Chekhov, Anton, *The Cherry Orchard* (Oxford's World Classics, 2008)
Chekhov, Anton, *The Seagull* (Oxford World's Classics, 2008)
Churchill, Caryl, *Far Away* (London: Nick Hern Books, 2003)

Corrie, Rachel/Rickman, Alan/Viner, Katharine, *My Name is Rachel Corrie* (London: Nick Hern Books, 2006)
Corthron, Kia, *Breath Boom* (London: Methuen Drama, 2000)
Crimp, Martin, *Attempts on Her Life* (London: Faber, 2005)
Crimp, Martin, *The Country* (London: Faber, 2000)
Crouch, Tim, *The Author* (London: Oberon, 2009)
Crowe, E V, *Kin* (London: Faber, 2010)
Davies, Nick, *Dark Heart: The Shocking Truth About Hidden Britain* (London: Chatto & Windus, 1997)
Delaney, Shelagh, *A Taste of Honey* (London: Methuen Drama, 1959)
Donnelly, John, *The Bomb: A Partial History (Little Russians)* (London: Oberon, 2015)
Drury, Jackie Sibblies, *Fairview* (London: Methuen Drama, 2021)
Eldridge, David, *Beginning* (London: Methuen Drama, 2017)
Eldridge, David, *Under the Blue Sky* (London: Methuen Drama, 2000)
Fisher, Mark, *Capitalist Realism* (London: Zero Books, 2009)
Fo, Dario, *Accidental Death of an Anarchist* (London: Methuen Drama, 1987)
Fugard, Athol, *The Island* (London: Faber, 1974)
Gieselmann, David, *Mr Kolpert* (London: Nick Hern Books, 2000)
Gill, Peter, *The York Realist* (London: Faber, 2002)
Gilman, Rebecca, *Boy Gets Girl* (London: Faber, 2001)
Green, Debbie Tucker, *Random* (London: Nick Hern Books, 2010)
Greig, David, *The Bomb: A Partial History (The Letter of Last Resort)* (London: Oberon, 2015)
Griffiths, Trevor, *Comedians* (London: Faber, 1979)
Gubarev, Vladimir, *Sarcophagus* (London: Penguin Plays, 1987)
Guirgis, Stephen Adly, *The Motherf*cker with the Hat* (New York: Dramatist's Play Service, 2012)
Handke, Peter, *Offending the Audience* (London: Methuen Drama, 1987)
Hansberry, Lorraine, *A Raisin in the Sun* (London: Methuen Drama, 2001)
Hare, David, *The Absence of War* (London: Faber, 2015)
Hare, David, *Via Dolorosa* (London: Faber, 1998)
Harris, Jeremy O., *Slave Play* (London: Nick Hern Books, 2021)
Hawkins, Samson, *Village Idiot* (London: Methuen Drama, 2023)
Hickson, Ella, *The Writer* (London: Nick Hern Books, 2018)
Holliday, Joyce, *It's a Bit Lively Outside* (Yorkshire Art Circus, 1987)
Ibsen, Henrik, *Hedda Gabler* (London: Oxford's World Classics, 2008)
Icke, Robert, *Oresteia* (London: Oberon, 2015)
Ionesco, Eugène, *The Chairs* (London: Faber, 1997)
Jordan, Anna, *Yen* (London: Nick Hern Books, 2016)
Kane, Sarah, *4.48 Psychosis* (London: Methuen Drama, 2001)
Kane, Sarah, *Blasted* (London: Methuen Drama, 2001)
Khan Din, Ayub, *East Is East* (London: Nick Hern Books, 1997)
Kushner, Tony, *Angels in America: Part One & Part Two* (London: Nick Hern Books, 1992)
Lee-Jones, Jasmine, *Seven Methods of Killing Kylie Jenner* (London: Methuen Drama, 2021)
Leigh, Mike, *Abigail's Party* (London: Penguin, 2017)
Littlewood, Joan/Theatre Workshop, *Oh, What a Lovely War!* (London: Methuen Drama, 1967)

Macmillan, Duncan, *People, Places and Things* (London: Oberon, 2021)
McDowell, Alistair, *Pomona* (London: Methuen Drama, 2014)
McDowell, Alistair, *X* (London: Methuen Drama, 2016)
McPherson, Conor, *The Weir* (London: Nick Hern Books, 1998)
Mamet, David, *Edmond* (London: Methuen Drama, 1996)
Mamet, David, *Sexual Perversity in Chicago* (London: Methuen Drama, 1996)
Massini, Stefano/Power, Ben, *The Lehman Trilogy* (London: Samuel French, 2022)
Mayenburg, Marius von, *Fireface* (London: Methuen Drama, 2000)
Miranda, Lin-Manuel, *Hamilton* (London: Little, Brown, 2016)
Mullarkey, Rory, *Mullarkey Plays: One: Single Sex; Tourism; Cannibals; The Wolf from the Door; Each Slow Dusk* (London: Methuen Drama, 2018)
O'Brien, Richard, *The Rocky Horror Show* (London: Samuel French, 1983)
O'Neill, Eugene, *Long Day's Journey into Night* (London: Nick Hern Books, 1991)
Orton, Joe, *What the Butler Saw* (London: Methuen Drama, 1969)
Orwell, George, *Why I Write* (London: Penguin, 2004)
Osborne, John, *Look Back in Anger* (London: Faber, 1957)
Owen, Gary, *Iphigenia in Splott* (London: Methuen Drama, 2016)
Payne, Nick, *Constellations* (London: Faber, 2021)
Payne, Nick, *One Day When We Were Young* (London: Faber, 2011)
Pinter, Harold, *The Caretaker* (London: Faber, 1991)
Prebble, Lucy, *Enron* (London: Methuen Drama, 2009)
Prebble, Lucy, *The Sugar Syndrome* (London: Methuen Drama, 2013)
Reiss, Anya, *The Acid Test* (London: Oberon, 2011)
Reiss, Anya, *Spur of the Moment* (London: Oberon, 2011)
Russell, Willy, *Blood Brothers* (London: Methuen Drama, 2001)
Russell, Willy, *Educating Rita* (London: Methuen Modern Classics, 2001)
Russell, Willy, *Our Day Out* (London: Methuen Drama, 1984)
Schwab, Werner, *Holy Mothers* (London: Oberon, 1999)
Shakespeare, William, *The Comedy of Errors* (London: Red Globe Press, 2009)
Shakespeare, William, *Hamlet* (London: Red Globe Press, 2009)
Shakespeare, William, *Henry IV: Part One* (London: Red Globe Press, 2009)
Shakespeare, William, *King Lear* (London: Red Globe Press, 2009)
Shakespeare, William, *Macbeth* (London: Red Globe Press, 2009)
Shakespeare, William, *The Merchant of Venice* (London: Red Globe Press, 2009)
Shakespeare, William, *A Midsummer Night's Dream* (London: Red Globe Press, 2009)
Shakespeare, William, *Othello* (London: Red Globe Press, 2009)
Shakespeare, William, *Richard III* (London: Red Globe Press, 2009)
Shakespeare, William, *Romeo and Juliet* (London: Red Globe Press, 2009)
Shakespeare, William, *The Tempest* (London: Red Globe Press, 2009)
Shakespeare, William, *Twelfth Night* (London: Red Globe Press, 2009)
Shakespeare, William, *The Winter's Tale* (London: Red Globe Press, 2009)
Shawn, Wallace/Gregory, André, *My Dinner with André* (London: Methuen, 1983)
Shinn, Christopher, *Other People* (London: Methuen Drama, 2000)
Simon, Neil, *The Odd Couple* (London: Samuel French, 2010)
Skinner, Penelope, *The Village Bike* (London: Faber, 2011)
Sondheim, Stephen/Laurents, Arthur, *Gypsy* (London: Nick Hern Books, 2014)
Sophocles, *Oedipus Rex* (London: Penguin Classics, 1984)

Soyinka, Wole, *Death and the King's Horseman* (London: Methuen Drama, 1975)
Stenham, Polly, *That Face* (London: Faber, 2008)
Stephens, Simon, *Herons* (London: Methuen Drama, 2001)
Stephens, Simon, *Motortown* (London: Methuen Drama, 2006)
Stoppard, Tom, *Rock 'n' Roll* (London: Faber, 2006)
Strindberg, August, *Miss Julie* (Oxford: Oxford's World Press, 2008)
Thorne, Jack/Tiffany, John/Rowling, JK, *Harry Potter and the Cursed Child* (London: Sphere, 2017)
Treadwell, Sophie, *Machinal* (London: Nick Hern Books, 1993)
Wade, Laura, *Posh* (London: Methuen Drama, 2010)
Waller-Bridge, Phoebe, *Fleabag* (London: Nick Hern Books, 2016)
Washburn, Anne, *Mr Burns* (London: Oberon, 2014)
Williams, Roy, *Lift Off* (London: Methuen Drama, 2001)
Williams, Roy, *The No Boy's Cricket Club* (London: Methuen Drama, 1999)
Williams, Roy, *Sing Yer Heart Out for the Lads* (London: Methuen Drama, 2004)
Williams, Tennessee, *A Streetcar Named Desire* (London: Penguin Classics, 2009)
Wood, Alexandra, *The Eleventh Capital* (London: Nick Hern Books, 2007)
Wynne, Michael, *The People are Friendly* (London: Faber, 2002)
Yanagihara, Hanya/Hove, Ivo van/Tachelet, Koen, *A Little Life* (London: Nick Hern Books, 2023)

INDEX

Plays and Playwrights

Abedi-Amin, Bam 166
Abigail's Party 71, 104, 108
Absence of War, The 71
Accidental Death of an Anarchist 74
Acid Test, The 123
Adventures of Foothead and Zobe, The 68, 75
Agbaje, Bola 166, 169
Albee, Edward 68, 88
Alison! A Rock Opera 121–122, 162, 181
All You Need is LSD 36, 39, 72, 98, 106, 136, 143, 152–153, 154, 161
Alvarez, Bosco 173, 174
Angels in America: Parts One & Two 36–37, 39
Anwar, Subika 166
Anything Goes 12
Arancibia, David 173, 174
Arden, John 35
Ashton, Zawe 166
Attempts on Her Life 99
Author, The 100

Baker, Annie 30, 109, 188
Baldwin, Nicola 166, 170
Bano, Alia 166, 170–171
Barnes, Luke 166
Bartlett, Mike 171, 177
Battye, Miriam 166
Beckett, Samuel 16, 35–36, 42, 72, 74, 78–79, 82–83, 92–93, 103, 129, 179, 181, 189
Beginning 36
Bennett, Alan 35
Berger, Emilia 173

Berkoff, Steven 35
Birch, Alice 166, 171
Birch, Brad xvii 40–41, 166, 190
Blake, Yve 166
Blasted 11, 108, 161
Blood Brothers 126
Bond, Edward 7, 107, 109, 129, 156, 162
Book of Mormon, The 190
Boy 26, 31–34, 39–40, 60, 71, 73, 77, 109, 130, 141, 143, 148, 151, 155, *155*, 158, 160, 162–163, *163*, 181
Boy Gets Girl 97, 103
Brealey, Lou 166
Breath Boom 129
Brecht, Bertolt 34, 42, 70, 79, 99, 129, 172
Briar Rose 67, 68
Brittain, Jon 166
Brunger, Jake 166
Brute 41
Buchner, Georg 7, 103, 187, 190
Bush, Chris 178
Butterworth, Jez 84, 95, 131

Calderon, Guillermo 175
Caretaker, The 190
Carol Singers, The 67
Carr, Marina 134
Carter, Pamela 166
Cartwright, Jim 106, 189–190
Cassenbaum, Nick 166
Cats 12
Chairs, The 194
Chaudry, Hammaad 166, 170–171
Chekhov, Anton 16, 36, 92, 92, 93, 103, 109, 120, 138, 171, 188
Cherry Orchard, The 16, 190

Churchill, Caryl 7, 31, 36, 38, 70, 75, 107, 134, 156, 169, 179, 187, 191
Coleman, Clive 103
Contreras, Daniela 173
Cook, Elinor 166
Corbett, Poppy 166
Corthron, Kia 129
Costa, Pierre 173
Coward, Noel 35
Crimp, Martin 99, 129
Crouch, Tim 100–101, 169
Crowe, EV 166, 170–171, 191

Daniels, Sarah 129
Davies, Molly 166, 170
De Angelis, April 171, 175
De-Lahay, Rachel 166–167
Delaney, Shelagh 194
Devotion 164, 165, 181
Dissection of a Rapist 15, 122, 127
Donnelly, John 30, 168, 190
Drury, Jackie Sibblies 100–101

Éclair-Powell, Phoebe 166
El-Bushra, Suhayla 30, 166
Eldridge, David 30, 36, 99, 134, 136–137, 162, 171
Emson, Kenny 166, 169
End of the World Extravaganza, The 15, 122

Farr, Gareth 166
Fo, Dario 99
Fosse, Jon 12
4.48 Psychosis 6, 134, 179, 190
Friel, Brian 36
Fritz, James 166, 171
Fugard, Athol 129

Gardini, Genna 174
Giddy Little Kippers 3, 130–131, 171
Gieselmann, David 36
Gill, Peter 34
Gilman, Rebecca 97
Graham, James 34
Green, Debbie Tucker 7, 31, 87, 169
Gregg, Stacey 166
Greig, David 175, 190
Griffiths, Trevor 129

Gubaryev, Vladimir 74
Guirgis, Stephen Adley 71
Gumede, Dominque 174
Gupta, Tanika 30, 168, 175

Halsall, Karis 166
Hamilton 34, 99
Hamlet 12, 79, 85, 96
Handke, Peter 12
Hanly, Sarah 166
Hansberry, Lorraine 106, 190
Happy Days 72, 82, 82, 93–94
Happy Hospital 62, 179
Hare, David 71, 87, 141, 169
Harry Potter and the Cursed Child 165
Hawkins, Samson 34
Hayes, Rob 166
Hearst, Elise 166
Hedda Gabler 79
Henry IV: Part One 70
Herons 196
Hickson, Ella 166, 171, 190
Ho, Ming 166
Hoichi the Earless 67
Holliday, Joyce 74
Holy Mothers 128
Hunter, Al 67
Huxley-Smith, Lucien 166, 171

Ibini, Matilda 166
Ibsen, Henryk 70, 79, 191
Icke, Robert 190–191
Iliad-ish, The 73
I'll Be the Devil 5–6, 39, 71, 109, 130, 136–137, 147, 161–162, 162, 181, 191
Innocent Creatures 48–49, 50, 52, 52, 71, 97, 181
Ionesco, Eugene 79, 129
Iphigenia in Splott 35
Island, The 129
It's a Bit Lively Outside! 74

Jalaly, Sonia 166
Jellicoe, Ann 35
Jephta, Amy 174
Jerusalem 84, 131

Jimenez, Claudia 173
Jones, Jasmine Lee 34
Jordan, Anna 34
Joseph, Yasmin 166
Juicy Fruits 7

Kahn-Din, Ayub 6
Kalawski, Andres 173
Kane, Sarah 6, 11, 108, 129, 134, 161, 190
Karasik, Daniel 166
Kaye Campbell, Alexi 171
Kelly, Dennis 6
Kendrick, Ellie 166
Kene, Arinze 166
Kin 170–171, 191
King Lear 69–70, 103, 105, 168, 190
Koohestani, Amir Reza 175
Kosar, Sarah 166
Krapp's Last Tape 103, 189
Kureishi, Hanif 30, 166
Kushner, Tony 36, 38

Laurens, Joanna 161
Le-Bert, Camila 173
Lehman Trilogy, The 33
Leigh, Eve 166
Leigh, Mike 71–72, 104, 108, 192
Lennon 74
Letter of Last Resort, The 191
Lewenstein, Rose 166
Lift Off 130
Little Life, A 178
Little Russians 190
Live Like Pigs 34
Living 26, 141, 177
Local 118
Loh, Daniel York 166, 169
Loneliness of the Long-Distance Runner, The 123
Long Day's Journey into Night, A 6
Longman, Simon 166
Look Back in Anger 31, 74, 129
Lopez, Robert 190
Lucky Dog 17, 26, 39, 44, 44–45, 71, 77, 83, 83, 88, 104, 109, 142, 148, 152, 181, 188
Lynn, Cordelia 166
Lynn, Isley 166

Macbeth 36, 69–70, 87–88
McDowall, Alistair 34, 103, 166
Machinal 190
McLean, Michael 166, 171
Macmillan, Duncan 166, 169, 191
McPherson, Conor 15, 88, 94–95, 95, 128
Made of Stone 6, 15, 26, 36, 39, 42, 106, 109, 118, 122, 132, 134–136, 141, 146, 148–149, 149, 153, 159–160
Majola, Simo Mpapa 174
Makubika, Mufaro 166
Mamet, David 75, 87, 172
Martinez, Florencia 173
Maserumule, Tau 174
Masheane, Napo 174, 174
Massini, Stefan 33
Matura, Mustapha 172
Mayenburg, Marius von 129
Merchant of Venice, The 67
Midsummer Night's Dream, A 58, 62, 66, 67, 69–70, 72, 77, 107–108, 181
Miller, Arthur 34
Miss Julie 196
Mitchell, Natalie 166
Moleba, Eliot 174
Molusi, Omphile 174
Mongiwekaya 174–175, 174
Moore, DC 166
Mother Courage and her Children 42, 44, 79
Motherf*cker with the Hat, The 71
Motortown 96
Motton, Gregory 171
Mr Burns 99
Mr Kolpert 36
Mullarkey, Rory 166–167, 190
Muthy, Nessah 166
My Name is Rachel Corrie 175

No Boy's Cricket Club, The 119
Norris, Luke 166, 169
Not I 36–37, 42, 72, 108

O'Brien, David 166
O'Brien, Richard 129

Odd Couple, The 106
Oedipus Rex 79, 105
Oettinger, Gerado 173
Offending the Audience 12
Oh! What a Lovely War 74
Okoh, Janice 166
On Raftery's Hill 134
One Day When We Were Young 170
One Man, Two Guvnors 161
O'Neill, Eugene 6, 103, 190
Oresteia, The 190
Orton, Joe 70, 103, 129, 156
Osborne, John 31, 75, 129, 163
Othello 70, 85, 105
Other People 130
Our Day Out 126
Owen, Gary 35

Park, Kyoung H 166
Parker, Trey 190
Parry, Margaret 166
Payne, Nick 37, 141, 166, 170, 173, 173, 175
Pearson, Deborah 166
Penhall, Joe 129
People are Friendly, The 34
People Places and Things 191
Peppa Pig's Fun Day Out 179
Pezhman, Arzhang 118
Pied Piper, The 67
Pilgrim's Progress, The 67, 137
Pinnock, Winsome 30, 168, 173–174, 174
Pinter, Harold 75, 104, 129, 179, 190
Pomona 34, 103
Posh 191
Potter, Dennis 72, 74, 181
Prebble, Lucy 33, 105–106, 169
Prime Controller, The 75, 119
Punter, Michael 30

Raisin in the Sun, A 106, 165, 190
Ramayana, The 58
Random 87
Rattigan, Terrence 35, 104
Ravenhill, Mark 30, 93, 129
Razia, Ambreen 166, 169

Redundant 26, 33–34, 42, 43, 44, 58, 72, 75, 104, 109, 122–123, 135–136, 142, 150–151, 151, 159, 163, 165, 170, 181, 188
Reiss, Anya 123, 141, 166, 170–171
Richard III 70
Rivera, Juan Andres 173
Road 189–190
Robyn Hudd: The Pantomime 73, 74
Rock n Roll 169
Rocky Horror Show, The 99, 129
Romeo and Juliet 67, 70, 73, 79–80, 82–83, 92
Roots 31
Russell, Willy 34, 126, 127, 134

Santos, Marcelo Dos 166
Sarcophagus 74
Saunders, Simone 166
Saved 7, 107, 109
Schey, Jonathan 166
Schwab, Werner 128
Seagull, The 74, 92, 92, 93, 103, 171, 188
Seven Methods of Killing Kylie Jenner 34
Sexual Perversity in Chicago 75
Shabangu, Nobantu 174
Shakespeare, William 11–12, 58, 62, 64–65, 67, 69–71, 75, 79, 95, 108, 128, 190, 192
Shawn, Wallace 29–30, 169
Shepard, Sam 171
Shinn, Christopher 30, 130
Sigarev, Vasily 175
Simmonds, Sarah 166
Simon, Neil 106
Sing Yer Heart Out for the Lads 34
Skinner, Penelope 166, 170
Solemani, Sarah 166
Sondheim, Stephen 74
Sophocles 79
Soyinka, Wole 71, 172
Spur of the Moment 123
Stalham, Dean 166
Standing at the Sky's Edge 135, 178
Stanic, Paula B 166
Starship Gaia 122, 131
Steel, Beth 166

Stenham, Polly 30–31, 35, 37, 141, 166, 177
Stephens, Simon 6, 30, 96, 106, 135, 166, 170
Stone, Matt 190
Stoppard, Tom 148, 169
Streetcar Named Desire, A 36
Strindberg, August 196
Sugar Syndrome, The 105
Sumbwanyambe, May 166

Talking About the Fire 87
Taste of Honey, A 34
Tempest, The 5–6, 8, 65, 67, 72, 178
That Face 30, 37
Thompson, Chris 166
Thorne, Jack 198
Thorpe, Chris 87
Toast 128
Tourism 190
Treading Water 122
Treadwell, Sophie 190
Twelfth Night 70

Ugalde, Begoña 173
Uncle Vanya 138
Under the Blue Sky 99
Upton, Judy 15

Via Dolorosa 87
Village Bike, The 170–171
Village Idiot 34
Vorozhbit, Natal'ya 175
Vundla, Mandi 174

Wade, Laura 191
Waiting for Godot 16, 71, 79
Waller Bridge, Phoebe 87
Washburn, Anne 99
Weir, The 88, 94, 95, 128–130
Wertenbaker, Timberlake 129
Wesker, Arnold 31
What the Butler Saw 103
Where the Shot Rabbits Lay 190
White, Joe 166
Whitney, Monsay 166
Who's Afraid of Virginia Woolf? 68, 88

Williams, Roy 30, 34, 119, 130
Williams, Tennessee 7, 36, 85
Winter's Tale, The 96
Wood, Alexandra 166, 169
Woyzeck 7, 103, 156, 157, 187, 190
Writer, The 190
Wynne, Michael 34

X 103

Yen 34
York Realist, The 34
Young Marx 103
Young Osama 136

Zeller, Florian 12

Films, Filmmakers and TV

Aguirre, Wrath of God 38, 96
Akerman, Chantal 98, 192
Alice in the Cities 192
Alien 103
Allen, Woody 30, 60–61, 73, 96, 175
And Now for Something Completely Different 60
Angel Heart 72
Annie Hall 61
Antonioni, Michaelangelo 71, 192

Bagpuss 19
Barry Lyndon 5
Bergman, Ingmar 71, 84, 84, 92, 100, 100, 192
Blackadder 60
Blazing Saddles 94
Brats 86–87, 86
Breaking Bad 71
Brief Encounter 106
Brooks, Mel 60, 94, 192
Brownlow, Kevin 60
Bunuel, Luis 104

Cat who Loved a Bath, The 77
Cat who Loved a Bath Pt Two, The 77
Chaplin, Charlie 34, 60–61, 69, 78, 181
Chytilova, Vera 71
Cinema Paradiso 73

Circus, The 60
City Lights 60
Clarke, Alan 72, 189
Clockwork Orange, A 46
Close-Up 98
Clueless 39
Come and See 191
Cries and Whispers 71
Crimes and Misdemeanours 73

Daisies 71
Dawn of the Dead 61, 170
Day the Earth Caught Fire, The 192
Do the Right Thing 73, 105, 105
Donen, Stanley 192
Don't Look Now 103
Downton Abbey 64
Dracula 61
Driller Killer 61

Empire Strikes Back, The 82
Ephron, Nora 108
E.T. The Extra Terrestrial 88
Evil Dead, The 61
Exorcist, The 61

Fanny & Alexander 192
Fellini, Federico 60, 118
Fellowes, Julian 64
Fight Club 94
Flying Circus, Monty Python's 27
Four Hundred Blows, The 106
Friends 85
Funny Games 99, 100

Ghostbusters 22
Gill, David 60
Godfather, The 96
Goodfellas 14, 73, 76
Great Dictator, The 60
Guest, Val 192

Haneke, Michael 71, 99, 100, 192
Hannah and her Sisters 61
Herzog, Werner 38, 96, 191
Hidden Fortress, The 192
Hitchcock, Alfred 102, 102, 104, 191
Horror at the Bloggs Motel 61
Horrors of the Forest 77

Immigrant, The 61

Jackson, Peter 91, 92, 108
Jim'll Fix It 59
Jurassic Park 71

Kelly, Gene 192
Kes 22
Kiarostami, Abbas 98
Kid, The 60
Kings of the Road 192
Klimov, Elem 191
Kubrick, Stanley 2, 5, 46, 85, 85, 106
Kurosawa, Akira 3, 133, 181, 193

Land of Silence and Darkness 191
Laughing Gravy 86
Laurel and Hardy 78, 80, 86–88,
    108–109, 129, 168
L'Avventura 71, 192
Lee, Spike 73, 105, 105
Leigh, Mike 71–72, 104, 108, 192
Leviathan 191
Little Miss Sunshine 82–83, 83
Loach, Ken 22, 191
Lord of the Rings, The 91, 92, 108
Love and Death 61
Lynch, David 39, 104, 174, 181, 192

Made in Britain 72
Magic Chocolate Box, The 77, 77
Magician, The 192
Manhattan 30
Mankowitz, Wolf 192
Marker, Chris 6
Marx Brothers, The 60, 68, 74
Match of the Day 96
Meantime 72, 192
Meyers, Nancy 39
Modern Times 60, 79
Monty Python 27, 30, 60, 95, 105
Monty Python and the Holy Grail
    61
Mulholland Drive 39, 84, 192
Music Box, The 78–81, 78–80, 84–86,
    89–91, 91, 93–96, 97, 99, 101,
    101–102, 104, 104, 105, 107,
    108, 138, 187
My Dinner with Andre 29

New Shmoo, The 19
News from Home 98, 193

Old Grey Whistle Test 21
Old Joy 190

Pasolini, Pier Paulo 108
Pennies from Heaven 72
Persona 84, 84, 100, 100, 192
Potter, Dennis 72, 74, 181
Psycho 102–103, 102, 160
Psycho 2 61

Raging Bull 71, 82–83, 83
Raining Stones 191
Ray, Satyajit 60
Rear Window 104
Reichardt, Kelly 190
Roach, Hal 78–80, 79, 87, 89–91, 97, 99, 101–102, 104, 108
Runners 76–77, 76, 119

Salo, or the 120 days of Sodom 108
Satantango 191
Scorsese, Martin 3, 14, 71, 73, 82, 83, 155, 192
Separation, A 191
Seventh Continent, The 71
Shining, The 106
Simpsons, The 36, 85, 149
Singin' in the Rain 192
Sleeper 61
Sopranos, The 71, 148
Spielberg, Steven 38, 71, 88
Star Trek 87
Star Wars 22, 71, 81–82, 81
Stranger Things 87
Streetcar Called Marge, A 36
Succession 71

Tarkovsky, Andrei 76, 138
Tarr, Bela 138, 191
Taxi Driver 192
Texas Chainsaw Massacre, The 5, 61, 149
This is England 126
Threads 19, 21, 181
Throne of Blood 133

Through a Glass Darkly 192
Top of the Pops 18, 60
Truffaut, Francoise 106
2001: A Space Odyssey 46, 85, 85

Uncle Buck 138
Unknown Chaplin 60
Usual Suspects, The 94

Vagabond 87
Varda, Agnes 87

Way Out West 86
Wenders, Wim 87, 192
When Harry Met Sally 108
White Ribbon, The 193
Wilder, Gene 192
Wrong Move 87, 192

Young Frankenstein 192
Young Ones, The 60

Zelig 61, 96
Zombie Flesh Eaters 61
Zvyaginstev, Andrey 191

People, Places and Things

Abbey Road (album) 39
Abe's Odyssey(game) 120
Across the Universe (song) 61
Age of Reason, The 68
Almeida Theatre 32–34, 40, 70, 99, 143, 155, 155, 163, 190–191
Amis, Martin 61
Andersson, Bibi 84
Animashawun, Ola 48, 130, 131, 166
Aristotle 168
Arnoldi, Ingeborg 43

Bacon, Joanna 149–150
Badger, Harvey 147
Bagnall, Nick 121
Ball, Amy 148–149
Barber, John Gordon 22, 22, 25, 181
Bassett, Linda 83, 88, 148, 152
Bausch, Pina 35
BBC Sound Effects: Death and Horror (album) 61

Beadle, Jo 73, 75
Beatles, The 5, 21, 39, 56, 59–60, 69, 181
Berliner Ensemble, The 42
Berry, Chuck 39
Billington, Michael 161, 165
Birds, The (song) 37
Blair, Tony 21
Brit School xv
Brook, Peter 62, 191
Brown, Ashleigh 147
Bruce, Deborah 149, 149, 159
Buether, Miriam 151, 160
Burgess, Matthew 74
Burial 155
Burke, Tom 162
Burton, John 87
Bush, Kate 39
Bush Theatre 171
Butler, Alan 24
Butler, Bea xvii 77, 77
Butler, Clara xvii 77
Butler, John 24
Butler, Joseph 25, 26
Butler, Judy (nee Barber) 20, 22–25, 23, 26
Butler, Matt xvii 2, 17–22, 18, 25, 26, 60–61, 74, 159
Butler, 'N' 118–119, 135, 142, 181
Butler, Terence 'Bill' 2, 20, 24–25, 24, 26
Byrne, David 177

Cardboard Citizens 167
Cardiac Arrest (song) 59
Carter, Billy 162
Cathcart, Clare 122
Cattle, Sarah 149, 150
Champion, Ian 63
Chapman, Graham 27
Chill Out (album) 119
Chisholm, Greg 149–150, 149, 159
Clachan, Lizzie 8
Clarke, Alan 72, 189
Clash, The 59
Clist, Sophia 77
Collective Psychosis of the 21st Century, The (album) 77

Collery, Brian 25
Collyns, Saskia 147
Combat 84 56
Connections Festival, NT 48, 131
Constable, John 39
Cooke, Dominic 33, 43, 129, 135, 142, 150–151, 151, 166–167
Cream 169
Crucible Theatre 67, 74, 167
Cruise, Tom 75
Cubin, Bill 86, 87

Daldry, Stephen 32, 74, 129, 172, 175
Dark Heart: The Shocking Truth about Hidden Britain 194
Davies, Nick 194
Devine, George 31, 129, 135, 163, 167, 177
Dodd, Ken 74
Dodgson, Elyse 130, 168, 172–176, 173–174, 176, 181
Drew, Amanda 103
Duke of York's Theatre 128
Dunkerly, Lucy 130
Durer, Albrecht 41–42, 41, 79, 133
Dylan, Bob 21

Eaton, Paul 74
Edge, Lucy 122
Elbow 37
Elen, Ffion 147
Elizabeth II (Queen) 167
Emin, Tracey 39
Evans, Roger 122

Faithful, Marianne 44
Featherstone, Vicky 175
Firth Park Comprehensive School 57–58, 61, 67–68, 75
Fisher, Mark 31
Fitzmaurice, Annie 154
Fleetwood Mac 47
Foot, Michael 21
Ford, Giles 149, 150
Fox, Frankie 60, 143, 155, 155
Fretwell, Marc 74
Fricker, William 151

INDEX

Garbiya, Huss 1, 14, 74, 123, 149, 150
Gaskill, William 129
Genesis (band) 21
Gilbert, Billy 89
Ginsberg, Allan 36
Glover, Brian 67
Goater, Michael 62
Goold, Rupert 32
Gormley, Colm 162
Graham, Abigail xvi 147
Graham, Stephen 126
Grass Hoppa 35, 118, 120, 121, 122
Gray, Ramin 5, 147, 161, 162, 191

Happy Mondays, The 75
Harper, Stephen 154
Harrison, Evelyn Mary 25
Harrison, George 58, 135
Hawley, Richard 178
Hazel, Paul 67
Hendrix, Jimi 120
Holder, Ruby 147
Horan, Julia 148–149
Howard, Trevor 106
Howl 36
Hunter, Jack 154
Hunter, Paul 143, 154
Huxley, Aldous 106
Hyman, Robert 6

Idle, Eric 27
Imperial War Museum 41
Innes-Hopkins, Robert 151, 151

Jackson, Michael 22, 38, 168
Jepson, Meg 58, 62, 64, 72, 77, 181
Johnson, Celia 106
Johnson, Robert 39
Jones, Terry 27
Joseph-Wright, Joden 147

Kafka, Franz 94, 122
Kalman, Jean 152
Kelleher, JD 162
Kelly, Leigh 164
Kent, Nicholas 190

Kinks, The 59
Kinski, Klaus 96
KLF, The 119
Krankies, The 74

Laden, Osama bin 136, 163
Lady Gaga 157
Larkin, Phillip 39
Leaud, Jean-Pierre 106
Led Zeppelin 21
Lennon, John 74
Liotta, Ray 14
Lizzimore, Clare 103, 147
Lloyd Webber, Andrew 12
Lovatt, Dave 120
Lowry, LS 31, 34
Lyndon, Nina 130, 166

McCartney, Paul 126
McClaren, Malcolm 56
Macdonald, James 83
McGonigal, Gracie 152
McLaughlin, Emily 130
Macliam, Edward 162
McNamara, Seamus 147
McQuillan, Clare 166
Made of Stone (song) 132
Madness 59–60
Madonna 18
Magical Mystery Tour (album) 59
Mannix, Aoife 130
Marlowe Theatre 8, 167
Marshal, Lyndsey 43, 151
Marx, Harpo 60, 68, 74
Mercell, Sophie 154
Merlin Theatre 65, 67
Metamorphosis 94, 98
Milne, Ryan 67–68, 72–73
Mitchell, Katie 134
Monk, Denzil 120
Morrison, Van 21, 25, 75
Moss, Nick 149–150, 159
Muck and Spit (song) 146
Murphy, Gerard 162
Murray, Martin 17–18, 20, 52, 59, 62, 181
Myles, Ciaran 61
Myles, Justin 20, 24–25
Myles, Penny 20

Natural History Museum 41
New Ambassador's Theatre 128
Nicholson, Jack 106
Night Boat to Cairo (song) 59
Night Bus (song) 155
Norton College 1, 73
Nottingham Playhouse 123
Notton, Simon 128, 129

O'Briain, Donnacadgh 147
O'Brien, Eileen 43
Odyssey, The 78
Oldfield, Ada J 23
Oldman, Gary 1
Oliver, Mark 164
O'Neill, Con 103
Orwell, George 8
Ovenden, Kate 147

Patten, Chris 167
Peggy Ramsay Foundation 29
Persad, Dan 77, 120–121, 121, 122
Persad, Joseph 122
Persad, Nathan 122
Persad, Rhydian 118, 120–122, 121, 134–135
Philip (Prince, Duke of Edinburgh) 167
Pink Floyd 21, 39
Porter, Cole 12
Potts, George 154
Pritchard, Sam 175

Red Riding Hood 38
Redding, Otis 106
Rego, Paula 44
Richards, Keith 44
Richie, Lionel 34
Rickman, Alan 175
Rickson, Ian 15, 26, 95, 128–129, 135, 159, 177
Risin' Still (song) 120
Robinson, Tom 21
Rolling Stones, The 39
Rose Bruford School of Speech and Drama 1, 77, 118–119, 122, 126, 150
Royal Court Theatre
  bar 118, 150
  commission fee 28
  and David Byrne 177
  discounted tickets 34
  Elyse Dodgson 172–176
  and Graham Whybrow 139
  and Ian Rickson 177
  'N' 119, 135
  and Polly Stenham 30
  rejection by 31–32
  script meetings 171
  and Simon Notton 128
  'The Matrix' 171
  ushering team xvi
  working class drama 30–31
  writing tutor 30, 33, 37, 41, 137, 161, 166, 168–169, 171–176
  Young Writers' Festival 15, 42, 118, 122, 126, 131, 134, 159, 177
  Young Writers' Programme xvi 30, 130, 166–167
Royal Court Theatre, plays
  Acid Test (Reiss) 123
  Attempts on Her Life (Crimp) 99
  Blasted (Kane) 11
  Boy Gets Girl (Gilman) 97
  Breath Boom (Corthron) 129
  Comedians (Griffiths) 129
  Constellations (Payne) 37
  Early Morning (Bond) 7
  Enron (Prebble) 33
  Far Away (Churchill) 36, 191
  Fireface (Mayenberg) 129
  4.48 Psychosis (Kane) 6, 134, 179, 190
  Gone Too Far! (Agbaje) 169
  Happy Days (Beckett) 82, 82
  Herons (Stephens) 196
  Holy Mothers (Schwab) 128
  I See You (Mongiwekaya) 175
  Jerusalem (Butterworth) 84
  Kin (Crowe) 191
  Lift Off (Williams) 130
  Live Like Pigs (Ardon) 34
  Local (Pezhman) 118
  Look Back in Anger (Osbourne) 129
  Motortown (Stephens) 96
  Mr Kolpert (Gieselmann) 36

My Name is Rachel Corrie (Corrie/ Vimer/Rickman) 175
Not I (Beckett) 36
Other People (Shinn) 130
Pomona and X (McDowell) 103
Posh (Wade) 191
Psychosis (Kane) 6, 190
Random (Tucker Green) 87
Road (Cartwright) 189–190
Rock n Roll (Stoppard) 169
Roots (Wesker) 31
Saved (Bond) 7, 107, 109
Seven Methods of Killing Kylie Jenner (Jones) 34
Spur of the Moment (Reiss) 123
Talking About the Fire (Thorpe) 87
That Face (Stenham) 30, 37
The Author (Crouch) 100
The Country (Crimp) 129
The Eleventh Capital (Wood) 169
The Island (Fugard) 129
The People are Friendly (Wynne) 34
The Rocky Horror Show (O'Brien) 99, 129
The Sugar Syndrome (Prebble) 105
The Weir (McPherson) 95
The York Realist (Gill) 34
Toast (Bean) 128
Under the Blue Sky (Eldridge) 99
Village Bike, The (Skinner) 170–171
Where the Shot Rabbits Lay (Birch) 190
Yen (Jordan) 34
Royal Court Theatre, plays by the author
　Alison! A Rock Opera 121–122, 162
　Boy 31, 141
　Faces in the Crowd 162
　Lucky Dog 83, 88
　Made of Stone 6, 15, 42, 118, 149
　Redundant 33, 43, 72, 151, 159
Royal Literary Fund 29
Royal National Gallery 41

Royal National Theatre 27–28, 34, 48, 109, 161, 178, 191
Royal Shakespeare Company 5, 28, 147, 162

Samad, Sharif 129–130, 132, 134
Sampson, Eva 146, 147
Sartre, Jean-Paul 68
Seber, Esme 147
Sex Pistols, The 56
Shaw, Khai 147
Sheffield Playhouse 141
Sheffield Youth Theatre, The 58, 62, 64–66, 165
Shepherd, Andrew 63, 66
Shield, Leroy 79
Shipbuilding (song) 21
Shut Up (song) 59
Sierz, Aleks 161
Silbert, Roxana 156, 157
Sillitoe, Alan 123
Sing if You're Glad to be Gay (song) 21
Smith, Jim 120, 121
Smith, Rae 103, 151
Smiths, The 61
Something Quite Nice about ISIS (song) 146
Sorrento's Cafe 48–49
Spread-Eagle Theatre, The 122
Stafford-Clarke, Max 129, 150, 172
Stanislavski, Konstantin 63, 150
Steinbeck, John 35
Stewart, James 104
Stone Roses, The 1, 39, 75, 132, 159
Stranglers, The 56
Syed, Humera 147
Synergy Theatre Project 33

Talisman (board game) 72
Tate Modern 41
Thatcher, Margaret 15, 21, 72, 190
Theatre Centre xv 164, 164
Theatre Royal Stratford East xv 119
Thriller (song) 22
Told By An Idiot xv 143
Tolkien, JRR 4, 91–92
Tomlinson, Ricky 191
Traveling Wilburys, The 169

Trinder, Simon 151
Twyman, Richard 173

Ullmann, Liv 84
Ultz 151

Viner, Katherine 175
Vitti, Monica 192

Wardell, Nancy 86, 87
Wares, Sacha 32, 40, 143, 151, 155, 160, 162
Wenger, Arsene 32
West, Fred & Rose 44
White Album, The (album) 59
Whitelaw, Billie 72, 82

Why I Write 8
Whybrow, Graham 139
Williams, Alan 83, 152
Wolf, Howlin' 21
Writers' and Artists' Yearbook, The 123–124
Wyatt, Robert 21

Yershon, Gary 152
Young Vic Theatre 100, 167, 171
Young Writers' Festival 15, 42, 118, 122, 126, 131, 134, 159, 177
Young Writers' Programme xvi 30, 130, 166–167

Zahir, Gigi 152